THE HOUSE OF ISLAM

A Global History

Ed Husain

BLOOMSBURY PUBLISHING
LONDON • OXFORD • NEW YORK • NEW DELHI • SYDNEY

BLOOMSBURY PUBLISHING
Bloomsbury Publishing Plc
50 Bedford Square, London, WC1B 3DP, UK

BLOOMSBURY, BLOOMSBURY PUBLISHING and the Diana logo are trademarks of Bloomsbury Publishing Plc

First published in Great Britain 2018
This edition published 2019

For legal purposes the Acknowledgements on p. 305 constitute an extension of this copyright page

A catalogue record for this book is available from the British Library

Library of Congress Cataloguing-in-Publication data has been applied for

ISBN: HB: 978-1-4088-7226-0; TPB: 978-1-4088-7227-7;
PB: 978-1-4088-7228-4; eBook: 978-1-4088-7229-1

2 4 6 8 10 9 7 5 3 1

Typeset by Newgen KnowledgeWorks Pvt. Ltd., Chennai, India
Printed and bound in Great Britain by CPI Group (UK) Ltd, Croydon CR0 4YY

For my daughters, Camilla and Hannah:
may you and your generation carry forth divine love, light and faith of the ancient prophets and philosophers.

When zealous Muslims burnt the books of Averroes, a disciple of his began to weep. Averroes said to his student, 'My son, if you are lamenting the condition of the Muslims, then tears equal to the seas will not suffice. If you are crying for the books, then know that ideas have wings and transcend aeons to reach the minds of thinking people.'

(Averroes/Ibn Rushd, 1126–98)

Contents

Introduction: Inside the House

Muslims are shaping world events and constantly feature in the news, yet few among us genuinely understand them, so that our behaviour tends to be based on ignorance at best, or half-truths at worse. This book surveys the foundations of the faith of Muslims and explains the design of the House of Islam. It describes how Muslims feel, practise and perceive Islam, and sets out to explore their minds and their worldview. I write as one born and raised as a Muslim in Great Britain. I am a Westerner and an observant Muslim. Caught between two worlds, I have learned to dovetail the two facets of my identity. This book is a reflection of that inner bridge between Islam and the West.

Globally, the Muslim population is 1.7 billion strong – that is to say that one in every five human beings is a Muslim – and there are fifty-nine Muslim-majority countries. By 2050, the Muslim populace is projected to grow twice as fast as the overall world population. After 2050, Muslims will probably surpass Christians as the world's largest grouping of humans based on a faith identity. While the global population is projected to grow by 35 per cent by 2050, the Muslim population is expected to increase by 73 per cent to nearly 3 billion, according to the Pew Research Center. Muslims have more children than members of other faith communities. Muslim women give birth to an average of 2.9 children, notably higher than the average of all non-Muslims at 2.2.

A convergence of five facts explains this worldwide surge in Muslim birth rates. Firstly, Pew estimates that Muslims in large numbers are approaching the stage of their lives in which to have children. The median age of Muslims in 2015 was 24, while the median for non-Muslims was 32. Secondly, more than a third of

Muslims live in the Middle East and Africa, regions of the world expected to witness the largest population growths. Thirdly, most Muslim countries still retain a very traditional understanding of the role of women as wives and mothers. Therefore the emphasis on motherhood is stronger than for others. Fourthly, the firm Muslim belief in sustenance for children coming from God means that there is often reliance on God for food, clothing and shelter. Finally, the cultural value placed on the birth of boys is, sadly, still greater than girls. Therefore, many families will continue to have children until a boy is born to carry the family name to the next generation. Unlike Catholicism, Islam does not prohibit birth control.

With the mass movement of people globally, and since refugees and workers come to Europe mostly from Muslim-majority countries, what happens inside Islam will have an impact on us all. Extreme forms of politicised Islam will act to disrupt the peace in our societies through increased tendencies of social separatism, confrontation, attempts at domination, and political violence inflicted through terrorism.

Currently, there is a global battle under way for the soul of Islam. Why? What and where are the battle lines? Who will win? And how does this affect the West? In different ways, my life has been spent at the forefront of this struggle.

I was born in London to Muslim migrants from British India. Mine was the first generation of Muslims born and raised in the West. My first book, *The Islamist*, recounts my teenage journey into international, religious radicalism and my subsequent rejection of it. I have lived through Islamism, Salafism and Sufism. Seeking to better understand Islam, away from militant Muslims, I spent two years studying Arabic and Islam with mainstream Muslim scholars in Damascus, Syria, from 2003 to 2005. I lived in a dictatorship where I was free to study for as long as I did not express political views in public. In private, we were continually suspicious of fellow students and even of our teachers – who was the informant? The deep knowledge of Islamic theology, history and philosophy of Syrian scholars was second to none. Without freedom, however, our education always felt partial, compromised, and lacking in the full rigour of students entitled elsewhere to ask tough questions.

Yearning to be closer to the source of Islam, in 2005 I moved to live and work in Jeddah, Saudi Arabia. I worked as a teacher with the British Council during the week, and at weekends I spent time in worship at Islam's holiest sanctuaries in Mecca and Medina. There, I prayed and interacted with Muslims from all over the world. My immersion in Arabic language, religion, culture and peoples was fulfilling to me, but back home in Britain my youngest sister escaped death on the London underground bombings on 7 July by minutes. When my Saudi students reacted by saying to me that Britain deserved this terrorism, that this was jihad against the infidels, I felt angry and a visceral need to return home to London. I knew that we had a battle of ideas ahead of us. When Saudis in their twenties, followers of the holy Quran, could not commiserate, but actually celebrated the misfortunes of the West; when young Muslims born and raised in the West killed themselves and their fellow citizens on London's public transport, the sentiments and convictions that led to such actions would not easily subside. Indeed, in recent years the thousands of radicalised European Muslims who have turned to terrorism in their attacks on France, Belgium, Holland, Germany, Norway, Canada and Denmark are offshoots of that same trend.

Back in Britain, I completed a postgraduate degree in Islam and Middle East politics. I then established a think tank in 2007, Quilliam, named after a Victorian-born Muslim, Abdullah Quilliam, to illustrate that Islam should not be associated in Britain with immigration or recent radicalisation. Led by Muslims to research and renounce radicalism, Quilliam was the the first of its kind in the world. It was controversial work, but it was necessary to take the lead and show how Islam was being politicised by Arab political anger. I believed it was my religious and civic duty to speak out against the political hijacking of Islam, my faith. Quilliam was successful in its countless media appearances, helping to change British government policy, briefing multiple European governments, speaking on university campuses across the Continent, and thereby compelling Muslim activists to rethink their confrontational anti-Western politics. But the backlash from objectors was strong. Death threats and physical intimidation are the default recourse of bullies who cannot win an argument. I felt that I needed to leave Britain for a while.

In late 2010 I became a senior fellow for Middle Eastern studies at America's leading foreign policy think tank, the Council on Foreign Relations. I lived in New York and Washington DC for four years, researching and writing about politics in the Arab world, national security, Islam and Muslims. The Council's members included professionals at the highest level of the US government, media, business and universities. I found myself in a unique position: a Brit, a Muslim, and an Arabic speaker explaining the challenges of the modern Middle East, and advising on America's policy options, to powerful audiences at the height of the Arab Spring uprisings. Conversely, I was interpreting the actions of the West for Arab and Muslim governments and civil society when I travelled to Egypt, Turkey, the Gulf and Pakistan.

I have the rare privilege of being an insider both in the West and in the Muslim world. This book draws from that source: the conversations, reflections and experiences of the last decade enabled me to better understand the House of Islam from the inside. A story I was told in Nigeria helps explain further.

An American billionaire arrived in a large West African village. Rather than announce donations from his philanthropic office, he was keen to see, feel, smell and assess Africa for himself. It was a Friday morning. He parked his jeep by the home of the local tribal chief, and they sat outside the simple house, which was dusty and dwarfed by the shiny black vehicle.

As the African chieftain and the billionaire exchanged pleasantries and drank coconut water, the American saw groups of children carrying large, empty plastic bottles off into the distance.

'Where are those kids heading?' he asked, struck by the sight. 'Shouldn't they be at school?'

'They are going to get water from the river for their families,' the chief replied. 'They go every week around this time. An hour to the river, and an hour back. School will begin when they come back in two hours.'

This was a eureka moment for the American. He identified a need, and thought like a Western businessman: his unique selling proposition would be to build water-well pumps in this and other nearby villages. The children would be able to go to school, get an education, and prosper. He kept his thoughts to himself, and when he returned to New York he instructed his charity to install the pumps with central government cooperation.

The charity employed consultants, engineers, and local experts to implement this 'strategic initiative'. It was strategic because, they kept reiterating at meetings, it would facilitate education and prosperity – the pumps were a vehicle for change.

A year later, the American returned to the African village on another Friday morning. The chief welcomed him, as did the village elders. With true African warmth of spirit, they thanked him for his contribution. But that was not enough. In the language of the corporate and charitable sectors of the West, this was an 'M&E' visit (monitoring and evaluation).

The water pumps looked new and clean. The American sat and made polite conversation with the villagers. Soon enough, throngs of children started to emerge from their homes with empty plastic bottles and the billionaire watched as they headed toward the pumps. But then they kept on walking. They continued walking as they had the year before: toward the river.

'But why?' protested the billionaire. 'Now they have water in the village!'

'Let us speak in confidence,' said the chief. He beckoned the American inside his house, away from their staff.

'My friend,' said the chief, 'your intentions are noble, but you did not ask us if we needed water in the village. Have you seen our tiny houses? Our families are large and many live together in the same bedroom. We send the children away to get water so that the husband and wife can be alone for a while and service their marital relationship!'

Even from his front-row seat, the American billionaire missed the insider knowledge, nuance, and realities of life in West Africa from *within*, and it did not occur to the chief to express them. In much the same way, the West today does not understand Islam and Muslims for who they are.

Western liberal individualism is all-pervasive: to question the West is perceived as backward and primitive. While the West prides itself on being progressive, Islam is now seen as the ultimate retrogressive religion. This is made worse by the daily provision of headlines from within Islam of extremism, terrorism, misogyny, and even slavery, which reinforce feelings of Western superiority.

When the Arab uprisings of 2011 took the world by surprise, overthrowing Western-backed governments in Tunisia, Egypt, Yemen and Libya, we were rightly in awe of a young generation of Arabs. They shouted that they sought *hurriyah*, *karamah*, *adala ijtima'iyah* meaning 'freedom, dignity, and social justice' across the region. Our impulse was to assume that these uprisings were secular. Our elites were programmed to think of 1789 and the French Revolution – at long last democracy had reached the Middle East. How wrong we were.

For those familiar with the Muslim world, the indicators were there. The Arab Spring protests were not held on Saturday nights, but on Friday afternoons. Why? Because that is the day for communal prayers. Every Friday Muslims went in their millions from the mosques to protest against their politicians. These were not radicals, but ordinary Muslims. The dead youth in Egypt and elsewhere were called *shahid* (pl. *shuhada*), martyrs, a word from the Quran that means those who died as witnesses for God. Verses from the Quran accompanied the photos of the dead.

Soon, Christians and Muslims were praying in public squares on Sundays and Fridays. In Egypt's Tahrir Square, Christians formed a protective ring around their Muslim brethren. We overlooked this religion-based energy until extremists appeared and hijacked the protests by burning churches and attacking the Israeli embassy in Cairo. In Tunisia they attacked the American embassy; in Libya they killed the American ambassador. That whirlwind of radicalism sweeping the Middle East found a home in the sectarian spaces of Iraq and Syria, in what our media mistakenly refers to as the 'Islamic State of Iraq and Syria', or ISIS. We award the self-styled caliphate a PR victory by referring to it as 'the Islamic State', even though we in the West do not feel we can pronounce on whether ISIS is Islamic or not.[1]

The West's miscalculations are widespread: whether it was mistakenly amplifying Khomeini's support base, tolerating intolerance from Muslims in the West after Rushdie, standing by and watching in Algeria as the military forbade Islamist democrats from taking power, failing to understand the religious sensitivities of basing US troops in Saudi Arabia, or ignoring warnings that removing a Sunni Saddam Hussein would invite a stronger Iranian Shi'a presence into the Middle East. The West is again blundering by supporting the imprisoning of Islamists en masse in Egypt after the ousting of the country's first Islamist president, Mohamed Morsi, in 2013. Did we learn nothing from the terrorism born of Egypt's torture prisons in the 1960s? We armed and supported Arab and Afghan Islamists to fight Soviet communists in Afghanistan in the 1980s, and they turned into al-Qaeda. Now we are supporting Kurdish communists killing Islamists in Syria.

Lawrence of Arabia promised the same Arab kingdom to multiple tribal leaders to encourage them to rebel against the Ottoman Turks. We actively buttressed Wahhabism in the last century against Turkish Sufism (did we know the difference?), and now we tear our hair in despair as Wahhabist intolerance spreads across the globe. More fighters are joining jihadist conflicts and targeting our own Western Muslim populations.

Again and again the West misreads the political trajectory in the Muslim world. The British government promised in the Balfour Declaration in 1917 a 'Jewish homeland' in Palestine. What peace have we brought to Jews or Arabs since then? The Hussein–McMahon correspondence of 1915–16 colluded to partition Arab lands and depose the Ottoman Turks from their territories. What peace have Arabs in Iraq, Syria or Egypt known except to live under nationalist–socialist dictators? The Sykes–Picot Agreement of 1916 gave birth to nation-states that we carved in Europe reflecting Westphalia. What do these borders mean today as transnational Islamists and jihadists override them in their organisations and operations? We helped popularise 'Ayatollah' Khomeini – there was no such formal title as Ayatollah, meaning 'sign of God', until the nineteenth century. He called himself Ayatollah, so we did, too. Why? He claims authority; we publicise, amplify, and help consolidate his position. We do not judge. The same principle is at play with ISIS today as in 1979. It matters not that the vast majority of Muslims recognise neither the authority of the Ayatollah nor of ISIS.

Religious extremism has gripped Iran's government since 1979. The West does not understand Iran's messianic creed of *Wilayat al-Faqih* (Rule of the Cleric), a form of caretaker government while waiting for their promised messiah, known as the infallible Mahdi. In the name of preparing for this perfect Mahdi, the clerical government justifies its tyrannical rule. For a thousand years, Shi'a Muslims had no such concept of clerics governing in absence of their Mahdi. They patiently waited for its utopia. Khomeini invented this power trick and now Iran seeks to influence other Shi'a communities around the world with this dogma of *Wilayat al-Faqih*. Iran's support for terrorism through its proxies Hezbollah or Hamas against Israel, or its attempt to acquire nuclear weapons are driven by an imaginary apocalyptic war with the West and its allies. The Iranian government has gained each time the West has blundered. In Iraq, after the removal of Saddam Hussein, today it is Iran that is strongest and controls several cities, including Baghdad. In Syria, after the West called for Assad's removal but failed to act, Iran murdered civilian protestors in the hundreds of thousands to consolidate the pro-Iran government in Damascus. If the West does not have the strategic stamina for the long fight necessary in Iraq or Syria, why take half measures and strengthen Iran? It is not only in the Middle East that the West falters.

We kill our own citizens with no recourse to the rule of law. In 2015, the UK's prime minister defended his decision to kill British Muslims in ISIS ranks with drone attacks. In 2012, the United States led the way by killing the American citizen Anwar al-Awlaki, again with drones – in yet another case, the presumption of innocence was waived, the rule of law ignored, and trial by jury denied. If we valued these hallmarks of civilisation, our armed forces would be prepared to die in their defence. With no arrests or trials and this new summary execution, the line between dictatorship and democracy grows thinner. Worse, in this way we fuel the fury of fanatics by confirming their global narrative: that they have no rights and no dignity, and must kill or be killed.

The West keeps on fanning the flames with sensational headlines, penalises the innocent majority with sanctions, and uses drone warfare to deal with symptoms, while ignoring the causes of the conflicts against and within the Muslim world. Our political leaders cannot think beyond five-year election cycles. They strategise for the short term while our extremist enemies think far longer-term.

The West cannot reverse the anti-Americanism that is widespread among the world's Muslims without acknowledging the deep emotions of betrayal, hurt, injustice and humiliation harboured by many – not just radicals. Like the American billionaire, our response is delineated through materialist lenses. We miss what is not in sight, but is all-powerful: feelings, narratives, and perceptions. In this, a chasm has opened up between the modern West and Islam.

Just over a century ago, writers and politicians referred to a global entity, Christendom. Today, that reference is limited to a handful of faith leaders. The deep influences of a strident secularism have chased religion out from the public domain in most parts of the West. What was Christendom has now become 'the West'. Modern, secular philosophers have taken the place of prophets. Jean-Jacques Rousseau (1712–78), godfather of the French Revolution, argued that man is a self-sufficient individual with absolute freedom. Defying tradition and religion, he had five children with his laundrymaid and abandoned every child to a hospice. Family meant nothing to Rousseau. Just as children had no right to a family, there was no divine right of kings or queens. Royalty was overthrown and modern liberty was born.

Modernity's unquestioning adherents regard the Enlightenment project with awe – a blind faith of sorts. We forget that these men were as flawed as their contemporaries and were not always the contrarian liberators we have come to believe. The British philosopher John Gray exposes their regressive thinking. Voltaire, Gray reminds us, believed in a secular version of the anti-Semitic creed of pre-Adamite theory. This was the idea, advocated by some Christian theologians, that Jews were pre-Adamites, leftovers of an older species that existed before Adam.[2] Immanuel Kant, the ultimate Enlightenment guru, asserted that there are innate, inherent differences between the races. He judged white people to 'have all the attributes required for progress towards perfection', Gray writes. Africans were 'predisposed to slavery'. Gray quotes Kant as writing: 'The Negroes of Africa have by nature no feeling that rises above the trifling.' Asians fared little better. John Stuart Mill in his *On Liberty* referred to China as a stagnant civilisation: 'They have become stationary – have remained so for thousands of years; and if they are ever to be farther improved it must be by foreigners.' His father, James Mill, argued in his *History of British India* that the natives could only achieve progress by abandoning their languages and religions. Marx defended colonial rule as a way of overcoming the apathy of village life. 'Progress' was the Enlightenment's salvation. Gray reminds us that: 'All had to be turned into Europeans, if necessary by force.'

Voltaire mocked Catholicism and Islam. Nietzsche declared God dead. Rousseau, Bentham, Voltaire, Mill, Nietzsche, Marx, Lenin and their worldviews are preponderant in the West today. Just as Jews and Muslims venerate prophets and cherish their tombs, so too does the modern, liberal West its philosophers. Rousseau was dug up by the French revolutionaries and reinterred in the Pantheon in 1794, a mark of highest honour in secular France. Bentham was embalmed and remains on display in Bloomsbury at University College London. Lenin, too, was mummified in Moscow.

There is, however, another, lesser-known West: that of Edmund Burke (1730–97). Not widely known beyond the Anglosphere, Burke was a British Member of Parliament and an Irishman. A devout believer in God, he took principled stances against the French Revolution and foresaw the troubles and terror unleashed by it. He viewed the radical attacks on the French monarchy and seizure of Church property as godless. To Burke, Rousseau and

Voltaire offered destruction and darkness. Burke's conservatism was based on religion; he hedged his support for the British monarchy with the need for greater parliamentary power. His political philosophy instituted the oldest political party in the world, the British Conservative Party.

Burke wrote in his seminal *Reflections on the Revolution in France* that: 'Society is a partnership not only between those who are living, but between those who are living, those who are dead, and those who are yet to be born.'[3] He stated that this social partnership connected 'the visible and invisible world'.[4] He considered our time spent on earth as stewardship of the planet's resources for the next generation, and our inheritance from the last generation. As such, he opposed tyranny and injustice against the creation of God. He therefore supported emancipation for the peoples of America, Ireland and India. In France, however, he swiftly concluded that it was the revolutionaries who were the tyrants, for they sought to remove all residue of tradition and impose on society new and abstract ideas.

If the modern West has greater alignment with Rousseau and Bentham, the Muslim world is with the conservative Burke. By conservatism I mean that Muslims strive to preserve the collectively inherited wisdom and goodness of the past. Burke echoed this sentiment in his *Reflections*: 'When ancient opinions and rules of life are taken away, the loss cannot possibly be estimated. From that moment we have no compass to govern us; nor can we know distinctly to what port we steer.'[5] But we have not made the connection between Burke, conservatism and the Muslim world – instead, we have tried to impose Rousseau, Voltaire and Marx through wars, propaganda, education and occupation since Napoleon's invasion of Egypt in 1798. We are yet to understand the power of conservatism for building lasting alliances with the Muslim world.

For example, when asked: 'Are there traditions and customs that are important to you, or not?', majorities in Muslim countries say: 'Yes' – Jordan 96%, Saudi Arabia 95%, Turkey 90%, Egypt 87%. Compare these figures with postmodern societies in the United States of America (54%), the United Kingdom (36%),

France (20%) and Belgium (23%).[6] These figures indicate that tradition, religion and custom are important in Muslim countries as diverse as Egypt and Turkey. If so, what are these traditions, what is this faith that unites more than a billion people around the world?

In contrast to a vanished Christendom, 'the Muslim world' still exists and is vibrant in its faith-based identity. A 2007 Gallup poll of more than thirty-five Muslim nations found that for 90 per cent of Muslims, Islam is an important part of daily life. From spirituality to food, dress code to bathroom etiquette, daily prayers to conduct with elders, a common civilisation and collective history bind Muslims together. From Morocco to Indonesia, Bosnia to Yemen, there is a presence of Islam in language, behaviour, prayers, architecture, food and habits that unite a people. There are, of course, linguistic, cultural, ethnic and political differences, but there is an underlying unity amid the diversity.

'You can always count on the Americans to do the right thing,' said Winston Churchill, 'after they have tried everything else.' Churchill's instincts about America were right then, and they are even more correct today. How many more wars, drone attacks and counter-terror operations will the West undertake? And how many more terrorist organisations will germinate in Muslim countries? The cycle of terrorism and counter-terrorism since 9/11 has not made our world safer. The West forgets that political violence is only a symptom of a much deeper malaise in the Muslim world that we have not fully grasped yet.

There are three dominant currents vibrating across the Muslim world. Every Muslim community feels these today, and has done so in various ways for several decades. Firstly, Arabisation, though the vast majority of the world's Muslims are not Arabs. Only 20 per cent of the Islamic world's population is Arab, but the conflicts and ideologies shaping global Muslim communities stem from Arab countries of the Middle East. Understanding the beating heart of Islam, the Middle East, is therefore vital to understanding the Muslim world. I will define Islam, Muslims, the Quran, and Sunni and Shi'a Muslims in the first chapters.

This disproportionate Arab influence on the Muslim world is driven by several factors: Islam was born in Arabia, the Quran is written in Arabic, the Prophet Mohamed was an Arab, Islam's primary history and personalities were in Mecca and Medina in Arabia, and Muslims around the world turn to pray toward Mecca five times a day. This piety, history, culture and geography matters. Wearing the Arab cultural dress of hijab for women; the centrality of the Palestinian conflict; the popularity of Arab Islamist authors among all Muslims – these, and many more, point to the Arab superiority pulsating through contemporary Islam.

A hundred years ago, Muslims in Turkey or India or Africa were culturally distinct, but now Gulf Arab culture is being adopted as a marker of Muslim authenticity and religious identity in dress, using Arabic religious terms in conversations, names of children, television-watching habits, popularity of Gulf Arab clerics, Muslim reading habits, and even styles of facial hair and female attire. This is not accidental: Saudi Arabia has spent an estimated $200 billion in the last seven decades building mosques, training and exporting clerics, and using its embassies to evangelise its own form of Arabised Islam.

Chapters 7 to 11 deal with the ideas, identities and consequences of this Arabisation that has been accompanied with a rise in levels of anger. Muslim discussions on the meaning and relevance of sharia, Sufism, Islamism, Salafism, Wahhabism, jihadism, and the reappearance of Kharijism are addressed in these chapters.

The second current is Westernisation and the loss of Muslim confidence: the entire Muslim world is being called to embrace secular, liberal, democratic forms of Western government. No other form of consensual government is allowed. If a state is not a democracy, the West will consider it to be an autocracy. Just as in the ancient world, if not a Greek then a barbarian. The West has not allowed for any global grey zones, no other forms of consensual or tribal government that allows for recognition of other civilisations. The North African scholar Ibn Khaldun (d. 1406) wrote about a social contract 200 years before Hobbes. Just as Arabisation has disoriented traditional Muslim equilibrium, so has Westernisation. Those that are not Arabised are often Westernised in name, musical tastes, dress, preference for Hollywood, corporate lifestyle, and use of the English language. Chapters 12 to

16 address the control, positive and negative, of this enduring Westernisation and its discontents in the Muslim world.

The third current is confusion between Westernisation and Arabisation, with efforts to straddle the two, as well as the emergence of hybrids of people who speak fluent English, drive American cars, dine at McDonald's, wear jeans and baseball caps, but want to establish a caliphate or support the destruction of Israel.

Despite the perplexity, as chapters 17 to 20 illustrate, Islam retains an extraordinary hold over its adherents. Muslims value much that has been lost in the modern West. But that does not entail inherent conflict – global openness and coexistence is possible.

What is to be done about the multifaceted malaise in the Muslim world? The conclusion of this book provides ideas for finding new ways forward for a better world.

Through the centuries, Muslims have been taught their sacred tradition of faith via oral transmission of storytelling. The Quran has chapters named after prophets and their stories. The great Sufis passed on their sagacity through tales. Muslims look to the past for validation and vision. Burke took a similar attitude: 'People will not look forward to posterity, who never look backward to their ancestors.'[7]

The modern West closes off the past, and imagines a future of 'creative destruction' as Joseph Schumpeter put it. This is rooted in an assumed belief in incessant progress. To Muslims, history and historic individuals are important: we look behind to look forward; we step back before jumping ahead.

When it comes to individuals and incidents that are household names for Muslims – the events in Karbala, historic personalities such as Rumi, Khayyam, Hafez, Ibn Arabi, Jahanara, Hasan al-Banna, to name a few – I have included details that give the reader a full grasp of the subject.

Most modern Western minds, for instance, find it difficult to believe in miracles, angels, the divine, or an afterlife. But for the fastest-growing group of human beings on the planet, these are vital beliefs. To better understand, let us suspend our prejudices.

PART ONE

A Millennium of Power

What beliefs and rituals have defined Muslims for the past fourteen centuries?

Why does the Sunni–Shiʿa historical divergence matter so much and continue to play out in today's world?

Can historical sharia law become reconciled with the modern world?

Why is Sufism so attractive and popular among Muslims?

I

What is Islam?

'Islam began as a stranger,' said the Prophet Mohamed, who founded the faith in seventh-century Arabia. 'One day,' he predicted, 'it will again return to being a stranger.' Indeed, Islam today is a familiar outsider in our midst in the West.

We use the English word 'religion' to describe Islam, but Islam is not a religion in the Western sense. The *Oxford English Dictionary* definition of religion is cold and alien to a believer in Islam: 'A state of life bound by religious vows; the condition of belonging to a religious order.' There is no mention of the afterlife, the most important and abiding aspect of faith that has a daily impact on the behaviour of a believer, nor is there reference to a divine text, or prophecies. The *OED*'s other explanations include belief in a 'superhuman' – such notions may resonate in the West, but make little sense to the believer in Islam. For an adherent of Islam, a Muslim, God is not a 'superhuman', but an infinite being, a force, an entity, that the finite human mind can never fully comprehend. But the rational Western mind refuses to accept the possibility that it is limited and cannot comprehend. From definitions onwards, we seem to be in constant friction with Islam because we seek to impose on it our history, definitions, expectations and concepts.

'The idea of religion as a personal and systematic pursuit was entirely absent from classical Greece, Japan, Egypt, Mesopotamia, Iran, China and India,' writes the historian Karen Armstrong.

> Nor does the Hebrew Bible have any abstract concept of religion; and the Talmudic rabbis would have found it impossible

to express what they mean by faith in a single word or even in a formula. The only faith tradition that does fit the modern notion of religion as something codified and private is Protestant Christianity, which, like 'religion' in this sense of the word is also a product of the early modern period.[1]

So what is Islam?

Islam is a way of life based on three facets: it is a feeling and a conviction in the existence of one God; it is a belief in the message of the Prophet Mohamed; and it is a path to salvation in the coming life. The Muslim refers to these tenets as *tawhid*, oneness of God; *risalah*, prophethood and the message of Mohamed; and *Akhirah*, the next life or eternity.

For the devout Muslim, Islam's divine touches leave an imprint on daily life. Love for God leads Muslims to imitate the Prophet Mohamed, who was the most beloved of God. Ritual duties that may seem burdensome for some feel light for those in love with the Divine. When a sincere believer awakes, she thanks God for bringing her a new day after a night's sleep. Throughout the day, in her standing, bowing, reciting, prostrating, and praising of God, she emulates the Prophet Mohamed. She puts on her slippers with her right foot first, as he did. In the bathroom, she enters first with her left foot and brushes her teeth from right to left. She leads with her right foot after her ritual ablution and stands facing Mecca to pray.

Everything from her *Halal* breakfast to her choice of modest clothes is influenced by Islam, as explained in the Quran and lived by the Prophet. Through each act, she experiences and tastes the joy of faith and feels her soul growing ever nearer to a state of peace. A materialist, sceptical mind cannot easily surrender or submit to such divine ways. The word Islam shares the same root as the Arabic *istislam*, or surrender, which also leads to another derivative, *salam*, or peace. Through surrender to God, therefore, the soul finds peace.

Islam and its adherents are still loyal to Arabic, the abiding language of the Quran and the Prophet Mohamed. Hardly any Christians today speak or pray in Aramaic, the language of Jesus, but every single one of the world's 1.7 billion Muslims prays in Arabic.[2] Calls to prayer in Arabic sound from the minarets of mosques in the world's Muslim communities, where the faithful even meet and greet each other with *salamu alaykum*, meaning 'peace be upon you' in Arabic. From Indonesia to Bosnia, Muslims' liturgical language is undiluted by the passing of time. That freshness and connection of Muslim roots to seventh-century Arabia is a blessing, and also a curse, as we shall see in later chapters.

When I lived in Damascus in Syria during 2003–5, I was intrigued to hear Syrian Christians use words such as *inshaAllah* meaning 'God willing', or *Alhamdulillah* meaning 'Praise be to God'. Having been born and raised a Muslim, I always assumed those popular Arabic words somehow belonged to us, but this was the city in which St Paul preached, the walls of the city marked his escape from persecution, and the biblical 'street called straight' in Damascus was full of Christian artisans and craftsmen. There, Allah was God. And God was Allah.

The God of Islam is not a different deity to that worshipped by Christians or Jews. Allah is merely the Arabic word for God. In seventh-century Arabia, the Prophet Mohamed called his fellow city folk in Mecca to abandon popular paganism and turn to worship the one God of Adam, Noah, David, Jacob, Joseph, Abraham, Sarah, Hagar, Isaac, Moses and Jesus. Muslims recognise and venerate Old Testament prophets, and believe in Jesus as a mighty messenger of the same God. Why, then, is there a need for Islam, a different pathway from Judaism and Christianity?

Mohamed was a merchant in the city of Mecca born in the year 570 into the noble Quraysh tribe, custodians of the ancient pilgrimage, the annual Hajj. His father, Abdullah, died six months before Mohamed's birth. His mother, Aminah, had dreams in her pregnancy that she was carrying a light inside her that lit up the palaces of Rome and Persia. When she gave birth, her handmaids reported something extraordinary; a child had been born who did not wail and cry as others do, but breathed calmly. Reluctantly, Aminah followed the expectations of the Quraysh tribe and sent her child to the desert for raising and suckling away from the clutter and clamour of Mecca.

The Quraysh valued the desert. Its vastness held secrets for nomadic Arabs. Newborns were often sent to the wilderness to be raised by Bedouin women. There, they breathed fresh air and spoke a purer Arabic. In the desert sands they were free from the corruption of Mecca, where pilgrims to the Ka'bah, home to 360 idols, polluted the poetic language of the Meccan Arabs.

In the year that Mohamed was born, Halima, a foster-mother from the respected Banu Sa'd tribe, arrived in Mecca late one night on a slow, frail she-camel. Her husband asked around, but the wealthier children had already been fostered. They were too late to find a child whose family would pay for his days of desert nursing. There was only Mohamed left.

Halima's husband wanted to postpone the search, but Halima was insistent. 'The baby boy looks blessed,' she said upon seeing Mohamed. 'Let us take him with us. Perhaps God will bless us because we were kind to him.' Not all Arabs were pagans – and many who worshipped multiple deities also believed in a chief god. Some were also known as *haneef*, or monotheists. Halima was one of them.

As they journeyed back to the encampment of Banu Sa'd, Halima started to see changes around her. 'Did you not notice the sudden health of our camel?' she asked her husband and travelling companions when they were back in their desert tents. 'Did you notice that she was faster? And have you seen that her udder is full of milk?'

Halima noticed more about Mohamed. When she breast-fed her own son and her new baby, she told the other women, Mohamed would only drink from one breast, leaving the other for Halima's son.

Halima and her family grew fond of this special child. The two boys would play together in the desert. One day, Halima's son came running to his mother.

'Mother, mother,' he shouted. 'My Qurayshi brother is being held by two strange men! Come!'

Halima rushed to see the young Mohamed looking shocked, but not troubled. The boys recounted how two men in clean white clothes approached Mohamed, laid him down, opened his shirt and washed his heart with holy water and ice. Though Mohamed seemed calm, Halima was worried. She had witnessed and heard of so many extraordinary things happening to this boy that she was no longer sure she could protect him. After much deliberation, she took Mohamed back to Mecca.

Mohamed once again lived with his mother, who secured the support of his grandfather and uncle.

Mohamed was not yet ten when his mother died in al-Abwa, a village near Mecca. Umm Ayman, his mother's helper, was with Mohamed at his mother's death. Years later, she recalled how the boy kept running back to his mother's grave, refusing to return to Mecca. Fifty-seven years later, at the Hajj pilgrimage, with thousands of companions and after his famous last sermon in Mecca, Mohamed returned to his mother's final resting place in al-Abwa. The orphan boy's inner wounds had not healed. Such was the sensitivity, humility and humanity of the man who would lead masses to the one God, Allah.

Soon, marked out as different from such a young age, Mohamed was joining his uncle on business trips to Syria. In Borsa, a town near Damascus, a Christian monk warned his uncle that the boy would face harm in years to come. 'Protect your nephew,' he urged, 'for he is destined for greatness.'

When Mohamed was in his twenties, the lady Khadija, a wealthy Meccan, asked him to take her caravan to Syria and trade on her behalf. A trustworthy manager, Mohamed returned to Mecca with a handsome profit, impressing her family with his business acumen. Soon Khadija, a forty-year-old widow, fell in love with her new merchant trader and proposed to him through her relatives.

With the marriage, Mohamed's reputation as a gentleman of high moral character was secured. His and Khadija's home became the depository of others' valuables. Among the Meccans, he became known as *al-ameen*, or the trustworthy one. He was the keeper of their credit notes and secrets. When there were disputes, people turned to Mohamed for fair arbitration. And yet, the more he was exposed to the city's clamour, corruption and chaos, the more he yearned for solitude. Was this a leftover from his desert childhood? Or had he observed the Christian monks leaving Mecca for their spiritual retreats?

When he needed time on his own, Mohamed would retreat to a cave in Mount Hira, in the suburbs of Mecca. Aged forty and father to three children, Mohamed was given to long periods of pondering the future of humanity, the absence of justice in Mecca, and the widespread worship of multiple gods. For Mohamed, these were signs of ingratitude to the creator, Allah. Meccan paganism worried him. Though Judaism and Christianity presented monotheistic alternatives at that time – indeed, Khadija's cousin was a Christian – Mohamed felt an inner calling for something else.

I have climbed Mount Hira and entered the cave in which Mohamed found solace. It is a steep, forty-minute ascent over a hard rock surface in the daytime Arab heat. The fissure in the mountain's topmost point is small and has adequate space for only one person to move within. The silence, the distance from crowds, and the long days and nights of meditation that he undertook command deep respect. From atop the peak, I could see the centre of Mecca and the Ka'bah, the House of God. The Prophet would have beheld these places as he climbed and descended Mount Hira.

On one such solitary night Mohamed saw someone appear on the horizon. The being, full of light in the dark, and imposing in kindness and majesty, commanded Mohamed to 'read'.

'I am not a reader,' Mohamed responded, fearful. 'I don't read.'[3]

Again the being asked Mohamed to read, and he refused. Then the angel knelt down, embraced Mohamed, and said: 'Read in the name of your Lord who created you. Created mankind from a clot of blood.'

The words that Mohamed repeated in rhyming, authoritative Arabic became the first words of Islam's central text, the Quran, which Muslims believe is a revelation from God.

'Who are you?' asked Mohamed.

'I am Gabriel. You are the last and chosen prophet of God. Go forth and warn your people. Read, in the name of your Lord . . .'

Mohamed shivered with fear, and started to sweat. He rushed out of the cave and headed back to Mecca. In the sky above, he saw the angel Gabriel over him, vast and resplendent.

Islam, the last of the world's three monotheistic faiths, was now born. The Prophet Mohamed continued the Abrahamic tradition of worshipping the one God of Abraham, Isaac, Jacob, Joseph, Moses, Aaron, Jesus, and others. He sought to return Meccans to monotheism. He never claimed to have founded a new faith; he was reaffirming and reviving the worship of one creator.

2

Origins of the Quran

When Mohamed was back home in Mecca, Khadija embraced him.

'Cover me, cover me,' he pleaded. Despite the Arabian heat, he felt cold and flushed with fever, and he questioned himself intensely. Was that really God's angel, or was the devil playing tricks on him? Mohamed doubted his experiences, but his wife did not. She was the first to reassure him. He was doing no harm, she said, and thus no evil would befall him. Keen to soothe him further, she called her Christian cousin, Waraqah bin Nawfal.

When Mohamed told Waraqah what had happened, his facial expression changed.

'It is he, indeed. For it is Gabriel, the messenger from God to his chosen ones.'

With Waraqah's confirmation that Mohamed was indeed God's prophet, Khadija immediately proclaimed: 'There is none worthy of worship except Allah, and you, Mohamed, are the Prophet of Allah.' It was the year 610, or thereabouts, and with this short declaration, the lady Khadija became Islam's first convert.

Soon afterwards, that same day, the Prophet again felt the heaviness of revelation. It was as if a weight was holding him down, and once again he started to recite:

'O thou wrapped up ... Arise and deliver thy warning. And thy Lord do thou magnify. And thy garments keep free from stain. And all abomination shun. Nor expect, in giving, an increase for thyself. But, for thy Lord's cause be patient and constant.'

In Arabic, these verses rhyme and appear in perfect grammar. For the next twenty-three years, God spoke through Gabriel to

Mohamed in this same poetic language. These revelations became the Quran, the sacred scripture of Islam.

Al-Quran, Arabic for 'the recitation', accompanies Muslims through life. Its verses are whispered into the ears of newborn babies. Its shorter chapters are memorised for daily prayers. In marriage ceremonies, the Quran's poetic Arabic tells Muslims of their marital duties. In the final moments of life, the holy book provides comfort as family members recite it around one's deathbed. Most Muslims see the Quran as the literal word of God revealed to the Prophet, but there has always been a debate about whether God 'spoke' those exact verses. Some Muslims believe that the melodic Arabic was inspired by God and then articulated by Gabriel and the Prophet.

When Mohamed had questions, Gabriel appeared with answers. The Quran is a dialogue, a conversation between the Prophet and God. Verse by verse, it quotes the Prophet as he uttered what Gabriel revealed to him: 'Say, He is God, The One and Only. God, the Eternal, Absolute. He begetteth not, Nor is He begotten. And there is none Like unto Him.' (Quran:112)

The Quran differs in many ways from the New and Old Testaments. It is not always coherent or thematic, jumping from theme to theme in a style that can seem inaccessible to a reader unaccustomed to the text. There are no neat paragraphs, no demarcated new beginnings with logical end points. Perhaps the closest analogy is the biblical books of prophecy, such as that of Isaiah.

Grasping this context is difficult for those who have never encountered anything quite like it. In the eighth century, John of Damascus, a rare chronicler and eyewitness of early Islam, mocked the Quran and accused Muslims of collecting stories from unorthodox Christians. A thousand years later, the French Enlightenment writer Voltaire dismissed the Quran as unscientific and full of contradictions. The Scottish thinker Thomas Carlyle, who admired the Prophet Mohamed as one of the 'great men' who changed the course of history, had difficulty with the Quran. He declared it 'toilsome reading', 'insupportable stupidity', and 'a wearisome confused jumble, crude, incondite; endless iterations, long-windedness, entanglement'. Despite his lack of comprehension he detected that 'sincerity, in all senses, seems to be the merit of the Quran'. Carlyle read it in English and therefore missed the richness of the poetic Arabic, but still he intuited the honesty of the Prophet.

Napoleon collected manuscripts of the Quran in Cairo when he invaded Egypt in 1798 and sent back copies of the original Arabic text to France. The words have never changed. There is no 'King James Version', or some Ottoman sultan's rendition of the Arabic text. Sunni and Shi'a Muslims, divided on so many issues, all agree on the Quran. The University of Birmingham's specialists have been studying Napoleon's eighteenth-century acquisitions. They date those Quranic manuscripts as far back as the seventh century, thirteen years after the death of the Prophet. Mohamed's close companion Amr ibn al-Aas, conqueror of Egypt, most likely brought copies of the Quran with him from Medina, the city in which the Prophet settled and preached. To Muslims, the university's findings are not surprising, but neither are they reassuring. They did not have doubts in the first place.

The Quran, Muslims believe, was the result of the miracle sent from God to the Prophet Mohamed and a society absorbed in the art of playing with words and poetry. Just as Moses surpassed pharaoh's magicians and Jesus outperformed the healers of Jerusalem, Mohamed outshone the poets of Mecca. No one could produce verses quite like it. Fourteen centuries later it remains unmatched. Committed to memory by the early believers, written down on parchments and paper by the Prophet's companions, the earliest Muslims, the Quran remains preserved as it was at the time of the Prophet.

Violent extremists cite the Quran today for their cause, but to most Muslims their holy book is anything but violent. All except one of its 114 chapters begin with *Bismillahi Al-Rahman Al-Rahim*, 'In the name of God, the most compassionate, the most merciful.' This daily recital and remembrance of God's mercy and compassion is intended to reflect in the behaviour of the believer. A popular chapter of the Quran is called *Al-Rahman*, The Most Compassionate, but no chapter title invokes war, violence, fighting or killing. Indeed, the Prophet was known for outlawing the common Arab use of the name *Harb*, meaning 'war', for newborns. The Quran's main emphasis reflected the character and the call of the Prophet: to be kind and compassionate. The Quran declares of the Prophet: 'We sent thee not, but as a Mercy for all creatures.' (Quran: 21:107) In an age of warfare and tribal rancour, the Quran was a call to peace.

The Quran's 6,236 verses are broadly divided in two parts: chapters revealed to the Prophet in Mecca, and then, after the year 622, those that were revealed to him in Medina. The Meccan chapters are rich in similes, allegories, and majestic prose that recall the greatness of the next life, a sublime reward for the trials and tribulations faced in this world. The Medina chapters, meanwhile, address the circumstances and conditions of being in Medina, the city-state of which the Prophet was now a worldly leader.

This context of the Quran's chapters is known among Muslim scholars as *Asbab al-Nuzul*: the reasons for revelation. Historically, a Muslim would never come to a conclusion on the meanings of verses without consulting a scholar on the whys and wherefores of a chapter or verse. That culture is changing among Muslims in the information age, where Google and readily available books empower the individual. The Quran, like other books, is becoming a manual. In fact, the context of the Quran is being lost, because every believer is able to access the text directly and become an 'expert'. With this modern ease of entry to the scripture, the old respect is being eroded.

My parents taught me that the Quran always belonged on the highest shelf, just out of easy reach. At home, our Quran was covered in expensive velvet or some other quality cloth. My parents were devout Muslims and their veneration for the Quran, both as a physical book and its message, was the lived reality of an Islam that had a deep impact on the lives of believers. In a recent conversation, Archbishop Justin Welby told me how he admired old Muslims he met in remote parts of Africa who uphold this practice. To convey a similar veneration for the divine, the Archbishop said, he had taken to placing his Bible on the top ledge, too.

In a way, this interaction of the inward conviction and the outward devotion embodies the central message of the Quran. The holy book rarely mentions belief or faith without an accompanying emphasis on doing good deeds. Among its greatest and earliest commentators were Imam Ali (d. 661) and Ja'far al-Sadiq (d. 675). Both emphasised the Quran's multiple meanings; they warned that the text was not to be read, nor its injunctions implemented, literally. Just as God is *Zahir* and *Batin*, outward and inward, His book also has inner and outer meanings. This aspect of the historically multidimensional Quran is beginning to be lost on many Muslims. The House of Islam is losing its connection with the Quran.

3

Who is a Muslim Today?

'Go to Yemen,' the Prophet instructed one of his closest companions, Muadh bin Jabal. 'Call the people to believe in one God. Inform them that we will be brought to account for our actions in this world. If they accept, invite them to pray. Advise them that the poor among them have a right to a small percentage of the riches of the wealthy.'

His words encapsulated the most basic element of Islam: believing in the one God and his messenger, Mohamed, the last of the prophets. Stating these facts is known as the *Shahadah*, or declaration of faith. As long as a person holds them dear, they are Muslim. That is, quite literally, the definition of a Muslim.

For centuries, these beliefs manifested in a rich, diverse Islamic culture that was created by Muslims that were united in their identity by sharing this common and cosmopolitan faith. The Oxford historian John Darwin captures this accurately:

> The cultural life of Islam (in the Ottoman Empire and beyond) was strikingly cosmopolitan. An educated man might seek his fortune anywhere between the Balkans and Bengal. The historian 'Abd al-Latif (1758–1806), born in Shustar at the head of the Persian Gulf, acquired his learning from scholars in Iran. But the hope of advancement took him to India, where his brother was already a physician in Awadh. He became the *vakil* (agent) of the ruler of Hyderabad to the Company government in Calcutta. His view of Indian history was Islamic

> not 'Indian'. For the Islamic intelligentsia, the idea of territorial patriotism to an Ottoman, Iranian or Mughal 'fatherland' was deeply alien. The nation state as the unique focus of loyalty was simply meaningless. In the Ottoman Empire, Muslims (like Christians and Jews) drew their identity from their scripture and religion, not from their language or a concept of race.[1]

Those attitudes have changed. The Ottoman Empire, which ruled vast territories for centuries, is no more. Still, though Muslims are much more nationalist today than they were in the Ottoman or Mughal past, they continue to share a strong, global, religious identity. But where do most Muslims reside in the world? And what does it mean to 'practise' or 'observe' Islam through the oft-cited 'five pillars' of the faith?

Islam was spread through a combination of Arab merchant traders upholding the moral character of faith in their business conduct (fair prices, not cheating, reliable); Arab conquerors expanding the borders of their power to prevent attacks and gain riches; some degree of missionary activity of evangelical Muslims; and most widely disseminated by the charisma and conviction of the mystical Sufis. Often times, it was an amalgamation of all of these strands that led to the speedy advance of Islam. Today, however, the growth of Islam is not due primarily to conversions, but high rates of fertility.

The world's 1.7 billion Muslims live in seven different cultural and geographic spheres. The first is the Arabic-speaking domain from Iraq to Mauritania, home to approximately 400 million Muslims. This is the oldest wing of the House of Islam. The Prophet himself resided in Arabia and sent envoys to neighbouring lands to invite them to join the Muslim community. Only 20 per cent of the Muslim world lives in this realm today. The poetic language of the Quran spread throughout these lands with the early Muslims. Iraq, Syria, North Africa and Egypt all adopted Arabic. Ethnically, therefore, these nations were not originally Arab, only linguistically. This distinction is now rarely made. In fact, the beating heart of Arab nationalism in the 1950s and 1960s lay in Cairo and Damascus, not Riyadh or Doha. Persians and Turks did not start speaking Arabic, though they did embrace the faith.[2]

The Persian sphere, consisting of modern-day Iran, Afghanistan and Tajikistan, is the second zone of the House of Islam. Here, the 100-million-strong population speaks Farsi, Dari or Tajik – different dialects of the same language. Persian Muslims usually have a strong feeling of affinity with the companion of the Prophet Salman al-Farsi (d. 656), the first Persian convert to Islam. As early as 636, the Muslims were engaged in conflict with the Persians, most famously at the Battle of Qadisiya (636–7). By 750, after more than a century of trade and taxation for protection of Persian municipalities by the Muslims, the Persian presence within Islam was strong enough to topple the Umayyad rulers and replace them with a new dynasty, that of the Abbasids, descendants of the family of the Prophet.

Today, Iran is home to the largest Shi'a Muslim population in the world. Of its 80 million populace, the vast majority are adherents of Shi'a Islam, with its greater emphasis on respecting the household of the Prophet. Away from Iran, and from Iraq, Lebanon, Bahrain and parts of Pakistan, Afghanistan and Azerbaijan, most Muslims are not Shi'a.

Sub-Saharan Africa, home to some 250 million Muslims, is the third zone. Islam first spread to Mali and Senegal in the seventh century. Several companions of the Prophet Mohamed were buried in Chad, pointing to an Islamic presence there in the first century of Islam. By the eleventh century, nearby Ghana had a powerful Islamic kingdom. Arabs and Persians traded and settled on the coastal areas of east Africa, Kenya and Somalia, bringing Islam to those regions. Islam only arrived in Nigeria, with its varied languages, somewhere around the tenth century. For Africans, Bilal al-Habashi, a beloved companion of the Prophet and the first African convert to Islam, has special resonance. Bilal was the first muezzin, the first to call people to prayer from the roof of the Prophet's mosque in Medina.

The fourth sphere is the Indian subcontinent. Mohamed bin Qasim, a general of the Umayyad Caliphate (661–750), conquered

Sindh in 710, but it was the gentle Sufis, with their music, miracles, mysticism and meditation, who spread Islam throughout India from the tenth century. Today, Pakistan, India, Bangladesh, Burma, Nepal and Sri Lanka make up this domain, which has the world's highest concentration of Muslims, around 400 million. The Mughal empire consolidated and codified Islam in this region from the sixteenth century.

The fifth concentration is Turkic. It spans around 170 million Muslims who speak mostly Turkish, but also include others of backgrounds such as Azeri, Chechens, Chinese Uighur, Uzbek, Kirghiz and Turkmen. Turks conquered and took Central Asia from the Persians in 1071 during the battle of Manzikert (Malazgirt, in present-day Turkey). This was the precursor to the Seljuk Muslim empire's conquest of Anatolia, which led to the Ottomans' eventual seizure of Constantinople in 1453. The Turkic sphere, care of the Ottomans, ruled over the entire Middle East for six centuries, dominating the Arabic-speaking hinterlands.

Sixth is the Malay area of South East Asia, which consists of Indonesia, Malaysia, Brunei, and sizeable minorities in Thailand and the Philippines. More than 200 million Muslims live here. Islam arrived relatively late in this location, incrementally from the thirteenth to fifteenth centuries. Sufi traders from Arabia, particularly the descendants of the Prophet from the Hadhramaut valley in Yemen, converted the first Muslims in this part of the world.

The seventh and final home for Muslims is in the West. Roughly 60 million of today's Muslims live in the West as minorities and new immigrant communities in, for example, France, Germany, Britain and the United States, but also as older, settled majorities in countries such as Albania, Kosovo and Bosnia.

But what does it mean to be a Muslim?

To be a 'practising Muslim' or an 'observant' one, a believer needs to act on his or her faith. And what should a believer practise or observe?

The Prophet taught that Islam is 'built on five'. Based on that hadith, or saying of the Prophet, Muslims teach and uphold the 'five pillars of Islam', actions that lend a feeling of unity and common purpose to believers from Indonesia to Morocco. A Muslim from Turkey or Bosnia may be white and Europeanised, but they will feel at home observing these ubiquitous rituals, whether in black Sudan or brown Bangladesh. Each one of the five pillars is mentioned in the Quran, meaning that they are broadly accepted by all mainstream Muslims.

The saying of and believing in the *Shahadah* is the first pillar. The second is the five prayers to which the Prophet referred. The first, *Fajr*, is at dawn. *Dhuhr*, the second, is at noon. The third, *Asr*, comes in the late afternoon, *Maghrib* at dusk, and *Esha*, the fifth and last, about an hour after sundown. These daily prayers are the milestones in a believer's day. They connect the faithful to the divine and remind Muslims why they are on this earth: to worship the creator, be upright with others, and prepare for their return to Allah when they die.

On his deathbed, the Prophet warned Muslims not to abandon their prayers. Turning to those surrounding him, he declared: '*Al-salah, al-salah* – The prayer, the prayer.'

The five daily prayers remain central across the Muslim world. The call to prayer or *adhan* fills the air as the muezzin invites believers to pray at the mosque. The Prophet taught that the rewards from God were higher in collective prayers, which strengthened this sense of Muslim community, or *jama'ah*. But a believer may also pray alone, whether at home or on an aeroplane. There is disagreement among the faithful as to when exactly these five daily prayers should be performed – some Muslims pray at five separate intervals, while others merge them. When the Prophet introduced the idea of daily prayers it was neither new nor odd. Standing, bowing and prostrating in worship were normal among Jews and early Christians, and still common in Catholic and Orthodox devotion.

Believers repeat the ritual of these prayers throughout their lives. First, while standing during prayers, they recite in Arabic the first chapter of the Quran, the short and oft-repeated *al-Fatiha*, or opening:

Praise be to God,
The Cherisher and Sustainer of the Worlds;

Most Gracious, Most Merciful;
Master of the Day of Judgement;
Thee do we worship;
And Thine aid we seek.
Show us the straight way,
The way of those on whom
Thou hast bestowed Thy Grace,
Those whose portion is not wrath,
And who go not astray.

Then, bowing, the believer says: *Glory to My Lord, Most Magnificent.*

And, finally, in prostrating: *Glory to My Lord, Most High.*

Arabs and Muslims of the East wear clothes that are comfortable to pray in, garments that are not too revealing when bowing and prostrating. Most non-believers do not observe the private moments of Muslim faith in the mosque. Worshippers wash their hands, face and arms before prayer. They wipe their heads, and clean their feet with water.

Prayer and the need for daily ablutions drove the advanced water technology of Muslim civilisations – the fountains and wells in the illustrious mosque courtyards of Córdoba. Society centred on regular prayer in other ways, too. The large mosques in Baghdad, Damascus and Cairo were built facing Mecca, as that is the direction in which Muslims pray. Marketplaces, hospitals and schools were then located around the mosques, because that was where the masses gathered for worship every day. Craftsmen and calligraphers won commissions to adorn the mosque walls with Quranic verses and poetry. In short, Muslim civilisation was built around the five daily prayers.

Giving alms, or *Zakah,* to the poor is the third pillar of Islam. Every Muslim is expected to give 2.5 per cent of their surplus wealth to the needy. This money is meant to fund schools, hospitals, orphanages, travel lodges and mosques. In the past, the money sometimes made it into state treasuries. Today, some Muslim governments administer *Zakah*, but most Muslims distribute it privately among those who are qualified to receive it.

The fourth pillar of Islam is perhaps the hardest to uphold, which also makes it the most satisfying. For an entire month of the lunar year, Ramadan, healthy Muslims fast from dawn to dusk.[3] During the day, drinking, eating, smoking and sexual contact are forbidden; Muslims in the hottest countries or the coldest do not let one drop of water pass their lips. When the sun goes down, there is a special joy as families and local communities break the fast together with dates and water as the Prophet Mohamed did. A feast follows the regular dusk prayer. After night prayers, there is an additional, longer prayer, the *Tarawih*, in which the entire Quran is recited over the course of the month.

The final and fifth pillar was once the hardest, but now, in a world connected by planes and trains, it comes with relative ease: the pilgrimage to Mecca, or Hajj. The airport at Jeddah feels like most other airports, and the motorway to Mecca is now laid with tarmac, busy with cars, and has road signs and advertisements. Throughout most of Muslim history, pilgrims would come on foot, horse or camel to this city in the Arabian desert. As they made their months-long journey, they recited: 'Here we are oh God, here we are at your service – *Labbaik, allahumma labbaik.*' Muslims still raise this chant, and in this there dwells a feeling of connecting to the Divine as they recall Abraham, Ishmael and Mohamed using these words. From Egypt, it used to take two months to reach Mecca. From India or Africa, it took four. As believers made their arduous journey, they relied on God for protection and a safe return home.

My visits to Mecca have always left me wanting to return again. It is still a commercial city, but the prayer-filled, serene quarters surrounding the Ka'bah fill every visitor with awe.

About 200 metres from the Ka'bah, Muslims walk up a small hilltop known as Safa where thousands of pilgrims congregate. From Safa, Muslims walk to Marwa, a nearby hill. Walking, sometimes running, between these hills, believers remember Hagar's search for water for the baby Ishmael. Hagar was Abraham's lawful lover, in addition to his wife Sarah, but Muslims refer to Hagar as his 'second wife'. Muslims all grow up knowing this story from parents, partly mentioned in the Quran and partly told by the Prophet. Hagar ran from Safa to Marwa seven times. Hagar was desperate and lonely, but she relied on God and her love of Abraham and Ishmael. This self-sacrifice brought her divine help. When she returned to check on Ishmael, a small well had appeared beside the infant. The Well of Zamzam still stands in Mecca today.

For millennia, pilgrims have drunk water from this well and remembered Hagar's trust in God, and His help for a pure-hearted woman, a lover of God and Abraham, in the Arabian Desert. Muslims are descendants of Ishmael. Our Jewish cousins are descendants of Isaac. We share the same patriarch in Abraham, who God promised in the Bible would have 'descendants as numerous as the stars in the sky'.[4]

In Mecca, where pilgrims poured in from all over the world, a believer would have met saints and scholars. The keepers of the Well of Zamzam would have poured water from precious jugs passed down through generations for the faithful, and the pilgrim would have walked barefooted through Safa and Marwa on paths that were not paved with marble as they are today. Male pilgrims wearing two pieces of unstitched cotton and women in modest clothes would have fulfilled the rituals of the Hajj that honour Abraham, Hagar and the Prophet Mohamed. After Mecca, Muslims would travel to see Medina, where their beloved Prophet established the first Muslim community, and his final resting place. There, they would stand before his tomb and recite poetry. They would visit the graves of his family and companions, feeling that link of faith through the centuries. Then, each pilgrim would slowly head homeward to Africa, India or Indonesia. The modern Muslim gets home much faster. They absorb the blessings of the Hajj and try to retain the spiritual uplift of the fifth pillar of Islam on their return to normal life. Those who have made the journey are known as *Hajji*, a title of honour.

The matter of who leads Muslims in upholding the five pillars causes angst among many Muslims, and confusion among non-Muslims. Muslims do not require religious leadership; Islam is not like Catholicism and has no equivalent of clergy or a pope. The Prophet stressed repeatedly that he bequeathed the Quran, his family and his own example as guiding lights for Muslims.

The survival, indeed the thriving of Islam for over a millennium, is ample evidence that the faith's spiritual core is mostly robust and intact. But in worldly, material, terms, Muslims are suffering from disunity and have no centralised political leadership as they did under the Ottoman and Mughal empires. Some Muslims crave a caliphate because of the glory and power associated with past Muslim civilisations. The so-called ISIS does not uphold this magnificence for most Muslims. When the Prophet died, his companions selected a caliph or leader in Abu Bakr, the Prophet's closest confidant and father of his favourite wife, Ayesha. The title caliph meant representative; Abu Bakr was seen as the Prophet's agent after his death.

That first period of the caliphate of the four caliphs after the Prophet's death lasted only thirty years, from 633 to 661. The governor of Damascus, Mu'awiya, gave rise to a new order by assuming the caliphate for himself after the assassination of the fourth caliph, Imam Ali, in 661. Known from 661 to 750 as the Umayyad caliphate, it was based in Damascus, as Islam expanded beyond the deserts of Arabia, and it was under the full control of Mu'awiya. By the ninth century, the Umayyad caliphate had disintegrated in the face of rival caliphates in Spain, subsequently home to a glorious Muslim civilisation in Andalusia. Soon, in the Arab lands, the Abbasids (750–1258) took political leadership of Islam from Baghdad. Then the Mamluks (1250–1517), headquartered in Cairo, overlapped with the Seljuks (1077–1307) in central Asia and then Iran. The Ottomans (1281–1924) ruled Arabia and central Asia, expanding into North Africa, and Eastern Europe by the sixteenth century. In parallel, the Safavids (1501–1732) ruled the Persian Muslims, and the Mughals (1526–1858) ruled the Indians. Throughout, there were other rivals for power, holdouts, and most importantly overlap in the smaller sultanates in India and South East Asia. Muslim sub-Saharan Africa, meanwhile, was divided into princedoms. Rarely, since the Prophet, has there been a single ruler of all the world's Muslims. Rivalry, competition and even warfare between caliphate claimants was the norm.

It is often assumed that Islam was 'spread by the sword', though perhaps this impression is influenced more by today's headlines than historical fact. The Prophet Mohamed returned to Mecca from Medina in 629 victorious. After years of killing, torture and boycott at the hands of the Meccan elite, he would have been fully within his rights by the standards of the time to raze their houses to the ground in revenge. Instead, he rode into Mecca on a mule, his head lowered in humility, and forgave the city's residents with a general amnesty. That same spirit, in general, continued among his people. The Oxford historian Peter Frankopan in his magisterial *The Silk Roads* writes:

> In fact, it appears that the Muslim conquests were neither as brutal nor as shocking as the commentators make out. Across Syria and Palestine, for example, there is little evidence of violent conquest in the archaeological record. Damascus, for instance, the most important city in northern Syria, surrendered quickly after terms were agreed between the local bishop and the attacking Arab commander. Even allowing for some poetic licence, the compromise was both reasonable and realistic: in exchange for allowing churches to remain open and untouched and for the Christian population to remain unmolested, the inhabitants agreed to recognise the overlordship of new masters. In practice what this meant was paying tax not to Constantinople and to the imperial authorities, but to representatives of 'the prophet, the caliphs and the believers'.[5]

Arab occupation of surrounding lands and leadership over Muslims did not last. Non-Arabs would come to dominate the Muslim world. The Ottoman Turks ruled Sunnis, for instance, for 600 years until the early twentieth century. After the end of Abbasid rule in 1258, it was the Turks, Indians and Persians that dominated Muslim history. The Ottomans, Mughals and Safavids were not Arabs, but their influence and institutions have shaped Islam.

Today, though 80 per cent of the House of Islam is not Arab, Arabs and conflicts in the Arab world set the global geopolitical and religious agenda. In fact, the Muslim world is undergoing a renewed Arabisation, led by Saudi Arabian-influenced

Salafism and the international activism of the Egyptian Muslim Brotherhood, as we shall see.

There were always multiple claimants to Muslim leadership, and the vying started very early in Islam's history. Only fifty years after the Prophet's passing away, the peace that he pursued was pilloried. Bloodshed and destruction began with the battle of Karbala.

4
The Sunni–Shi'a Schism

The word 'Karbala' evokes emotions in every erudite Muslim. Karbala, now a major city in central Iraq, is where early Muslims clashed over the future of the caliphate. The battle that raged there – or rather the massacre there of the Prophet's progeny in 680 AD – is a raw wound for most Muslims. Shi'a and Sunni interpret moments of Islamic history completely differently. Where Shi'a see the Prophet declaring that Ali was his successor, Sunnis see something else entirely.

The divergence between Shi'a and Sunni was a direct result of the Prophet not declaring a successor. Nothing has created a more profound division among Muslims than this. How could he name a replacement? There were to be no prophets after him; Mohamed was the last of God's messengers in the Abrahamic line of monotheism. Within a century of his passing, however, Muslims loyal to the Umayyad caliphate would kill the Prophet's own grandson, Imam Husain, at Karbala, along with his seventy-two travelling companions.[1]

This 1,200-year-old split had its roots even before Karbala, however. Disagreements over who would succeed the Prophet sowed seeds of bitter division soon after his death. As Ali, the Prophet's son-in-law, cousin and close friend, made the burial arrangements, Abu Bakr, Mohamed's good friend and father-in-law, met with the Prophet's companions to discuss who should lead the Muslims. Over three decades, during the reigns of Abu Bakr as first caliph (632–4), then Omar (634–44), and then Othman (644–56), ever-increasing numbers of Muslims would come to believe that Ali should be caliph. When the Prophet died, however, many thought that 28-year-old Ali was too young to lead. Others thought he was too pious and mystically minded for the dark arts of politics. Still, some Muslims insisted that Ali, not Abu Bakr, was the Prophet's rightful first heir. Ali's followers were known as *Shi'at Ali*, or supporters of Ali. Indeed, the word Shi'a means 'community' or 'supporters' in Arabic. After Ali, the Shi'a backed his sons, the great imams Hasan and Husain, and then their children.

To this day, Shi'a maintain loyalty to Ali's bloodline, while Sunnis stress allegiance to the Prophet. Ali was married to Fatima, Mohamed's beloved daughter. They were tied to the Prophet, as were their children. Shi'a Muslims claim that to love the Prophet is to love his family. Their opponents, however, claimed that Islam concerned meritocracy, not lineage.

This is not an abstract theological and historical dispute: Muslims are still living through this unresolved quarrel. Lesley Hazleton's powerful book *After the Prophet* captures this conflict accurately – I have drawn from her and my own teachers. Across the Islamic world, the Sunni–Shi'a dynamic drives politics, protests and conflict, as is evident from just the past fifty years. Shi'a symbolism, for instance, fuelled the 1979 revolution in Iran. Ayatollah Khomeini (1902–89), the figurehead of the mass opposition to Shah Mohammed Reza Pahlavi (1919–80), referred to the monarch as Yazid, the name of the caliph who killed Imam Husain. In the Iran–Iraq War in the 1980s, Karbala and Husain's martyrdom took centre stage in propaganda efforts inside Iran. That Shi'a ethos of sacrificing oneself in pursuit of justice gave birth to the first Shi'a Muslim suicide bomber who drove a truck into a US base in Beirut in 1981.[2]

Saudi Arabia has made opposing the Shi'ism of Tehran a central plank of its foreign policy since 1979. The Saudi state was born in 1932, mired in blood spilled by its founder, Mohamed bin Abdul Aziz al-Saud, who, under Sunni Salafi influences, killed

Shiʿa Muslims in the eastern provinces of Arabia and sent Saudi forces to ransack the shrine of Imam Husain in Karbala. Hardline reformist Sunnis, known also as Salafis, consider tombs an emblem of polytheism and consider the physical destruction of shrines to be a virtue. To date, 95 per cent of the oldest buildings in Mecca that stood for more than a thousand years have been demolished.[3] Shiʿa Muslims make up the largest religious minority in Saudi Arabia, yet they are banned from gathering in the mosques of Mecca and Medina.

In January 2016, Saudi Arabia beheaded an influential Saudi Shiʿa cleric, Sheikh Nimr al-Nimr, amid accusations that he had called for self-rule in the oil-rich Shiʿa-dominated Saudi eastern province. Iran and Saudi Arabia then severed diplomatic ties. Several Saudi allies followed suit, taking the side of the Sunni kingdom against the Shiʿa republic.

In Pakistan, suicide blasts and other attacks have targeted innocent Shiʿa in a major sectarian surge over the last ten years. Pakistan was founded by Muslims from Shiʿa backgrounds, including Muhammad Ali Jinnah, the country's founder, an Ismaili Shiʿa, yet anti-Shiʿa rhetoric in the media, mosques and schools has fed an increase in Sunni extremist violence. Thousands of Shiʿa have been killed in the past decade. Millions of Shiʿa Pakistanis live in fear.

In parts of Iraq and Syria, a civil war is under way between Sunni and Shiʿa, abetted by countries and organisations that identify as Shiʿa and support Bashar al-Assad on one side, and regional Sunni backers supporting rebels on the other. The Damascus regime is led by the Alawi Shiʿa sect, which is named after Ali. Iran, Iraq and Hezbollah provide money and manpower to bolster Syria's government, as well as preparing thousands for martyrdom in that fight. They are also invested in protecting shrines in Syria sacred to Shiʿa.[4]

In contrast, Sunni Turkey, Saudi Arabia, Qatar, and the most extreme of the world's Salafi-jihadi fighters support insurgents who claim to represent Syria's Sunni majority. This war was not sparked by the Sunni–Shiʿa schism, yet the conflict has taken on the dynamics of the divide. As regional powers chose their sides in Syria, identity, faith and history made their inevitable appearance.

The removal from power in 2003 of Iraq's Saddam Hussein, a Sunni dictator in a Shi'a-majority country, led to Iran growing closer to Iraq's new Shi'a government. The rise of ISIS and al-Qaeda's Sunni extremists inside Iraq, as well as their attacks on Shi'a shrines and prominent Shi'a figures, is driven by a sectarianism that few in the West or outside Muslim-majority countries truly understand or feel.

Sunni Muslims mostly live in blissful ignorance of Shi'a attitudes towards those the former venerate. No figure epitomises this divide more than the Prophet's youngest wife, the Lady Ayesha. Sunni Muslims universally revere her for several reasons. She was the daughter of Abu Bakr, the Prophet's best friend. From Ayesha we know of the Prophet's private habits as a husband and lover. Muslim men for generations have tried to emulate the Prophet based on Ayesha's teachings. The Prophet loved her dearly. Her strong personality, wit and beauty made her his favourite. It was in her chamber, resting his head on her thighs, that he breathed his last breath. Sunnis know her as *Umm al-Mumineen*, mother of the believers.

A verse of the Quran provided Ayesha with that epithet. But it was not easily attained. Ayesha travelled with the Prophet often, and joined his expeditions. One day, on one of these excursions, she left the caravan to attend a call of nature in the desert. Then Ayesha lost her necklace, a gift from Mohamed, beside a bush and went to retrieve it. Unaware that she had yet to return to her camel-top carriage, the convoy continued home to Medina. As Ayesha waited for the convoy to return for her, a young companion of the Prophet, Safwan, passed by and took the mother of the believers back to Medina on his camel. The people of the city started spreading rumours that she was having an affair with Safwan. The Prophet himself was in some sadness as Medina murmured, and he avoided spending time with his beloved wife. Months went by. Ali encouraged the Prophet to leave Ayesha and end his troubles. She never forgave Ali for this unwanted counsel.

Soon, God absolved Ayesha of any wrongdoing. Gabriel came from the highest heavens proclaiming her innocence. The Quran declares her *mubarra'a*, or blameless. For Sunni Muslims, she could do no wrong. God was her ultimate guarantor of purity and fidelity to the Prophet. Her love of the Prophet, and his dedication to her, returning to his Lord while resting on her, gives her an unrivalled status in Sunni Muslim hearts and minds.

Ayesha would go on to battle Ali, riding at the head of 10,000 soldiers to contest Ali's claims to the caliphate. For this and her general dislike of Ali, the Shi'a have constantly cursed Ayesha and her father Abu Bakr. At the mausoleum of the Prophet in Medina, Muslims visit Ayesha's chamber, where the Prophet died and was buried. There, beside his resting place, are the tombs of Abu Bakr and Omar. Sunni Muslims hail the Prophet, and the first caliphs Abu Bakr and Omar. Many Shi'a Muslims greet the Prophet with prayers of peace and curse the latter two.

Where Sunni Muslims venerate Ayesha, the Shi'a tell a very different story. For them, Ayesha aimed to secure the caliphate and power for her father, Abu Bakr. To do so, she administered poison and killed the Prophet. For a thousand years, this stunning Shi'a claim, capable of sparking serious conflict, has been written in books and taught by Shi'a clerics. Most Sunni Muslims have turned a blind eye for the sake of communal coexistence, but in the age of Twitter and free-flowing information, this accusation, heinous to Sunnis, is being revived by Shi'a leaders, who depict Ayesha, her father Abu Bakr, and others as murderers. 'The greatest pain is the loss of our Holy Prophet. Equally painful is the fact that he was murdered, yet we can't publicly discuss it,'[5] says one tweet by a well-known Shi'a scholar. It is only a matter of time before a populist Sunni cleric highlights such Shi'a beliefs, which are deeply offensive to Sunni Muslims. The fire of Sunni–Shi'a fighting still risks spreading, and spreading further yet.

What exactly happened in Karbala? Why are Sunni and Shi'a still fighting?

The Prophet's two grandsons, Hasan and Husain, were loved and popular in Mecca and Medina, Islam's home cities. Sons of the Prophet's pious daughter, the Lady Fatima, and the gallant Imam Ali, they were born a year apart, in 625 and 626 respectively. The companions of the Prophet often saw the five relatives together. Collectively, the Prophet and the believers called them

Ahl al-Bait, or 'People of the House'. The Quran refers to the Prophet's family as being purified by God, meaning that they were not as prone as others to sinning and fallibility. The Prophet would cover them under his shawl to pray together. In the mosque, Hasan and Husain would jump on their grandfather's shoulders as he stood in prayer. He would kiss and hold them tightly, as though he knew that calamity lay ahead for his grandsons.

In March 632, the Prophet stood before a vast crowd of Muslims on Mount Arafat near Mecca and delivered what we now know as his farewell sermon or final address. 'Lend me an attentive ear,' he began. 'I know not if after this year I shall ever be among you again.' Addressing the believers, numbering tens of thousands, he warned against racism and said that no Arab was superior to a non-Arab. Piety, not skin colour, was the only thing that marked one man as superior to another, he told the crowds. In Islam, social ascendance is based on faith and devotion. He called on the Muslims to treat women well, reminding them that women had rights over their men. He reaffirmed in his speech that the life and property of a believer were sacred, and not to be violated by force or vigilante groups, as was the practice of pre-Islamic tribal Arabs. After him, he reminded the Muslims, there would be no other Prophet. And he said that he was leaving two touchstones as guides for Muslims, the Quran and the *Ahl al-Bait*. He then lifted his blessed face to the heavens and asked: '*Allahumma hal ballaght?*', meaning: 'My Lord, have I conveyed your message?' The Prophet's heart, mind and soul connected the worldly and the divine. He was a vessel for transmitting the transcendental, not for ordaining who was to lead the Muslims after his death.

The Prophet had named no successor at the sermon, for nobody could assume his office. But that is not how the Shi'a recall history.

On his journey back to Medina, at a well in the desert called Ghadir Khumm where he and his companions were resting, the Prophet pointed to Ali. 'To whomever I was a master, Ali is their master,' he said. Was the Prophet now naming a successor? If so, why do this in front of a smaller crowd, and not before the vast crowds in Mecca? The word he used was *mawla*, which is also Arabic for tribal protector, overlord, friend or patron.[6]

Within the year, the Prophet fell ill with flu and the Muslim community was concerned about his well-being. One day, he left his wife Ayesha's room, where he was resting, and headed for the prayer niche where he usually led worshippers. Abu Bakr, the imam in that evening's prayer, began to step back when he saw the Prophet. Mohamed smiled and insisted that Abu Bakr continue. In this key point of Muslim life, the Prophet wanted Abu Bakr to lead. Sunni Muslims see this as the Prophet choosing Abu Bakr as his successor.

Ali was only twenty-eight years old when the Prophet died. Abu Bakr was a seasoned, wise and widely respected 61-year-old man. Ali's supporters might have felt snubbed, but Abu Bakr lasted only two years as the first caliph of Islam, ruling from 632 to 634, when he died naturally. After him, Omar was selected as second caliph by a group Abu Bakr had nominated to choose who would follow him. Omar ruled for ten years, from 634 to 644, until a Persian servant angered by the Muslim conquest of Persia assassinated him. After him, the elderly and aristocratic Othman ruled for twelve years, from 644 to 656, until rebels opposed to his policies killed him. And then, finally, Medina's elite chose the great Imam Ali as caliph. He ruled from 656 until 661. He was killed by the Kharijites, the first extremist sect within Islam opposed to Ali's arbitrations and peacemaking between warring factions of Muslims. These four caliphs came to be known as the *Rashidun*, or the rightly guided, among Muslims. After Ali, it was widely accepted – and expected – that the mantle of leadership had returned to the *Ahl al-Bait*, and that Imam Hasan would govern after his father.

But the cunning governor of Damascus, Mu'awiya, who was appointed by Othman and controlled vast wealth and armies of men, kept Hasan from his rightful place. Hasan was cajoled into conceding any claims to the caliphate. To prevent bloodshed and further discord after the killing of three of the first four caliphs of Islam, Hasan agreed to live a life of scholarship and prayer in Medina, on condition that after Caliph Mu'awiya, Islamic rule would return to the Prophet's family. His brother, Imam Husain, would become the sixth caliph of Islam and he would govern from Medina, the city of the Prophet.

From his new and famously lavish home in Damascus, Caliph Mu'awiya agreed to Hasan's concessions and vowed to honour Husain as the leader of the believers. Muslims assumed that Mu'awiya was preparing to hand the reins back to the much-loved Husain, but he maintained control of the Islamic empire for twenty years. In the meantime, Mu'awiya's son Yazid was gaining a reputation for corruption and cruelty. The normally reticent Syrian historian Ibn Katheer (d. 1301) confirmed what people around the soon-to-be caliph Yazid said: that he was frequently drunk. He liked keeping the company of young boys, a euphemism for paedophilia. He held bear fights. He kept several monkeys as pets, which he blindfolded and mounted on horses to see what havoc they would wreak. He did not seem like a believer in the faith of the Prophet Mohamed.

What Islam was this? the Muslims asked.

Mu'awiya was taken ill in the year 680. Rather than honour his word that Imam Husain would become caliph, he wrote letters to his regional governors, ordering them to pledge allegiance to his son, Yazid. They followed the order. In April 680, Yazid was proclaimed caliph from Damascus.

The news reached Husain in Medina. His supporters in several cities in what is now Iraq sent him saddlebags full of letters pledging allegiance to him, not to Caliph Yazid. What was Husain to do? Yazid's governor in Medina was ordered to arrest him. Husain gathered his family members and headed for Mecca, his ancestral city, to meet more allies, friends and supporters. Letters and delegations from Iraq, at that time the second home of Islam after Syria, kept pouring in. From Iraqi cities, large armies of Muslims urged him to come and lead them. In Mecca, Husain's supporters rejected Yazid, but the new caliph sent word: 'If Husain was tied to the walls of the Ka'bah, he is not safe – we will kill him.'

Not wishing to bring more war and death to the sacred city that had persecuted his grandfather a generation earlier, Husain left Mecca in September 680 and headed for Iraq, where thousands had written to him pledging support. 'Hurry to us, O Husain,' they pleaded. 'The people are waiting for you, and are committed to none but you. Take your rightful place as the true heir of the Prophet, his grandson, his flesh and blood through Fatima, your mother. Bring back power to where it belongs, to Iraq. We will drive out the Syrians under your banner. We will reclaim the soul of Islam.' Husain sent his own delegation to Iraq, and they confirmed that an army of 12,000 men was ready. For twenty years, since his father Caliph Ali's murder, he had waited patiently.

Since his grandfather's death when he was an infant, Husain had lived his entire life in the shadow of caliphs. Now in his mid-fifties, he and his household were the custodians of his grandfather's faith. He left Medina accompanied by his own family. Eighteen of the women and children were his and his brother's immediate family members. Husain's instinct was not to trust Caliph Yazid, not to leave behind the great-great-grandchildren of the Prophet.

As he left Medina for Mecca, and then Mecca for Iraq, Husain kept saying: 'I do not seek harm, or corruption of this nation, but I seek justice. We must do what is right and end what is evil. I want the message of Islam, granted by my grandfather, to proceed.' This was Husain at his best. It was also a manifestation of an ideal Islam, pursuing justice and freedom from tyranny against all odds. The days ahead would be full of sacrifice, pain and tears. In the darkness of night, Husain turned to his seventy-two travelling companions and gave them permission to leave. 'It is night and you can leave me without embarrassment of being seen to be leaving my family and me. None shall know; and I forgive you. So please leave without discomfort.'

His companions refused to abandon him, however, and Husain was intent on reaching Iraq, despite the dangers that lay ahead. 'The hearts of Iraqis may be with you,' warned a messenger who rode from Kufa, capital of his father Ali's years as caliph, to meet Husain. 'But I fear their swords belong to Yazid. I ask you by God to return to Mecca.'

Mecca's governor, meanwhile, fearing for Husain's life, sent messages pleading with him to return and offered 'safe conduct, kindness, generosity and protection'. Husain was the grandson of Mohamed. The Prophet Mohamed taught his family and companions that once a prophet puts on his armour for war, he never returns home. He fights to be victorious in this world, or a martyr in the next. Husain replied: 'The best guarantee of safe conduct is from God. Man journeys in darkness, and his destiny journeys towards him.'

Still other messengers caught up with Husain and his companions as they travelled toward Kufa. Fear was widespread. Husain must retreat, the messengers told him, and wait for a better time to make his move. His father, Imam Ali, had accepted arbitration. His elder brother Hasan had opted for abdication. But Husain was determined neither to arbitrate, nor abdicate. He wanted to rejuvenate Islam with his blood. For Muslims today, both Sunni and Shi'a, Imam Husain's journey to Iraq is the finest illustration of courage, self-sacrifice, and the pursuit of justice.

Three weeks after leaving Mecca, Husain had almost reached Kufa. It was from this city on the banks of the Euphrates river that he had received the bulk of messages of support. Kufa had been the capital of the Islamic caliphate under Imam Ali. The Kufans wanted the caliphate returned to the Prophet's family, and to them; they did not support the tyrants of Damascus. Their pledge was to the Prophet, to Imam Ali, to the dynasty of which Husain was now the standard-bearer.

It was night when, 20 miles from Kufa, Husain and his companions stopped to rest, preferring not to enter the city in darkness. When news reached the city that the Prophet's grandson was nearly at the gate, the governor, loyal to Caliph Yazid, sent one hundred men to warn Husain and his companions to retreat.

The warrior who led that battalion is famous in the annals of Islamic history. His name was Hurr Al-Riyahi, meaning 'free', and he approached Imam Husain under orders from Kufa's governor. He did so as a valiant man, however, his shield reversed in a gesture of peace. Disobeying his governor's orders, Hurr could not bring himself to arrest the Prophet's family. With his soldiers behind him, he begged Imam Husain to return peacefully to Mecca, or pledge allegiance to Yazid.

'No, by God,' Husain answered. He stood on his saddle, his head held high, and addressed the soldiers from Kufa:

> I will neither give my hand to a tyrant like a humiliated man nor flee like a slave. May I not be called Yazid. Let me never accept humiliation over dignity. I have here two saddlebags full of your letters to me. Your messengers brought me your oath of allegiance, and if you now fulfil that oath, you will be rightly guided. My life will be with your lives, my family with your families. But if you break your covenant with me, you have mistaken your fortune and lost your destiny, for whoever violates his word, violates his own soul.

Muslims still recall Husain's moving speeches. The Shi'a memorise and recite them every year when they commemorate the catastrophe of Karbala. In a clear reference to Caliph Yazid and his governor in Kufa, Imam Husain roared: 'The goodness of this world is in retreat, and what was good is now bitter. Can you not see that truth is no longer practised? That falsehood is no longer resisted? When that is so, I can only see life with such oppressors as tribulation, and death as martyrdom.'

There was nothing left now for Imam Husain to inherit. No pledges, no weapons, no wealth, no power, not even an organised mass following. Nothing at all. Yazid and the Umayyad caliphate controlled every reach of society. Husain had only one weapon: his own death. For him, martyrdom was not a loss. It was a choice to be *shahid*, a witness, to meet his Lord in death, to return to his father, mother and grandfather having stood up to an unjust caliph in Yazid.

Hurr was unable to arrest Imam Husain, but he could not allow him to enter Kufa, either. Husain helped the warrior by turning away from the city, but he did not head back to Mecca. Instead, he walked north for three days, leading his small caravan in the desert heat towards a no-man's-land. Within sight of the cool blue waters of the Euphrates, he led them further on.

News soon reached the governor of Kufa that Hurr was escorting the family of the Prophet away from Kufa, but not detaining them. Outraged, the governor sent a four-thousand-strong force of cavalry and archers headed by a monster of a man, Shimr. The troops had a very clear mission: to put Husain's family under siege in the terrible heat, denying them all access to the river. Surely thirst would force Husain to capitulate.

The location of this siege would become known as Karbala, literally 'place of *Karr* and *Bala*', or 'trial and tribulation'. The site where thousands of soldiers of Yazid's corrupt caliphate trapped Imam Husain and his seventy-two companions in the blistering sun has come to stand for truth against falsehood.

Over the next seven days Husain gave rise to a new history. His suffering forms the basis of *Ashura*, an annual commemoration in which Shi'a mourn Husain's pain and loss with *Taziya*, or passion plays. Husain's suffering is also recalled by Shi'a and non-Shi'a alike in the Muslim fight for self-worth. His actions and attitudes, his serenity under siege, are inspirational for Muslims.

Husain's nephew Qasim, son of Imam Hasan, who was travelling with the caravan, knew that the group's destiny was martyrdom in Karbala. He carried a letter his father wrote on his deathbed, which read: 'A day will come when Islam will need to be saved by giving blood. My brother Husain will need you. On that day, be there with him and represent me.' Led by Qasim, several other members of the Prophet's household rode into the enemy ranks and faced certain death. The most painful of memories for Muslims is that of Husain's six-month-old son, Ali al-Asghar, racked with thirst in the burning heat.

Imam Husain held the thirsty, crying child up to Shimr and Yazid's guards and said: 'You are at war with me. This infant has done nothing wrong.' Before Husain could finish, a three-headed arrow pierced the helpless baby's neck. Husain returned to the tent holding the tiny, blood-soaked corpse. When the baby's crying ended, the women began to wail. This was the last day of the siege.

That night, Imam Husain turned once again to his companions. Totally composed, he said: 'All of you, I hereby absolve you from your oath of allegiance to me, and place no obligation upon you. Go home now, under cover of darkness. Use the night as a camel to ride away upon. These men of Yazid's want only me. If they have me, they will stop searching for anyone else. I beg you, leave for your homes and families.'

But no one moved. With their dry mouths and hoarse voices, one of Husain's companions said: 'We will fight with you until we reach our destiny.' Others offered to renew their pledge, but vowed never to leave the grandson of the Prophet. Visibly moved, but tranquil, he spoke: 'Then call upon God and seek His forgiveness. For our final day will be tomorrow.' He recited a verse of the Quran known to all Muslims, recited when death or difficulty visits us: 'To God we belong and to God is our return.'

That night, Imam Husain donned white cotton. This was his burial shroud. He applied melted myrrh and put on perfume. Tears fell on the parched faces of the family of the Prophet, for this was the end.

In the morning, Imam Husain bid farewell to the women of his family and mounted his white stallion. With a small band of warriors surrounding him, he charged fiercely into enemy lines. 'By God I have never seen his like before or since,' one of Yazid's soldiers would remember. 'The foot soldiers retreated from him as goats retreat from an advancing wolf.' Still, as he advanced, the enemy force kept up its attacks. By the time he fell to the ground there was an arrow in his shoulder and thirty-three knife and sword wounds on his body. His mount rode back to the camp alone. Imam Husain was no longer physically alive, but spiritually he captured the Muslim mind for ever.

Not content with killing him, Shimr's men chopped off Husain's head and impaled it on a spear. Then, with the women and children as captives, Shimr sent the family of the Prophet marching unveiled, dishonourably, to surrender to Caliph Yazid in Damascus. Husain's eloquent sister Zeinab now led the caravan, holding Husain's one surviving son, Zain Al-Abideen. In front of hundreds of witnesses in the court of the caliph, she proclaimed:

'O Yazid, do you believe that you have succeeded in closing the sky and the earth for us and we have become your captives because we have been brought before you in a row? And that you have secured control over us? You are boastful and happy. Wait for a while. Do not become so joyful.'

She then recited verses of the Quran, reminding Yazid how much oppressors ultimately lose, in this world and the next. Indeed, after all the precious blood spilt on his behalf, Yazid ruled for only three years, from 680 to 683.

The killing of the grandson of the Prophet sent shockwaves across the Islamic world. Rebellions broke out in Mecca and Medina, and Yazid subdued them with brute force. The caliph's army laid siege to Mecca, and bombarded the holy site of the Ka'bah, setting it on fire with catapults. His forces also attacked Medina, raping many women in the city of the Prophet. Such was the Muslim-on-Muslim violence inside the Prophet's own city, within only a century of his dying.

Meanwhile in Damascus, Zeinab stood daringly before Yazid in the caliph's court. She chastised him for veiling his own womenfolk, while the daughters of the Prophet were paraded before Damascus without honour. Lady Zeinab retired into the suburbs of Damascus until her death in 682. She lived with a group of believers and, loyal to Imam Ali and Husain, continued to teach and remember the lessons of Karbala.

Her nephew, the great Imam Zain Al-Abideen, grew up and became, true to his name, the 'prince of the pious'. He was also known as Imam al-Sajjad, or the imam 'who habitually prostrated'. Among all Muslims, Sunni and Shi'a, this man's legendary piety led to the birth of Sufi orders and spiritual chains of authority that still survive. Muslims today continue to practise his teachings. He returned to Medina, where he taught a select group of Muslims, died in the year 713 and was buried in the city. More than a thousand years later, in 1925, his shrine was destroyed by the modern Saudi government under orders from Salafi clerics who deemed such veneration of the Prophet's family as a form of polytheism. Saudi destruction of historical Muslim sites fuelled tensions with mainstream Muslims and particularly the Shi'a. Turkish and Iranian hostility to Saudi Salafism is born from such Saudi acts of obliteration.

Zeinab's dazzling tomb stands in Damascus today. In the Umayyad Mosque, the prayer niche of Zain al-Abideen lies at the corner of the grave where Yazid buried Imam Husain's head. An endless march of Muslims visits these shrines and remembers Karbala. And for Shi'a and Sunni alike, Karbala was not 1,200 years ago. It feels as if the massacre happened in our lifetimes, that we failed to come to Imam Husain's aid. This guilt still tugs at the Muslim conscience. The Iranian government has sent soldiers to Syria to protect these graves from demolition at the hands of violent Salafis such as ISIS.

However, while both Sunni and Shi'a feel this guilt, it manifests itself in very different ways. When most Sunni Muslims are asked about Karbala, they feel regret, remorse, and distress that the Prophet's beloved grandson was killed by other believers. But Sunnis do not grasp the intricacies of what happened. Sunni Muslims fear *fitna*, or dissension, and this leads to the obscuring of a painful history.

For Shi'a Muslims, it is the opposite. They hold on to every detail of Karbala. Shi'a life, clothes, colours and creed reflect that catastrophe. The majority of observant Shi'a wear black clothes. Women wear black robes, and men who claim descent from Ali wear black turbans and robes, still in mourning for the death of Imam Husain. Hezbollah's Hasan Nasrallah, Iraq's Moqtada al-Sadr, and Iran's Khameini mostly reflect this trend, as do the millions of women who wear a black chador in Iran or Afghanistan to cover their chins, foreheads and the rest of their bodies with the same black wrap. Sunni women generally tend to wear a headscarf as separate clothing to the *abaya* or gown.

Shi'a Muslims believe that Imam Husain's son, Zain al-Abideen, became their imam after Husain died. And from father to son, this imamate passed until the twelfth imam went into occultation or spiritual hiding in 873. Hence most Shi'a Muslims are known as *Ithna Asharis*, or Twelvers, because they believe that, including Ali, there were twelve imams. Breakaway sects such as the Ismailis or Alawites believe in a different number of imams. While Sunni Muslims believe that only the Prophet was protected from flaws, Shi'a believe that these imams, part of the household of the Prophet, were also free of faults. Shi'a Muslims live in anticipation of the last imam, also referred to as the Mahdi, a mythical figure who appears at the end of times and, with Jesus, will bring peace to a troubled earth. Iran's former president Mahmud Ahmedinajad kept an empty chair in cabinet meetings for the Mahdi.

Most Muslims believe that those the Prophet referred to as next of kin were his immediate family. Shi'a, however, give a fifth of their income to those they consider descendants of the Prophet, their religious guides. They follow the Quranic injunction that a fifth of the spoils of war, or a fifth of the Muslim treasury, should go to the Prophet's family, a practice known as *khums*, literally meaning 'a fifth'. Today, this ancient practice funds thousands of Shi'a scholars in the great cities of Qom in Iran, Najaf in Iraq and Syria's capital Damascus, as well as smaller Muslim communities around the world.

When Shi'a Muslims pray, they press their foreheads on a piece of flat stone extracted from the soil in Karbala. In their prayers and rituals, the remembrance of the Prophet and the family of the Prophet feature frequently. When Shi'a faithful visit tombs and shrines in the Middle East, they mourn, cry and recite sad verses to remember Karbala. Sunni Muslims generally do not undertake such elaborate rituals.

Among Arab Sunni Muslims, especially in Saudi Arabia and the Gulf, the pejorative term for Shi'a is *Rawafid* or 'the rejectors'. The name stems from Shi'a dismissal of the first three caliphs of Islam. This slander of the Shi'a has been part of the modern Arab Muslim lexicon since the 1790s, when Salafi extremists from today's Saudi Arabia raided Karbala and other Shi'a-dominated cities. Al-Qaeda, ISIS and other violent Salafi jihadi movements use this exact word to describe Shi'a Muslims when justifying their mass murder.

If Shi'a customs and prayers seem strange to Sunnis, then to Shi'a their Sunni brethren seem tyrannical, unthinking, disloyal, and worse, supporters of murderers. Sunni Muslims recognise the caliphs Abu Bakr, Omar and Othman as 'rightly guided' caliphs, thereby rejecting Imam Ali as Mohamed's successor. Sunni Muslims recognise the realities of that period, and see the Umayyad dynasty, however flawed, as a caliphate and as part of a legitimate continuum.

There are many Shi'a grievances against the Sunni majority. However, Sunnis, who have been the stronger group both numerically and militarily throughout Islamic history, have mostly been tolerant of the Shiʿa. Where this tolerance did not exist, in rare instances of history, the Shiʿa created the dogma of *Taqiyya*, the legitimate concealment of their faith in order to prevent persecution.[7] Most Sunnis have no knowledge of the doctrine of *Taqiyya*, although since 9/11 anti-Muslim American pundits have accused activist Sunni Muslims of *Taqiyya* in wishing to convert the West to Islam (wrong allegation and incorrect community). This is another example of those outside the House of Islam misunderstanding what happens inside. The rivalry between Iran and its allies, and Saudi Arabia and its Gulf allies, has metastasised into the Syrian war. But this war between Sunni and Shiʿa is yet to peak.

The emotions of Karbala live on. The potential for conflagration and conflict is still worse than anything the world has witnessed in Iraq, Syria, Lebanon, Yemen and Pakistan. What can heal this centuries-old wound? If anything can stop further intra-Muslim bloodshed it is a return to a deeper, fuller understanding of the sharia, the Islamic pathway that the majority of Muslims, both Sunni and Shiʿa, hold sacred.

5

What is the Sharia?

As the Prophet's companions left for Yemen to call people to worship God, he appointed Muadh bin Jabal to head the small delegation. The Prophet had concerns. If there were differences between the groups or the people they would meet in Yemen, how were they to settle disputes? he asked.

'By referring to the Quran,' Muadh replied.

'And what if the answer is not in the Quran?' the Prophet asked.

'By consulting your ways [or *Sunnah*] here in Medina,' answered Muadh.

'And what if my *Sunnah* has no precedent for your question, dear Muadh?'

'I will exercise my own reason and judgement, O Prophet of God,' responded Muadh.

The Prophet smiled and praised God for Muadh's precise answer. Muadh was among the most knowledgeable and upstanding of the Prophet's companions. The answer he gave before setting out to Yemen embodies the spirit of sharia, or Islamic law.

When facing tough questions that require guidance, a Muslim refers to the Quran and the Prophet. If an answer is not found, then a Muslim exercises their independent reasoning, or *ijtihad*. But what does it mean in practice to interpret the holy texts? And why is sharia so controversial, and so feared in the West? Is there a way in which sharia can find a conciliatory place in the modern world?

The word sharia means 'path to water' in Arabic, a mark of a people with a nomadic heritage. Something so basic, so simple, has become complicated through centuries of accumulated Muslim scholarship and commentary on scripture. The absence of sharia as state law in most parts of the Muslim world now drives a widespread political cause, a protest movement of modern Islamists. Their success can be measured by the popularising of the call for sharia as the perceived solution to the problems besieging the Muslim world.

In 2011, just after the revolution in Egypt, the largest Arab Muslim nation, a survey found that 87 per cent of the population wanted sharia to hold official legal authority.[1] In Egypt, 88 per cent of people and in Jordan 83 per cent supported the death penalty for apostasy. Eighty per cent of Egyptians said they favoured stoning adulterers, while 70 per cent supported cutting hands off thieves. In 2012, when the new parliament drafted a constitution, the second article confirmed that the primary source of legislation would be 'principles of the Islamic sharia'. For puritans, that clause was interpreted as a major defeat: the 'principles' were not sufficient; their demand was full sharia as law. This approach was the result of eight decades of popular activism by the Egyptian Muslim Brotherhood, embedding in the public imagination the idea that 'The Quran is our constitution.' Now, anything other than the Quran as 'the constitution' is seen as betrayal. Bowing to this sentiment, the Saudi monarch, King Salman, in 2015, in his first major speech, declared that Saudi Arabia's constitution was the Quran. What does this mean in reality? The political freedom to question the king or the puritans with impunity is not yet available in most Arab lands.

Islamists have clung to this obsession with the 'law of God' since Imam Ali was killed in the name of the idea that 'rule is for God alone'. In fact, as secular and 'man-made law' has become dominant in the West, Muslim activists have rallied under the sharia.

The first generation of Muslims had either direct access to the Prophet Mohamed, or one degree of separation. Questions of guidance that were not answered in the Quran were easily resolved directly by the Prophet himself or his companions. There were quandaries, but the solutions were within reach. If early Muslims continued to quiz the Prophet about personal life or matters that he felt were too worldly, he would often remain silent. At other times, he mildly reprimanded those who wanted answers to all the minutiae of life. '*Istafti qalbak*'– Ask your heart – he would say. The conscience was as good a guide as he to any moral dilemma. Famously, the Prophet taught his companions: '*Antum a'lamoo bi umoori dunyakum*': You know best about the affairs of your world.

Muslim scholars would later see this as strong evidence that Islam did not seek to control every aspect of a believer's life. Instead, Islam sought to provide broad principles of good morality, as in the Quran and as lived by the Prophet. But such breadth of view threatened the coherence of the new faith. The Quran was revealed in Mecca and Medina, when the Islamic community was still relatively small. Within a hundred years, however, Islam was an empire stretching from Spain to Central Asia. The battle of Karbala with its powerful centres lying in Kufa and Damascus showed that Mecca and Medina had become marginalised geopolitically within the Muslim world.

With the growth of the empire, the Prophet's Islam became increasingly complex. From the eighth to the tenth centuries, Muslim thinkers expended much intellectual energy on this challenge: was it possible to devise a legal system to administer the empire, while maintaining local customs and tribal agreements, and remaining true to the Quran's teachings and the Prophet's life? The result of this search was the complex codification of the sharia.

Muslim jurists developed five responses to questions that the faithful might ask them, which were categorised in five ways. '*Wajib*', or obligatory acts, such as prayers or almsgiving, were rewarded by God in the next life. '*Mandub*' denoted acts rewarded by God that are not compulsory, such as keeping streets clean. '*Makruh*' referred to acts it is preferable to avoid, but which are not sinful, such as smoking cigarettes. Acts that merited punishment from God in the next life, such as murder or theft, were '*Haram*'. Permissible acts were '*Mubah*' or '*Halal*'. These classifications have stood the test of time, and in mosques across the Muslim world today imams answer queries from the faithful by selecting among *Wajib, Mandub, Makruh, Haram* or *Halal*.

Historically, the vast majority of Muslim jurists agreed, as have most Muslims, with the principle that everything is *Halal* except for a few limitations. This was not dissimilar to St Paul's teaching that: 'All things are permissible, but not all things are beneficial.' But the rise of literalism and extremism (as will be discussed in the chapter on Salafism) among Muslims globally has resulted in an important shift. Now, for Muslim puritans and their followers, everything is prohibited – *Haram* – unless it is specifically permitted. Their slogan is: 'Every action requires scriptural evidence.'

Along with this demand from puritans for a fundamental change in attitude, Muslims face another major imposition. The Islamist agenda aims to enforce their interpretation of sharia through state law. For Islamists, *Haram* acts should be punished by the state in this world, as well as by God in the next. This is the difference between Islamists and ordinary Muslims. Most Muslims agree, for example, that drinking alcohol and homosexuality are forbidden by the sharia (although both practices are open to permissive interpretations). For Islamists, these acts should be made illegal and punished by the state in this world. This was not the historical attitude of most Muslims, however. We know this because in 700 years of Ottoman history there was only one case of an adulterer being stoned in public. The outrage it caused was such that it never occurred again under Ottoman rule. Through hundreds of years of history, Muslims understood that *Haram* was not to be made state law, but left to the believer's conscience.

When the Salafi puritanism of forbidding everything unless it is expressly sanctioned by scripture is combined with Islamist legalism, the result is totalitarianism and fascism. Muslim leaders with moral courage and intellectual clarity have not shied away from identifying this as a form of fascism. For example, Salman bin Hamad al-Khalifa, the Crown Prince of Bahrain, has repeatedly warned of emerging 'fascist theocracies' unless we understand, define and counter this danger.[2]

The sharia is far more complex and constructive than mere binary prohibitions and permissions. When ordinary Muslims yearn for more sharia, they are reflecting an inner craving for the complexity and compassion they have encountered when putting questions to the *ulama*, the learned scholars of Islam. But that experience should not be translated into headlines that portray Muslims as fanatics wanting stonings and amputations.

Sunni legal experts refer to four sources to answer questions put to them by Muslims. A judgement, or fatwa, can only be reached after consulting all four. The first is the Quran, and though it prescribes behaviour on matters of marriage, divorce and inheritance, it does not address other details of life. Why should it? And indeed, if God wanted other details included, surely He could have included them. Muslims have debated whether the Quran is sufficient as guidance in life, but the first two centuries of Islam, when the empire was consolidated and laws codified, left Muslims with an appetite for more than the Quran. That legacy of wanting more than the Quran remains with Muslims today.

The second-most important source is the traditions of the Prophet Mohamed, meaning his sayings (hadiths), approvals and actions. Muslims know these as the *Sunnah*, or 'ways'. The Quran teaches Muslims that if they wish to draw closer to God and to love God, they should emulate the ways of the Prophet. The difficulty is in knowing whether the Prophet really said the things attributed to him.

Some of the most popular hadiths among all Muslims today include:

'He who has not thanked humans has not thanked God.'

'To honour an old person is to show respect for God.'

'Heaven lies at the feet of your mothers.'

'God is beautiful and He loves beauty.'

'The key to paradise is prayer.'

'No person is a true believer unless he desires for his brother human that which he desires for himself.'

These hadiths, for instance, do not contradict the Quran, and seem fully in keeping with the spirit of the teachings of the Prophet. Such Quran-compliant hadith material is popular among Muslims and used widely in citations of books, sermons and other religious materials. But there are other alleged hadiths calling dogs and women filth, and condemning Jews, homosexuals and Christians, the authenticity of which is questionable. This matters because it directly influences Muslim belief and attitudes towards dogs, women, homosexuality, Jews and Christians. Verifying and questioning certain hadiths, therefore, is more than an academic exercise.

There are records of the Quran being written at the time of the Prophet, but the early caliphs forbade the writing of hadiths, which were mostly written 200 years after the Prophet died. They feared that Muslims would equate the Prophet with God, or the hadiths with the Quran. The caliph Omar punished and then banished to Bahrain a prominent hadith collector, Abu Hurayrah, for documenting alleged actions and sayings of the Prophet. The emphasis must be on the Quran.

And yet, despite these precautions, most Muslims wish to obey the Quran and *Sunnah*. The Islamist and Salafist movements around the world focus on these two strands of sharia. However, very little thought is given to the fact that the hadiths were written so long after the Prophet's passing. Worse, there is very little criticism of the content of the hadiths. For example, the Quran does not mention stoning adulterers to death, killing apostates, or throwing homosexuals from tall buildings. Nor does it mention men growing their beards and wearing short robes, or women covering their hair. All these actions are derived from alleged sayings of the Prophet. Muslims have lost the courage to question hadiths that do not align with the Quran.

Are these practices right or even necessary today? Were they originally cultural or religious? Apostasy was treachery – but why is it upheld now with death as penalty for apostates, when people are free to proselytise and, equally, to apostasise? What benefit is there if a woman who covers herself is just as likely to be molested in Cairo as one who does not wear the veil? Re-examination or questioning of recorded hadiths has been abandoned in favour of a suspension of intelligence on these issues. This has become the norm among most Muslims. Adversely, hadith content, or *matn*, is not cross-referenced for logical validity and consistency with the Quran. As long as the *sanad*, or chain of narration – the provenance – is considered to be accurate, then a hadith is accepted.[3]

This method has led to thousands of fabricated pseudo-hadiths entering the Muslim consciousness.

The third additional source of the sharia is analogy, or '*Qiyas*'. When jurists encountered a situation for which there was no previous precedent in the Quran and *Sunnah*, they reached a new conclusion on the basis of *Qiyas*. The Muslim jurist Imam Abu Hanifa (d. 767), founder of one of the main Islamic schools of law, introduced this element of human reasoning into Islamic legal thinking. He based it on the instructions the Prophet gave to Muadh when he set off for Yemen. For example, *Qiyas* is applied to the Quranic prohibition on drinking wine, expanding it to forbid the use of cocaine and other drugs. In the absence of a clear reference in the scripture, the scholars use *Qiyas* as guidance for believers.

The last supplementary source is the consensus of the Muslim community, or '*Ijma*'. The Prophet was thought to have declared that his community would not agree on an error. In an attempt to maintain Islamic practices, *Ijma* became the fourth strand of the sharia. The application of *Ijma* is found, for example, in how and when Muslims pray. Among scholars, however, there is debate on precise definitions of *Ijma*: should it be the *Ijma* of ordinary Muslims, or only the leading scholars, for instance?

These four sources of the sharia – the Quran, *Sunnah, Qiyas, Ijma* – are agreed upon by the vast majority of Sunni Muslims. They were pioneered and systematised by Abu Hanifa and his students. But as with any human endeavour, not everybody agrees on everything. Most Muslims today believe that the Quran and *Sunnah* are the main sources of the sharia, the former being indisputable, the latter open to debate. But adherents of other schools of Islamic law suggest that *Qiyas* is too heavily influenced by logic and Islam's early Greek-influenced logicians, the Mutazilites. Meanwhile, the school of Imam Malik (d. 795) rejects *Qiyas* altogether, preferring to follow the practice of the people of Medina, the city of the Prophet.

Along with these four, various schools of thought refer to other sources of sharia. These include '*rai'i al-sahabah*', or an opinion of a notable companion of the Prophet; '*Urf*' or '*Aada*', meaning customs or habits; '*sharia man qablana*', or the laws of those who went before Muslims; and '*sadd al-dara'i*', which means blocking pathways to wrongdoing. For many Muslim jurists, all these depend upon on yet another source: *Istihsan*, meaning good or beautiful. Juristically, *Istihsan* is a way of exercising personal opinion in order to avoid rigidity or unfairness as a result of the literal enforcement of law. *Istihsan* might, therefore, be called juristic preference or discretion. *Istihsan* aims to serve ideals of justice and what is in the public interest.

These principles come from references in a number of places in the Quran that seek to reassure Muslims that Islam is about *Yusr* – ease – not difficulty, which is *Usr*. Muslims cite verses of the Quran such as: 'God intends felicity and ease for you and He does not want to put you in hardship' when seeking sharia rulings. All of these Islamic legal precepts are woven into the assorted schools of law, or *madhabs*, to which the vast majority of Muslims adhere.

For Sunni Muslims, four great imams have led these schools of thought. They were Imam Abu Hanifa (d. 767), Imam Anas Malik (d. 795), Imam Idris al-Shafi'i (d. 820) and Imam Ahmed bin Hanbal (d. 855). Hundreds of schools of thought on the sharia developed over the centuries, but these four stood the test of time. Between them, they govern and instruct the vast majority of today's Muslims. These jurists are not abstract academics: they are household names that form part of mainstream Muslim identity. After first identifying as Sunni, the majority of Muslims will be adherents of one of these four schools.

Imam Abu Hanifa was of Persian origin. Born in Kufa, he helped build the city of Baghdad, where he died. His school, the Hanafi, is considered to be the first school of interpretation and is closest to the time of the Prophet. He focused on incorporating logic into the sharia. He was very popular among Muslims in the past, and remains so. The Ottomans and Mughals were Hanafis. Muslims from the Indian subcontinent and Turkosphere are still mostly Hanafis, and therefore the followers of this imam form easily the majority of the world's Sunni Muslims.

Imam Malik came from Medina. He died there, and based his school of sharia on the observed practices of the city's inhabitants. His approach was conservative. The Maliki school is popular mostly in North and West Africa. Imam Malik taught his students to stand in prayer with their hands at their sides.

Imam Shafi'i came from Gaza and died in Cairo. He completed and perfected methods of jurisprudence. The Shafi'i school is hugely popular among Egyptians, Malays in South East Asia, and Indonesians. The Hanbali school derived from Imam Hanbal, who came from Baghdad, and has a very strict interpretation of the sharia. It is based solely on the Quran and hadiths. Most of its few adherents are in the Arabian Gulf.

All four are approaches to the sharia that help a believer live life as a Muslim. In essence, they are methodologies that emphasise logic and analogy (Hanafi), practices of the people of Medina, the city of the Prophet (Maliki), or rigorous emphasis on hadiths (Shafi'i), and opinions of the companions of the Prophet (Hanbalis). These great imams did not always reach final conclusions, but bequeathed methodologies their students used to advance and apply sharia at all times.

Let us consider how the traditional methodology of a *madhab* works in reality. In the modern world, most people assume that all alcohol is completely forbidden for all Muslims. I don't drink alcohol, but I recognise Islamic opinions of past scholars that allow for drinking. The perceived prohibition stems from the meaning of the word *khamr*, forbidden in the Quran and widely assumed to mean alcohol. Early Hanafi scholars of the Quran sought precision and were convinced that *khamr* only applied to wine, not to other alcoholic drinks.[4] They therefore permitted ales, beers and spirits to be consumed in moderate proportions. Other jurists from alternative schools argued that these drinks cause intoxication, can lead to social and bodily harm, and therefore must be forbidden. The Ottoman caliphate embodied Hanafi teachings, and to this day raki, an alcoholic beverage, remains Turkey's national drink. There was a distinct lack of absolutism and banning of alcoholic drinks in the past. Indeed, some religious scholars and caliphs drank alcohol, and others did not. A genuine pluralism and flexibility of opinion thrived.[5]

Present-day Muslims have lost the sophistication of the principles and variables of the four *madhabs*. Historically, among those who took an interest in these schools of thought, the differences were about methodology. Today, the infighting among the schools' adherents can be observed in mosques. This derives from two sources: widespread ignorance about the role of the *madhabs*, and the rise of Salafi literalism. Traditionally, Muslims adopted the schools' methods to understand an answer to a question of religious observation. Now, in the name of the Salafi clarion call to 'return to the sources', a generation of Muslims is deeply suspicious of following a *madhab*. But since most Muslims undergo no formal training on the underlying philosophical principles, the place of these great schools has been reduced to the equivalent of bickering between rival clubs.

One typical argument centres on the way that Muslims pray, and particularly where Muslim men place their hands when standing before God. A Hanafi places his hands across his navel, a Maliki rests them at his sides, and a Shafi'i places them on his lower chest. To a Salafi, the obsession with rituals and outward examples of faith means that all three are wrong. The Hanbali placement on the chest is closest to Salafi practice. According to their literal reading of hadith, hands must be placed firmly on the upper chest.

What is overlooked is that the Hanafi, Maliki and Shafi'i each have their own evidence and valid reasoning for where, why and how they place their hands. This may seem a minor detail, but the Salafi disregard of other traditional schools of Islamic law leads to daily battles in mosques fought where Salafis evangelise against the *madhabs*. An assault upon an Islam of age-old pluralism is under way. This happens away from the glare of cameras. Very few outside the House of Islam understand the conflict.

Row upon row of men praying in ISIS and al-Qaeda videos do so in this Salafi way. When other Muslims see this they worry, and feel helpless in not being able to persuade Salafis of the flaw in their literalist ways. But the rest of the world sees only Muslims at prayer. The detail with which to demarcate ally from enemy is lost.

In the past, despite polemics and fierce intellectual debate between the schools, Muslim jurists recognised and respected each other's validity. Known as *ikhtilaf* – disagreement – books on sharia are filled with footnotes and side-notes on which scholar disagreed with his teacher and why. One hadith alleges that the Prophet said: '*Ikhtilafu ummati rahmah*' – 'Disagreement among my nation is a mercy.' Scholars dispute the validity of this hadith, but early Muslims believed it was a reflection of the Islamic spirit of knowledge. This inherent pluralism within Islam was best summarised by the twelfth-century Hanafi scholar Abu Hafs Nasafi when he said: 'Our school is correct with the possibility of error, and another school is in error with the possibility of being correct.'

Throughout history, political authorities tried to impose absolutism on Muslim societies, but failed. Just 147 years after the city-state of Medina became a home for the Prophet, Imam Malik disagreed with the caliph. The governor of Medina had him whipped naked and dislocated the shoulder for his writing hand. Despite the cruelty of the caliph's governor, the uncompromising stance and independence of Imam Malik left an imprint on Muslim societies that still cite this incident. The inherent pluralism within Islam survived from its earliest days. Imam Malik died as a result of the punishment inflicted.

Today, once again, there is a global attempt, led by Saudi Arabia, to impose only *one* approach to Muslim belief, worship, and even dress. For example, religious police in the mosques of Mecca and Medina confiscate material from pilgrims that does not comply with Wahhabism or Salafism. This attempt to eradicate a millennium-old Islamic pluralism bolsters the rise of al-Qaeda, ISIS, al-Shabab and other violent movements that seek to impose their strict, literalist reading of sharia on those around them. The tools to uproot this intemperance already exist within mainstream Islam. A better understanding of the depth, diversity, and nuance of the sharia is the answer to the present day's extremism and violence.

The greatest contextualisation of the sharia and its applicability in the modern world germinated from the Maliki school. Aside from its popularity in Africa, it was also popular in Islamic Spain. There, in Granada, it was Maliki jurists, such as Imam al-Shatibi (d. 1388), who crystallised Islamic law with the legal theory of *Maqasid al-Shariah*, or the Higher Objectives of the sharia. Shatibi taught, and others accepted, that literal compliance with scripture is the proper course in acts of personal worship, or *Ibadat*, while consideration of the *Maqasid*, or higher aim, is called for in worldly or social dealings, or *Mu'amalat*. In other words, Muslims should abide by the spirit of the law and not the mere letter of the law.

Today, the Muslim world's leading scholar of scholars, Shaikh Abdullah bin Bayyah, has been teaching the importance of these loftier aims. The Higher Objectives or *Maqasid* of the sharia are five: to conserve life, faith, family, intellect and property. Taken as a whole, the Quran and hadith seek to preserve these spheres. The *Maqasid* of sharia is to preserve property, not to amputate the hands of thieves. Sharia is not about whipping fornicators: its higher aim is to conserve the family. In sum, *Maqasid* is concerned with the wisdom behind the rulings of the sharia.

Other Muslim scholarly giants articulated this conservative and deeper approach to sharia before and after al-Shatibi. They include Imam al-Juwayni (d. 1085), Imam Ghazzali (d. 1111), and others. The historian and sociologist Ibn Khaldun, a Maliki scholar, also wrote of the *Maqasid* in his renowned series of books, *Al-Muqaddimah*, as a fact of Muslim life. This was not controversial or anything extraordinary when it was first introduced, but knowing that prominent early Muslim thinkers advance the theory helps root it more deeply for Muslims today. Ibn al-Qayyum al-Jawzi (d. 1350), a strict jurist from Syria, wrote:

> The foundation of the sharia is wisdom and the safeguarding of people's welfare in this life and the next. In its entirety it is

> about justice, mercy, wisdom and goodness. Every rule which replaces justice with injustice, mercy with its opposite, the common good with mischief, and wisdom with folly, is a ruling that does not belong to the sharia, even though it might have been claimed to be according to some interpretation.

The early imam Sufyan al-Thawri (d. 778), reflecting this inbuilt compassion within the sharia, taught: 'If you see a man doing something over which there is difference of opinion among scholars, and which you believe to be forbidden, you should not forbid him from doing it.' Even the strictest of imams, the founder of the exacting Hanbali school, Imam Ahmad, was committed to this diversity.

Today, along with Shaikh bin Bayyah, the power of this pluralist approach is on display elsewhere, too. During the Arab uprisings in 2011, parliaments in places like Tunisia and Egypt debated whether the Salafi approach of *Tatbiq* or legal implementation, a literalist application of sharia punishments, or the *Maqasid* view championed by conservatives such as Shaikh Rachid al-Ghannouchi in Tunisia worked best in the modern world. The appeal, credibility and methodology of the *Maqasid* approach was such that even Saudi Arabia's prominent and unofficial scholar Shaikh Salman Al-Audah, a former mentor to Osama bin Laden, called on Muslims to abandon literalism and embrace the *Maqasid* of the sharia.

The *Maqasid* method allows Muslims in the West, and the vast majority of the world's Muslims who live in countries that do not approach the sharia literally, to thrive. That is because, according to this way of thinking, any government that upholds the Higher Aims of the sharia is, in fact, Islamic by default. By that definition, Britain and America are fully Islamic because they conserve life, faith, family, property and the intellect. The West is already Quran-compliant. Therefore, though no Western states formally uphold sharia as law, there is in fact a full civilisational alignment. The Soviet Union in contrast would not be compliant with this approach because of its attempts to ban prayers and religious observance. China forbids Muslims from growing their beards, gathering for religious occasions, fasting in Ramadan, and even forbids the use of the name 'Mohamed'.

With the *Maqasid*, Muslims can credibly question and overturn rulings on killing apostates or blasphemers. With such extreme laws promulgated in several Muslim countries, minorities face intolerance and sometimes oppression, and Muslims are prohibited from changing faiths. But the Quran openly declares that 'there can be no compulsion in faith'. To literalists – and based on the time when schools of law or *madhabs* were created – apostasy was the same as treachery. But today, faith is not the same as nationality. When people choose to convert from Islam to Christianity, they are not inherently plotting against a state or Muslim communal welfare. *Maqasid* allows us to debate this. Some Muslims see this approach as an imposition of liberal secularism. What it actually does is help conserve the sharia and society by making it easy to be pious.

This approach is that of the Muslim mainstream consensus. The Ottoman Empire, and the vast majority of Muslim scholars throughout history, including Sunni Islam's highest seat of learning, Al-Azhar University and Mosque in Cairo, have all used this method to build *Ijma*, or Muslim consensus, against literalism. Today, the vast majority of the world's fifty-nine Muslim majority nations does not flog, whip, stone, amputate, or uphold slavery – with the exception of Iran, Saudi Arabia, and parts of Indonesia and Nigeria. Salafism and Islamism seek to break that consensus, however (see chapters 8 and 9). This is a symptom of our modern age: the empowerment of the individual over tradition, the sovereignty of the self over collective wisdom, has bred this iconoclasm.

Throughout Muslim history, scholarship on scripture was a specialised discipline. The scholars known as *Mufassir* studied Quranic commentary; the *Muhaddith* had expertise on hadith verification; the *Mu'arrikh* were dedicated historians; and the *Faqih*, or jurisprudents, had their area specialisms, but drew from the others to make rulings. The *Muhaddith* were like pharmacists, while a *Faqih* was a general practitioner. When people went to the *Faqih* with questions, he or she selectively drew on hadiths. They did so with training, by asking the right questions or by cross-referencing the Quran, the hadith, and history.

Modern Muslims, however, feel confident in accessing the primary sources, bypassing the *Faqih* and their *madhab*-based methodology. This has contributed to eroding the spirit of Islam. Homosexuals were not thrown off cliffs at any point in Muslim history; the Quranic arguments for compassion and kindness superseded an alleged hadith about punishing homosexuality. Mostly, Muslims turned a blind eye to homosexuality. (American–Muslim scholar Scott Siraj al-Haqq Kugle has written persuasively on the rights of gay, lesbian and transgender Muslims.)

In Islamic tradition, actions were not undertaken on the basis of a single hadith; they were placed in the context of a number of sources. When leaders of today's puritanical organisations, who are not trained Islamic scholars, access the hadith, they lose this wider context and the result is many of the actions in Saudi Arabia and ISIS-held territory: executions, flogging, sexual slavery, burning prisoners, and a commitment to perennial warfare.

In sum, prohibitions in the Quran are few and conclusive. Examples include specific bans on murder, stealing or cheating in business dealings. The bulk of the sharia is a man-made attempt, through interpretations and commentary on scripture, to provide an ethical basis to life. Imam Bukhari undertook the greatest of hadith collections for Sunni Muslims, 200 years after the Prophet died. This was also mostly a masculine province. Islamic scholarship was and is dominated by men, with all the inherent problems that entails. The Prophet's wife, Ayesha, is credited with 2,200 hadiths overall, but only 128 appear in Bukhari's work.

For a thousand years, male Muslim scholars debated and perfected the elements of the sharia. This process of human reasoning and deliberation on areas that the Quran did not address, or even where there was a Quranic reference, is known as *ijtihad*. Muslim civilisation and scholarship thrived as *ijtihad* allowed for new interpretations and new ways in which to respond to new realities. This openness and flexibility lay at the core of Islam even as it was being codified.

But not all Muslims took their orders from the rulebook. The state and its apparatuses maintained security and law, but the Muslim masses were and remain drawn to the mysticism and freedom of the Sufi brotherhoods. They sought the inner significance of the sharia – the *Batin*, the esoteric, not just the rules and rituals of the exoteric, the *Zahir*. That inner dimension of Islam is Sufism.

6

Who is a Sufi?

The Sufis tell a story of three men who went to a mosque to pray while a group of people stood outside watching. As the first man walked into the mosque, he saw the crowd, and carefully left his shoes at the door so that they could observe that he was faithfully following the rule of taking one's shoes off when praying. The crowd murmured appreciatively and praised God for the man's religiosity. Inside, he performed his prayers in textbook fashion: standing correctly, bowing perfectly, prostrating himself diligently. The crowd peeped in and witnessed this, and he rose even further in their estimation.

A second man, also known to be deeply pious, then entered the mosque. He too removed his shoes, but he carried them with him into the mosque. He too prayed diligently and meticulously. When the two men left the mosque, the crowd engaged them both in earnest debate. Which was correct: to leave one's shoes outside the mosque or carry them inside?

Meanwhile, as the pious men debated their respective positions with the crowd, a nondescript character slipped in quietly by the side entrance of the mosque, unseen by anyone. He quietly prayed and humbly left. Only God knew of his prayers, his intentions and his spiritual state, but that was all that mattered to him. He had no interest in people's praise, and no regard for external trivialities such as what to do with one's shoes while praying. This last man was the Sufi. An aspiring Sufi seeks only to please God, and does so in secret as often as possible. A Sufi shuns the temporal world and its banalities.

To understand the Sufis is to grasp the heart and soul of Islam. Sufis and Sufism are, essentially, Islam's greatest secret. Idries Shah's extraordinary book *The Sufis,* first published in 1964, introduced Sufism to the modern West. This powerful current within the Muslim world is hidden from most outsiders, not intentionally, but because very few non-Muslims either understand it or are willing to grasp the immaterial, metaphysical element in Islam's appeal for its believers. However, the Sufis have given real life and spiritual depth to Islam and to the religious experience of generations of Muslims.

Sufism is about the *Batin*, or esoteric, the inner secrets of the Prophet, the Quran and the sharia. Whereas the scholars of the sharia, the *ulama*, focus on when to pray, where to place the hands, and how to stand, bow and prostrate oneself, the Sufi masters are instead concerned with the state of the worshipper's heart and soul when standing before God. The sharia specialists are intent on explaining the Quran; the Sufis are, in their words, 'not interested in the love letter, but the lover Himself', and so immerse themselves in love, miracles and pious devotion.

There are four explanations of the origin of the term 'Sufi'. The first is that next to the home of the Prophet in Medina was a place known as the Suffa, where the most dedicated of his disciples spent all their time in study and service to Islam. The *ahl al-suffa*, 'the people of the Suffa', were known for their abstinence from material and worldly things, and their nickname later evolved into 'Sufis'. Another explanation is that the name comes from *safa*, an Arabic word for purity and cleanliness, because of the Sufi aspiration to be spiritually cleansed from the corruption of the world. Alternatively, 'Sufi' may be derived from the Arabic word *soof*, or *suf*, meaning 'wool', because, in abstaining from the wealth and splendour of the early Umayyad caliphate, many of the Sufis wore humble, inexpensive clothing made of wool. The fourth suggested derivation stems from the Greek word *sophia* (wisdom), as many of the early Sufis were seen as lovers of wisdom, or philosophers.

Sufi Muslims are an eclectic bunch, ranging from the very strict in observance of sharia to the very lax, from dancers and dervishes (originally a Persian word referring to those who relinquish the world and seek divine love) to serious scholars, and from the highly secretive to the exceptionally transparent. Most take instruction from teachers of the mystical orders – such as the vast, globally popular Naqshbandi, Qadiri and Chishti schools – while others roam freely and just follow their hearts. However, they all share in common a deep love for the Divine and a vibrant attachment to the Prophet Mohamed (who is spiritually alive to the Sufis); and they possess an otherworldly charisma that touches those who open their hearts to being taught. Their tranquillity is real and brings serenity to those who meet them – like sexual attraction, difficult to explain yet palpable to those who experience it. The Sufis and their masters radiate stillness, divine energy. A visit to a Sufi shrine or to a living master embeds calmness in the soul of the visitor.

The Sufis' contribution to the spread of Islam was to conquer entire new lands, not with the sword but with their love, miracles and esoteric teachings, and by living pious lives among the masses. Sufi travellers often made long journeys in response to dreams in which they saw the Prophet instructing them to call people to God in India, Africa, central Asia, Turkey and Indonesia. For example, the twelfth-century founder of the Chishti order in India, who came originally from eastern Persia, saw in his sleep the Prophet commanding him to call the people of India to worship the one God.

The Sufis today have hundreds of millions of Muslim followers and mosques spread across the globe – but they do not make news headlines. We constantly hear of al-Qaeda, the Taliban, ISIS and Boko Haram, but most people in the West know little or nothing of the incomparably larger and centuries-old Muslim Sufi orders of the Naqshbandi, Chishti, Qadiri, Shadhili, Tijani, Rifa'i, Mevlevi, Cerrahi and dozens of others. This chapter will delve into civilisations in Persia, India and Turkey, and how leading Sufi personalities thrived across the Muslim world. Through learning more about Rumi, Khayyam and Princess Jahanara, we will enhance our understanding of the ubiquitous spirit of the Sufis inside the House of Islam.

The presence of centuries-old *dergahs* – shrines built on the tombs of Sufi masters – and *khanqahs* – Sufi hospices and meeting-rooms – in every major Muslim city bears testament to Sufism's deep emotional and spiritual appeal. A traveller to Cairo, Mombasa, Khartoum, Xinjiang, Fez, Delhi, Lahore or Istanbul will see, even in our doubt-ridden times, devoted Sufis gathered at these *dergahs* and *khanqahs*, and will witness the influence the Sufi masters have on the practice and beliefs of ordinary Muslims today. Many of them are household names, and their continuing influence can be found in contemporary Muslim attitudes, art and poetry, and rebellion against the rise of modern Islamist radicals.

Konya, in Turkey, is one of these ancient cities that still draw countless thousands of devotees. There, in his mausoleum, sleeps Jalaluddin Rumi (1207–73), a renowned Muslim poet and Sufi master who founded the Mevlevi order, more popularly known in the West as the 'whirling dervishes', because his adherents dance in remembrance of the divine. Rumi had lived in Konya since the age of five, after his family fled Balkh, in today's Afghanistan, to escape the Mongol persecution. He is known as 'Rumi', meaning 'Roman', because Konya was in Anatolia, formerly part of the Byzantine or eastern Roman empire.

The Seljuk sultans of Anatolia welcomed Rumi's father, Baha'uddin Walad, as a professor at a sharia seminary. Rumi himself studied in the great cities of learning of the time, Damascus and Aleppo, and by 1244, as his father's son and as a scholar in his own right, he commanded an academic following in Konya and had a reputation for being upright and erudite. But all that was set to change.

A wandering dervish from Persia, Shams of Tabriz, had arrived in town. Rumi's fame and stature were such that he had little time for lowly dervishes – for Rumi, it was his books, lectures and students that mattered, not conversing with vagabonds, however inwardly alive to God they might be. Shams of Tabriz had other ideas.

Rumi was sitting one day near a fountain in Konya, talking to his students, with a precious, rare copy of the *Ma'arif*, a mystical tract written by his father, open on the fountain ledge. Shams walked up to Rumi, interrupted the gathering, and pushed the *Ma'arif* and other books into the water. 'What are you doing?' Rumi asked, aghast that one of the few extant copies of his father's masterpiece should be ruined in this way. 'O Rumi, you won't understand unless you start to live what you have been reading about,' Shams replied. 'But if you want, I can retrieve the books, and you will find them to be dry.' And so he did: Shams pulled the books out of the water, dry and with no trace of moisture about them.

Rumi had read about miracles, but never before witnessed one. He recalled his father's teaching – 'Listen to those who yearn achingly for God' – and realised that such a person was standing before him. An ambassador of the divine presence had reached Rumi, and Rumi knew it, felt it. Thirteen years after his father's passing, and three years before Rumi's fortieth birthday, the sober professor was about to shed his old self and emerge anew – but it would not be easy, or without scandal.

Soon after that, Shams of Tabriz approached Rumi in the bazaar in Konya and posed the question: Who was greater, the Prophet Mohamed for teaching '*Subhan Allah*' ('Glory be to God') or a venerated early Muslim saint, Bayazid Bistami (d. 874), who declared: '*Subhani*' ('Glory be to me')? Bistami had experienced divine unity with God and believed he had merged with the Divine, so that his glory was the glory of God. Shams's blasphemous question left Rumi speechless.

It was an uncomfortable moment for Rumi's students, to see their esteemed theology professor silenced by a travelling dervish. But with Shams's help Rumi soon learned the answer to the question: the celebrated Bistami had had only a taste of the Divine, and melted in its ambience, whereas Mohamed returned from the Divine presence again and again to teach humans how to get closer to their Source. Rumi now yearned for this knowledge of the Source.

The two key influences on Rumi's life, his Afghan father Baha'uddin and now the Persian Shams of Tabriz, gave Rumi wings. Both were from the East, had memorised the Quran in its entirety, taught people religious and mystical knowledge, and uttered profanities. Most importantly, both bequeathed their spiritual secrets to Rumi.

Rumi started spending more and more time alone with Shams. He could not stop asking him about the higher secrets of Sufism, the flaws of the path, the trials of progress in God's love, maintaining equilibrium while swimming in deep oceans of spiritual awareness, and the ways in which the human ego could be crushed.

Shams never spoke of Rumi as a disciple, and Rumi was not allowed to refer to Shams as his teacher. It was a meeting of equals, or at least that was how Shams insisted on presenting their relationship. When speaking to Rumi's students and sons, Shams was full of praise for the professor. Shams saw Rumi as a perfect human, the best possible reservoir for the secrets Shams had gathered as a Sufi traveller about the loving, why-less and how-less, approach to God. Shams had travelled vast distances to teach his insights to a mind and soul as deep as Rumi's.

Shams spoke less positively, however – in fact he was downright rude – about other people in Konya, apart from Rumi's students and family. He had only scorn and contempt for their spiritual laziness, and his sharp tongue and blunt rebukes did not endear him to them.

Meanwhile, Rumi was starting to make obscure statements in public such as: 'I was raw, I was cooked, I was burned', and other mystical utterances that made sense only to those who knew something of the journey to God. Perhaps rebuking those obsessed with the sharia, he wrote: 'Out there, beyond ideas of wrongdoing and rightdoing, there is a field. I'll meet you there.' And, alluding to the human search for the divine: 'What you seek is seeking you.' What did it all mean? The public were baffled, and horrified.

Shams and Rumi now became inseparable, spending months locked away in meditation, study and the exchanging of divine secrets. Rumi's neglect of his professorial duties aroused anger and jealousy among his colleagues and students. Who was this dervish who dared to take away their teacher? Worse was Shams's rudeness – not that he cared for popular approval. The light that

Shams had carried from the East had found a home. His dreams had sent him to Konya to find Rumi, and their scandalous association was set to change Muslim spirituality – Sufism – for ever.

Rumi had now been set alight within, and could no longer go back to dry book-knowledge and the mere rituals of religion. Under pressure, he returned to the seminary, but he would be seen there holding on to a pillar and slowly walking round it, again and again, murmuring love poetry, yearning for the Divine. His students looked on, and blamed the foreigner Shams for so corrupting their teacher. Shams urged Rumi to violate every code, every sacrosanct behaviour, so that in their eyes he became nothing, and predictably was cursed for it – but in Divine eyes Rumi would become everything, committed only to the love of God, seeking acceptance only in heaven. He killed his ego's desire to please others and be liked and respected, and he did everything society forbade: he sang, he danced, he was free.

This delirious, ecstatic style of Sufism is still alive today. The Turkish author Elif Shafak's bestselling book *The Forty Rules of Love* taps into people's enduring love for Shams and Rumi. The *Qawwali* singers of Sufi devotional music in Pakistan and India are YouTube sensations in the Indian subcontinent. Bollywood movies are peppered with Sufi shrines and poetry, and the Sufi values of valour and spirituality, reflecting the extent to which most Hindus in India do not see Sufism as alien to their own identity or ideas. Many Sikhs, Hindus and other Indians have a sense of mystical affiliation with the Muslim saints of Delhi and Bombay, and visit their tombs.

And Rumi's poetry is a top seller in America, because he speaks to that inner yearning of the human soul that within Islam only the Sufis understand:

Come, come, whoever you are.
Wanderer, worshipper, lover of leaving.
It doesn't matter.
Ours is not a caravan of despair.
Come, even if you have broken your vows a thousand times.
Come, yet again, come, come.

This Sufi message of hope and renewal has survived many centuries already, and will no doubt endure many more. But Rumi's was only one example of Sufi practice. The modern West too easily associates Sufism with his Mevlevi order's whirling dervishes, while ignoring the much broader and deeper dynamics of Muslim mysticism. The Sufis have had a far more wide-ranging impact on Islam, and today most of the world's Muslims are either Sufis or at least deeply influenced by Sufism.

It was Sufis from the Hadhramaut valley in Yemen, for example – six traders of the Alawi order – who spread Islam throughout Indonesia. The largest Muslim nation in the world today follows Sufi ways, venerating the Prophet with million-strong congregations joining in the *mawlid*, commemorating the Prophet's birth and life, and the collective *dhikr*, or gathering to glorify God.

In India, Pakistan, and Bangladesh it was the great Sufis of Ajmer Sharif and Delhi who brought millions to Islam with their meditation and miracles, outdoing the Hindu yogis. Later, the Mughal emperors were deeply influenced by this Sufism and renovated and revived the great shrines of the Sufis.

In Iraq, the Sufi Abdul Qadir al-Jilani (d. 1166) and his students founded the Qadiri order that is widespread across the Muslim world today. He was born in the Jilan province of Persia, and his mother sent him to Baghdad to study Islam. Sufis tell the story that she gave young Abdul Qadir food for the journey and sewed a large amount of cash into the lining of his shirt. His outer robe concealed his hidden wealth. On the way to Baghdad, the caravan was attacked by bandits. Their leader asked the boy if he had anything of value, or knew if anyone else in the convoy did. The young man opened his shirt and handed over the hidden cash. 'You have what you want of this world,' he told the thieves. 'Now give us safe passage to the wealth of knowledge in Baghdad that will give us the bounties of the next world.' Moved by Abdul Qadir's sincerity and single-mindedness, the robbers joined him and went with him to Baghdad. There they became the first students of the Sufi Qadiri order, which is now prevalent in the Middle East, India and Pakistan.

In Africa, the spread of Islam was greatly assisted by wandering Sufi dervishes who won fame by performing miracles. As in India, the Sufis in Africa did not disrupt local customs and traditions unless they contradicted Islam. Their understanding of the sharia was that everything was permitted unless specifically forbidden. Dance, music, dress, architecture, languages and landscape were left alone – their only purpose was to impart spirituality and a connection to the Divine among the masses. The Sufis sought to influence the *Batin*, the inner being, knowing that once that was touched, faith would manifest itself in the *Zahir*, the outward.

Beyond Indonesia, India, Iraq and Africa there was also Osman Ghazi, the Sufi founder of the Ottoman Empire. In the year 1300 he was leading an army of his Turkic warriors in Anatolia, accompanied by a Sufi dervish. Osman, from whose name we get 'Ottoman', would not lead an army into battle without his Sufi spiritual masters present. On one such military expedition, he dreamed that the moon came out of his Sufi guide's mouth and passed into Osman's own chest. Then a great tree sprang forth from the warrior's breast, its branches spreading over the whole world. Seven centuries later, Sufism remains the lifeblood of popular Muslim practice in Turkey and the Turkosphere across the Balkans and central Asia.

Unfortunately, in every area of human activity there is scope for rivalry, power politics and intrigue, and of course Sufism is no exception: at times it has harboured a degree of corruption and seen its good name exploited. The popularity of Sufism in Egypt, Nigeria and Pakistan has meant it getting embroiled in the vices of those fragile countries. There are Sufis who keep their distance from power in all three countries, but there are also powerful men who are members of Sufi orders.

In Egypt, the pious and popular (former) grand mufti Sheikh Ali Gomaa openly supported the military and government after they deposed President Mohamed Morsi in 2012, and provided religious justification for the killing of hundreds of Muslim Brotherhood members. In Pakistan, Sufi *pirs*, or teachers, and their students have sometimes been frauds. Their vast network of property ownership and political influence in garnering votes has besmirched the name of dervishes who are supposed to distance themselves from the *dunya*, the temporal world. And in Nigeria, the trust demanded by Sufi instructors has often been abused, when parents have handed sons over to live with their Sufi teacher, only for the master to send the children out to beg all day, claiming he is 'teaching them to combat the ego'. These Mujiri children (a derivative of the Arabic word *muhajir* or 'migrant') are now attached to several militias across northern Nigeria.

By and large, in developing Muslim countries like these, where Sufis have become corrupted, or Sufi scholars have been co-opted by the state and lost their independence, the middle classes have turned elsewhere for guidance: to the emerging Islamists and Salafists, among others. In their rejection of Sufism, Islamists and Salafists have created a version of Islam that is functional and robotic about acting in accordance with scripture, but is devoid of beauty. In this respect they have killed the soul of Islam, Sufism, with its veneration of the Prophet, its appreciation of beauty in poetry, art and architecture, and its commitment to coexistence with other faiths.

Iran was once home to this vibrant Sufism. The Islamist government in Tehran today, together with its allies in Hezbollah in Lebanon and the governments of Iraq and Syria, promotes a version of the faith that is a world away from the joyous freedom of the Sufis. Yet one of the pioneers of Sufism was the celebrated Persian scholar and poet Omar Khayyam.

Rare is the literary bookshelf in the West that does not have a copy of the famed *Rubaiyat* of Omar Khayyam, a collection of quatrains celebrating love, divinity, wine, and living life to the full. Khayyam was a devout twelfth-century Sufi Muslim scholar, poet and astronomer who loved drinking wine – forbidden in Islam – but was also intoxicated with love of the Divine. Edward FitzGerald's inspired nineteenth-century English translations of Khayyam's wild, euphoric poetry, published only two years after the trauma of the Indian revolt against British rule in 1857, helped to recast England's perception of the Muslim East.

Across America, FitzGerald's translations of Khayyam's masterpiece led to dining and drinking clubs being named after this great

Muslim scholar. It should be noted, however, that the Khayyam that FitzGerald unearthed, and with whom he dazzled the nineteenth-century literary elite, was not the whole Khayyam. FitzGerald's selective translations were driven by detestation of his own zealous, preacher brother – which led FitzGerald to remove Khayyam's religious side, and present the English-speaking world with only a truncated Khayyam.

Be that as it may, FitzGerald gave Khayyam's work a new lease of life and returned him from England, via America, back to his native Persia with added fame, stature, and now also recognition in the West. Iranians visited their medieval ancestor anew, and named streets and schools after him. His verses still play on the lips of young Iranians; the theocrats aren't happy about it, but they would not dare to outlaw the hugely popular Khayyam. So why, 900 years after his death, is he so important in the Muslim world, America and Britain?

Abul Fath Omar ibn Ibrahim Khayyam (1048–1129) was born in the district of Shadyakh in the old city of Nishapur in Khurasan, the eastern province of today's Iran. Omar's father Ibrahim was a *khayyam*, a tentmaker. Poor and without connections, how could an illiterate tentmaker educate his son? Like many piously raised Muslim boys then and since, young Omar had already memorised much of the Quran, so his father presented him to the imam at the local mosque. There he learned Arabic grammar and Quranic exegesis, and acquired basic religious knowledge.

Once firmly grounded in religion and Arabic, Khayyam moved on to another master, with whom he learned mathematics, astronomy and cosmology. The tentmaker's son possessed intellectual abilities that surprised his teachers, and he was accepted among the 'best of the best', being mentored by the teachers of princes and the nobility. Yet Khayyam never lost sight of his humble roots.

The Muslims of the time were fascinated by astronomy. Their reading of the Quran, with its reflective verses on the stars and galaxies, made them want to learn about the secrets of the universe. Study of the stars yielded a means of navigation for travelling merchants, and precise calculations of daybreak, dawn, noon, sunset and so on helped to regulate prayer times. From Ibn Hazm in Andalusia to Omar Khayyam in Persia, there was no shortage of Muslim contributors to the science of astronomy, but Khayyam's contribution was outstanding.

By tradition, higher learning was acquired through travel, study and *ijazah* (licence) from other masters. Khayyam travelled to Isfahan, where his fame as a leading astronomer and mathematician had reached the court of the Seljuk kings. In 1076 the king Malik Shah commissioned Khayyam, with several assistants, to work on a new imperial calendar. For three years he worked meticulously to produce the *Taqwim Jalali*, the most detailed calendar ever produced. It etched the name of Omar Khayyam on the Iranian national psyche, and remains Iran's time-honoured official calendar.

Soon afterwards, Khayyam went on the Hajj, where he was received by other scholars as an *allamah*, or scholar extraordinaire. Everyone had heard of his writings and scientific treatises, even if they had not actually read them. In Mecca, like other Muslim pilgrims, he would have worn two white shrouds to remind him of death, and fulfilled the rituals of the Hajj, from circumambulating the *Ka'bah* seven times to walking between two hills in commemoration of the sacrifices of Hagar for her son Ishmael. The spiritual experience stayed with Khayyam for life, and his encounters on his travels with scholars, merchants, clerics and judges helped form the rebel he was to become with the passing of time.

In the royal courts Omar Khayyam was an outsider – he was not born of the nobility. And his observations were acute. Little wonder, then, that the poetry that was to pour from his pen has become the succour of the underdogs, the anti-establishment Sufis, and lovers of pleasure through the ages.

Khayyam's *Rubaiyat* – 'Quatrains' – is a collection of 1,200 verses. FitzGerald's genius was to edit the lines and present their most pertinent themes in an impassioned English rendition that aroused a sense of urgency and passion for life, joy and freedom from the clerical reprimands both of Khayyam's time and of our own. Khayyam wrote freely, openly, about the taverns, wine and cups of Nishapur in the twelfth century, bringing to life for us a period in history. The drinking of wine is for Khayyam waking from the slumber of our lives. His opening lines in the *Rubaiyat* are:

Awake! for Morning in the Bowl of the Night
Has flung the Stone that puts the Stars to Flight:
And Lo! the Hunter of the East has caught
The Sultan's Turret in a Noose of Light.
Dreaming when Dawn's Left Hand was in the Sky,
I heard a Voice within the Tavern cry,
'Awake, my little ones, and fill the Cup
'Before Life's Liquor in its cup be dry.'

With his emphasis on drinking wine, metaphysical or otherwise, Khayyam communicates a variety of themes and messages that give us an insight into Khayyam the Sufi, the dissenter, the free thinker, the flying soul. In the lines below he is downplaying the importance of this mortal life, and pointing out its fleeting nature, a key Sufi theme intended to move human hearts away from a focus on this world to love of the Divine:

The Worldly Hope men set their Hearts upon
Turns Ashes – or it prospers; and anon,
Like Snow upon the Desert's dusty Face
Lighting a little Hour or two – is gone.

And again, emphasising the ephemeral nature of worldly existence, Khayyam invites us to go with him and abandon the learned to their empty talk:

Oh, come with old Khayyam, and leave the Wise
To talk; one thing is certain, that Life flies;
One thing is certain, and the Rest is Lies;
The Flower that once has blown for ever dies.

But go where? Like Jalaluddin Rumi, Khayyam leads us to seek unity with the Divine:

> There was a Door to which I found no Key:
> There was a Veil past which I could not see:
> Some little Talk awhile of ME and THEE
> There seemed – and then no more of THEE and ME.

This was not the Sufism of masters and disciples, but the wild Sufism of divine love: free of rules and guidance, and diving onto and into the divine fire again and again. And in this all-enveloping consumption, the lover and beloved become one. Here is Khayyam on his reliance on God, after a night of drinking:

> In tavern rather I to Thee confide
> Than pray without Thee at the Pulpit-side;
> O Thou, who art creation's First and Last,
> Now burn or bless me as Thou may'st decide.

Despite the focus on Omar Khayyam's love for wine and drinking, there is no doubt that he was a devout Sufi Muslim. Khayyam's philosophical and scientific treatises all started and finished with praise for the Prophet and thanksgiving to God. Some have argued that he was merely adhering to the norms of his time, but such a view does not hold up to scrutiny – there was more to Khayyam's religiosity than beginning each piece of writing with a prayer.

Toward the end of his life Khayyam fell ill, and when scholars wrote to him with scientific questions he wrote back saying that he was ill, and 'may God grant us and our brothers a good ending'. This 'good ending', or *husn al-khatimah*, was a prayer that the Prophet and generations of Muslims have made before and since. A close observer of Khayyam, his son-in-law Imam Muhammad al-Baghdadi, recorded Khayyam's last day in detail:

> He was studying the *Shifa* [the celebrated biography of the Prophet Mohamed, then recently published] while using

> a golden toothpick, until he reached the section on 'unity and multiplicity'. He marked the section with his toothpick, closed the book, and asked his companions to gather so he could state his will of testament. When his companions gathered they stood up and prayed, and Khayyam refused to eat and drink until he had performed his night prayer. He prostrated himself, putting his forehead on the ground, and said: 'O Lord, I know you as much as is possible for me; forgive me, for my knowledge of you is my way of reaching you' – and then died.

This was the 'good ending' he wanted.

So one of our greatest scholars, poets and Sufis was a drinker – as were many others before and after him, including caliphs. Let the drinkers drink, and let the rest of us abstain. It is not the business of governments or clerics to interfere and condemn people to be flogged in the name of their literalist Islam. Wherever that happens, hypocrisy reigns. I have seen this at first hand in Saudi Arabia and Pakistan, where the elite drink wine and whisky imported from Europe and Russia, but poor lorry drivers and village folk who drink homemade concoctions languish in prison or are flogged in public.

For a millennium, from the eighth to the eighteenth centuries, Muslims lived out their faith by venerating their Prophet, reciting the Quran, observing the sharia and enjoying the ecstasy of Sufism. These were the mainstays of Muslim life. The evidence surrounds us in every Muslim city, in poetry praising the Prophet and Quranic calligraphy engraved in the walls of major buildings, honouring the saints and fortifying the Hajj routes for hundreds of years. There were tensions between the worldly and the other-worldly, between Sufism and literalism, and caliphal dynasties and rivalries. But a balance was found in honouring the sharia, praying, giving *zakah* (alms) and going on the Hajj, but doing so in the Sufi spirit of love, devotion and purity. The survival of Sufi orders, books, music and gatherings in *dergahs, khanqahs* and *zawiyas*, shrines and meeting-rooms, speaks to us of continuity through a long age of this Muslim way of life.

However, the tensions between the spirit and the letter of the law, between mysticism and literalism, eventually came to a head in a way exemplified by the court struggles of the Muslim Mughals in seventeenth-century India. The struggle between mysticism and literalism, as fought out then between two princes, with their Sufi sister as arbitrator, continues to this day.

Princess Jahanara Begum was the favourite daughter of the Indian emperor Shah Jahan (1592–1666), a Sunni Muslim ruler closely aligned with the Sufi Chishti order of India. Jahanara was seventeen years old when, in 1631, her mother, Shah Jahan's favourite wife (of three), died, plunging him into deep mourning that brought him close to mental collapse. He vowed to create a magnificent mausoleum – the Taj Mahal – for his deceased wife that would testify to his love for her, and glorify her Creator.

Hindus cremated their dead, and orthodox, literalist Muslims forbade ostentatious 'worshipping at graves', which they feared could smack of idolatry. So the building of elaborate mausoleums for Muslims in India was chiefly influenced by Sufi Islam. When completed, the Taj Mahal was a triumph of Mughal Muslim architecture, complete with its own mosque, and with Quranic verses inscribed throughout in Arabic calligraphy, together with Sufi symbolism and poetry.

Shah Jahan's most loved children, Jahanara and her younger brother Crown Prince Dara Shikoh, were both drawn to Sufi mysticism too. Dara Shikoh's Sufi mentor was a leading mystic from Lahore, Baba Mian Mir, who had excellent relations with the Sikh community, rivals of the Muslims. At Dara Shikoh and Jahanara's request, Baba Mian Mir laid the foundation bricks of the great Sikh Golden Temple in Amritsar.

Dara Shikoh, enthused by his Sufi teacher's spiritual openness, went further. He translated the Hindu Upanishads – considered by orthodox Muslims to be blasphemous and idolatrous – into Persian, the lingua franca of Indian Muslims at the time. Dara Shikoh even claimed that the Upanishads were God's 'most perfect revelation', and saw no contradiction between the deeper messages of early Hindu scripture and that of the Quran. The prince's closest friends included Sikhs, Hindus, and even Sarmad the Jew, a wandering Jewish mystic who was verbally abused by anti-Semitic Muslim clerics of the time. In all of this, the princess supported Dara Shikoh, claiming 'my brother and I are one soul in two bodies'.

As the emperor's preferred daughter, Jahanara was at the heart of the imperial dynasty, and a wise and constant counsellor to both her father and her brother, the crown prince. She was instrumental on more than one occasion in ensuring that this Muslim empire was not threatened from within. Jahanara was a *hafizah*, meaning that she had committed the Quran to memory. She was fluent in Arabic and Persian, and probably Hindi as well – it was she who reintroduced her father to his old love of Hindi music after her mother died, as she tried to console him in his months of grieving. When he appointed her as Princess of the Court, the First Lady, it was the first time a daughter, and not a wife, had held such a prominent position in a Mughal court.

She also became increasingly drawn, in public and private, toward Sufism. At first she was a disciple of the Qadiri order of Baghdad, under the guidance of a living local teacher, Mullah Shah Badakhshi (d. 1616). Badakhshi testified in his writings about the princess that 'she has attained so extraordinary a development of the mystical knowledge that she would be worthy of being my representative – if she were not a woman'. Badakhshi's teachings of humility and love for God and godly people stayed with the princess, but being a Qadiri Sufi did not stop her turning to the Chishti order too.

The Chishtis had a strong presence among Muslims in India at the time, and still do today. The order was founded by Muin ad-Din Chishti (d. 1236), and his tomb in Ajmer, near Delhi, was a regular place of pilgrimage among Muslims then, as now. Chishti's appeal extends, interestingly, beyond Muslims: Hindus and Sikhs in India also visit the shrine of this Sufi to be connected to something of the afterlife, the metaphysical. Also at these shrines there is *Qawwali* Sufi devotional music, mastered and popularised by globally renowned musicians such as Nusrat Fateh Ali Khan.

When I visited Ajmer in 2012, the keepers of the shrine showed me the damage done in recent bombings by literalist Muslims, who consider this multicultural gathering an abomination. Yet despite the threat to their lives, devotees of the Sufis from Sikh, Hindu and Muslim backgrounds continue to gather in their millions, united in their shared commitment to the Divine.

As Jahanara continued to counsel her father in court, she also threw herself into writing about Sufism. In 1640 she completed a book entitled *Confidant of the Spirits*, a biography of Sheikh Muin ad-Din Chishti highly regarded among scholars of the time for its impeccable sourcing and research.

In November 1643 she went to Chishti's mausoleum with her father. The First Lady and her emperor father's visit to the most important and popular Sufi shrine in India was partly for purposes of protocol and to consolidate support among the populace, but for Jahanara it was more significant. She was no longer a mere student of Sufism, but was deeply enthralled by it. She wrote about her attachment to the tomb, referring to herself as 'this lowly *faqeera*', a Sufi term for someone who is spiritually needy and yearns for God's riches to be bestowed on them. She wrote about the various places in the mausoleum that she visited, and how she was touched deeply by the sanctity of the Sufi who was buried there, with an extraordinary humility and veneration:

> With an hour of daylight remaining, I went to the holy sanctuary and rubbed my pale face on the dust of that threshold. From the doorway to the blessed tomb I went barefoot, kissing the ground. Having entered the dome, I went around the light-filled tomb of my master seven times, sweeping it with my eyelashes, and making the sweet-smelling dust of that place the mascara of my eyes.

India's First Lady had a brush with death in 1644, when the 31-year-old princess attempted to put out an accidental fire that had engulfed a servant, and her flowing silk garments, perfumed with oil, caught fire. Six of her maids rushed to put out the blaze on Jahanara's body, and in the process inflicted further damage. She nearly died. Two of the maids did die, as a result of their own wounds. The emperor brought in the best doctors from Persia and Europe to attend his daughter, including a physician from the royal court of England.

It was at this point, just as the princess looked weakest, that she emerged at her strongest. In her fragile state, she struck her heaviest blow for Mughal power by using her position as the most senior princess in court to broker peace between her father and her warrior brother, Aurangzeb. For years, there had been rivalry and suspicion between them. Aurangzeb had put their father under house arrest in Agra as he fought Crown Prince Dara Shikoh for control of the empire. Aurangzeb's battle cry was to liberate his father from 'the infidel, Dara Shikoh' and others. By reconciling Aurangzeb and the emperor, Jahanara made it possible for Aurangzeb to win over leading courtiers and consolidate his path to the Mughal throne. It was this one action that put Aurangzeb in his sister's debt, and when he did eventually become king in 1658 (until 1707), he would look to Jahanara for counsel.

Not only did the Sufi prince Dara Shikoh lose the war for succession to the Mughal throne, but he was put on trial for apostasy and dishonouring Islam with his liberal utterances of praise for Hindus, Sikhs, Jews and others. The victorious Aurangzeb sent Dara Shikoh's head to the now frail emperor Shah Jahan, who was traumatised by seeing it.

So Aurangzeb won the throne, but Dara Shikoh's words at his trial have been preserved, and still serve as inspiration to Muslims and others seeking to stand up to the literalists. When asked in court if he could consider himself a Hindu or Sikh, he responded robustly:

> Of course I couldn't, because I am Muslim, but my humanness is shared with anyone and everyone. If we choose to love one special person, does it mean that they are the only person worthy to be loved? 'To you your faith, to me mine.' 'There is no compulsion in religion' – straight from the Quran. We cannot force our religion on others ... our duty as Muslims, whose God tells us that there is no obligation in religion, is to allow all faiths to flourish. Is that not what our empire is built on, the very reason the Mughals are great? We were the minority; who were we to

> march in to new territories and impose our creed on a massive majority of different faiths? Babur knew that. Akbar the Great knew it; Jahangir knew it ... Akbar's genius was to harness traditions, and his reward was a vibrant, prosperous kingdom. Akbar made his governors read poems by Rumi!

To the very end, Dara Shikoh kept advancing a pluralist, Sufi vision of the Mughal approach to power, every element opposed by his stronger younger brother Aurangzeb. Despite protesting: 'Of the twenty references to apostasy in the Quran, not one prescribes death!' he was subsequently killed by Aurangzeb's henchmen.

Amidst the bloodshed of Aurangzeb's rule, the Sufi princess survived and tried, unsuccessfully, to be a force for peace and reconciliation. She nevertheless continued to enjoy influence in court: the new king had not forgotten his sister brokering peace with their father. But as a Mughal princess and high lady of the court, she was not to be married. A husband might threaten the throne, and so, to keep lovers at bay, rumours were put about that the emperor poisoned all suitors. In her memoirs, she wrote passionately about her relationship with a Hindu lover – a relationship she did not consummate but promised to continue in the next life. She lobbied her brother to annul the old laws of Akbar the Great that forbade the princess to marry. Prince Dara Shikoh had agreed that if he became king, he would overturn the ban. But Aurangzeb was only too keen to ensure that outsiders did not marry into the royal harem.

Whatever the truth about her emotional life, we do know that Jahanara had a penchant for wild nights, and this troubled Aurangzeb deeply. A Venetian observer of the Mughal court wrote:

> The princess was fond of drinking wine, which was imported for her from Persia, Kabul and Kashmir. But the best liquor she drank was distilled in her own house. It was a most delicious spirit, made from wine and rosewater, flavoured with many costly spices and aromatic drugs. Many a time she did me the favour of ordering some bottles of it to be sent to my house, in sign of gratitude for my curing people in the harem ...

> The lady's drinking took place at night, when various delightful pranks, music, dancing were going on around her. Things arrived at such a pass that sometimes she was unable to stand, and they had to carry her off to bed.

In 1666, Emperor Shah Jahan died. Jahanara lamented her father's passing with words reminiscent of the Sufi poet Rumi's lines on reeds:

> I cry from grief like a reed, with only wind
> to grasp;
> I burn from sorrow like a candle, but only
> smoke rises from my head.

Her grief may have been for something more than just her father's death: the family legacy, the Mughal inheritance, was under threat. As she and other members of the family laid the late emperor inside the Taj Mahal, beside her mother, the liberal and inclusive intellectual and artistic spirit of Sufism was under threat from the militantly orthodox Aurangzeb.

Despite her father's and brother Dara Shikoh's deaths, and due to her own popularity inside the royal court and among the general populace, as well as Aurangzeb's trust in her, Jahanara remained First Lady of the Mughal empire. But her liberal instincts could not persuade the new emperor. The days of Jahanara's father and his grandfather, Akbar the Great – who had attempted to establish *deen-e ilahi*, a syncretistic mixture of Hinduism and Islam – were over.

Aurangzeb wanted to move away from the Islam of shrines, art, music, drinking and the rest. His rule was to be defined by a more literalist understanding of scripture. Aurangzeb banned court music, court poetry, and even the keeping of an official chronicle, saying this was too vainglorious for a pious Muslim. He abruptly ended his daily balcony appearances before his subjects – the Indian practice of Jharokha Darshan – on the grounds that this could be idolatrous. He went on to forbid alcohol, cannabis, and sexual relations outside wedlock.

Aurangzeb's literalism seems to have stemmed from his upbringing as a child. While Dara Shikoh and Jahanara were mentored by Sufi-inclined spiritual Muslims, Aurangzeb was fostered as a prince by literalist Muslims – though in later life he was critical of his own teachers, arguing that they had focused too much on ritual and not enough on how he could be a better warrior or monarch.

His sister Jahanara claimed in her memoirs that Aurangzeb had had a Hindu female lover at a younger age. He allegedly drank wine with her to prove that he would bend to her will and love her regardless of rules and social expectations, but somehow their relationship still broke down. Aurangzeb never quite forgave himself for his 'sins', and his revived literalism may therefore have been a form of penance. Ultimately, in his determination to be different from his Sufi elder brother and Sufi-influenced father, he opted for what they opposed: puritanical religion.

The permissive spirit of the Mughals thus came to an end, and was never revived again in India. Aurangzeb's ideas, attitudes and legacy were to set the scene for the bloodbath in 1947, when nearly 2 million Muslims were killed during the partition of India to create Pakistan. Dara Shikoh's instinct was to live among, and love, Hindus and Sikhs as God's people; Aurangzeb's was to ensure that Muslims always had the upper hand, that his religion reigned supreme.

In 1679, Princess Jahanara confronted her brother in public, and argued – in court – that he should apply 'the same law for all, as the same God rules over all'. One hundred and fifteen years previously, their great-grandfather Akbar the Great had decided that Hindus and Muslims were equal in India, and no special tax would be levied on the country's Hindus, despite the Quran's calling for a *jizya* poll tax on protected non-Muslims who lived in a Muslim-controlled state. Akbar had argued that although *jizya* had been useful in the Arabian context of the Prophet's day, it was not relevant to the India of his time, and few Indian Muslims, even Muslim clerics, disagreed with him. His great-grandson Aurangzeb, however, took a more literalist approach, and enforced the *jizya* tax on India's Hindus and Sikhs. Like all literalists, he justified his stance by quoting verbatim from the Quran.

How can reason ever win in the face of brute force combined with claims of godly validation? And must everything that is mentioned in the Quran be 'established' in society? If so, since the Quran mentions slavery repeatedly, should Muslims reintroduce that practice, too?

Aurangzeb's sister pleaded with him to abandon his rigid approach and undermining of their family traditions. In public, the Venetian chronicler Niccolao Manucci records, Aurangzeb 'bade her goodbye and turned his back on her, a movement that cut the princess to the very quick'. For the First Lady of the Mughals – daughter of the creator of the Taj Mahal, granddaughter of Jahangir, great-granddaughter of Akbar the Great – this abandonment by her own brother was a deep humiliation. Eighteen months later, in 1681, aged sixty-seven, Jahanara died.

If she had wanted, Jahanara could have been buried beside her beloved parents inside the Taj Mahal. Instead, she opted for a simple tomb close to the grave of a Sufi master in Delhi. Having helped her father build the Taj Mahal in all its glory, in the end she abandoned worldly pomp and power and was buried in a simple mausoleum among poets and spiritual seekers, under a tomb inscription that I read when I visited her graveside in Delhi:

> Let no rich canopy cover my grave: this grass is the best covering for the tomb of the faqeera [poor in spirit], the humble, transitory Jahanara, disciple of the holy men of Chisht, daughter of the emperor Shah Jahan (AD 1681)

The public battle of Jahanara's time between opposing strands of Islam saw the victory of literalism over mysticism. That battle rages today. Most people in Pakistan have heard of Aurangzeb and venerate him deeply, but very few know of his elder brother Dara Shikoh. Aurangzeb ruled with power and might, but by working to erase Sufism, the compassionate soul of Islam, from his court and circle of influence, he gave birth to a fanaticism that led to Mughal decline and Muslim losses in India.

Jalaluddin Rumi, Omar Khayyam, Dara Shikoh and Jahanara, the legendary Sufi figures we have met in this chapter, were all children of proud, confident Muslim civilisations in Turkey, Persia and India. But their poetic, mystical and pluralistic vision came under growing attack both from within Islam and, before long, and still more ominously, from further afield.

PART TWO

The Rise of Anger

Why did the loss of Muslim empires lead to the rise of political Islam?

Why did Salafis or Wahhabis emerge as a force of hatred against mainstream Muslims?

Why do jihadis persist in their violence despite global retribution?

Can radical Muslims kill and maim in the name of Islam and remain within the fold of the faith?

7
A Hundred Years of Humiliation

There was once a civilisation that was the greatest in the world. It was able to create a continental superstate that stretched from ocean to ocean, and from northern climes to tropics and deserts. Within its dominion lived hundreds of millions of people, of different creeds and ethnic origins.

One of its languages became the universal language of a large part of the world, and the bridge between the peoples of a hundred lands. Its armies were made up of people of many nationalities, and its military protection allowed a degree of peace and prosperity that had never been known. The reach of this civilisation's commerce extended from Latin America to China, and everywhere in between.

And this civilisation was driven, more than anything, by invention. Its architects designed buildings that defied gravity, and its mathematicians created algebra and algorithms that would enable the building of computers and creation of encryption. Its physicians examined the human body and found new cures for disease, whilst its astronomers looked into the heavens, named the stars, and paved the way for space travel and exploration. Its writers created thousands of stories – stories of courage, romance and magic. Its poets wrote of love, when others before them were too steeped in fear to think of such things.

> *When other nations were afraid of ideas, this civilisation thrived on them and kept them alive. When the censors threatened to wipe out knowledge from past civilisations, this civilisation kept it alive and passed it on to others.*
>
> *While modern Western civilisation shares many of these traits, the civilisation I'm talking about was the Islamic world from the year 800 to 1600, which included the Ottoman Empire, the courts of Baghdad, Damascus and Cairo, and such enlightened rulers as Suleiman the Magnificent.*
>
> *Although we are often unaware of our indebtedness to this other civilisation, its gifts are very much part of our heritage. The technology industry would not exist without the contributions of Arab mathematicians. Sufi poet–philosophers like Rumi challenged our notions of self and truth, and leaders like Suleiman contributed to our notions of tolerance and civil leadership.*
>
> *Perhaps we can learn lessons from this example: it was leadership based on meritocracy, not inheritance. It was leadership that harnessed the full capabilities of a very diverse population, which included Christian, Islamic, and Jewish traditions.*

Not the words of a Muslim leader, but of the successful US businesswoman Carly Fiorina, then CEO of Hewlett-Packard, ending her speech 'Technology, Business and Our Way of Life: What's Next?' in Minnesota in September 2001.

Fiorina was right to highlight the theme of leadership. The Quran confirms that Muslims are expected to take a lead in the stewardship of God's creation, and for centuries the Muslim psyche expected them to assume this higher position of responsibility. But no more.

Islam first spread across the Arab world through trade, spiritual perseverance and military success. For the first hundred years after the passing of the Prophet Mohamed, to be a Muslim was to be part of the ruling class, the victorious and powerful force that was Islam. In the eighth and ninth centuries, Muslims were the new ruling order in the Middle East. The Syrian Christian writer John of Damascus, observing the entry of the Muslims into the Levant in the eighth century, wrote of their zeal, but also their efficiency in collecting taxes. When Christians and others wanted to convert, the Umayyad caliphs of that period refused, preferring the higher taxes collected from non-Muslims in return for their *dhimmi* (protected) status. Yet over time, the Syrians, Egyptians and others came to believe in the elite Muslim creed, and adopted the conquerors' lifestyle, faith, and even Arabic language.

To be Muslim was to be powerful and expansionist, as the empire kept on conquering new territories. In the ancient world, if a people were not advancing and conquering, they were liable to be conquered. 'Kill or be killed' was the mantra of antiquity. Islam, in its simplicity of belief in the one God and the message of the Prophet, overturned the rule of Christianity in the East – the Copts of Egypt, the Najranis of Arabia, the Orthodox in Jerusalem – and soon the eyes of the Muslim armies were set on Constantinople, capital of the Byzantine empire. Although Jerusalem fell to the Crusaders in 1099, Saladin retook it for the Muslims in 1187, and the Ottoman Sultan Mehmet seized Constantinople in 1453. The Ottomans even laid siege to Vienna, in the heart of Europe, in 1529, and then again in 1683. In the West, an offshoot Umayyad dynasty brought Muslim rule all the way to North Africa and Spain. It was not until the fifteenth century that the Spanish expelled Jews and Muslims, and Catholicism reigned supreme.

In these great battles of ideas and peoples, Islam and Muslims were for a millennium largely unbeatable, and their inner core of faith, ideas, trade and territory was secure. Even the great scourge of the Mongol invasion of the Middle East, in the mid-thirteenth century, appeared to be reversed when the Mongol warriors from the central Asian steppes, having destroyed Muslim armies and cities, within a century embraced Islam. Their descendants created the Mughal Muslim dynasty in India and Afghanistan, while their Ottoman cousins ruled Turkey, the Balkans, North Africa and much of the Middle East. Such was the power and confidence of Islam. No set of ideas or army could defeat Muslim superiority.

And then everything changed.

In 1789, the French Revolution was proclaimed against the monarchy in the name of liberty, fraternity and equality. France witnessed the overthrow of a repressive royalty, attacks on the clergy, the ransacking of churches, discarding of tradition, and veneration of godless thinkers such as Voltaire and Rousseau. It was Voltaire who had entertained audiences by writing plays for French theatre mocking Muslims and their Prophet 'Mahomet' (rather than Mohamed) as the founder of a barbarian sect, an imposter, a scoundrel and a fanatic. A brash, new, modern, civilisation grew from the corpse of European Catholicism – and within a decade sent its emissary to the Muslim world.

The French moved into Alexandria with battalions of scholars, who built a library of modern European literature and a printing press with Arabic type (the first encroachment on the sacred art of Quranic calligraphy). As Muslims looked on bewildered, 29-year-old General Napoleon Bonaparte, a true child of the French Revolution, marched into Cairo. Where was the European intellectual response that defended faith, tradition, monarchy and family? When the French arrived in Alexandria in Egypt on 1 July 1798, the Islamic world would not have been aware of the British philosopher Edmund Burke's faith-based and principled repudiation of the French revolutionaries' iconoclastic zeal.

When Muslim armies had conquered cities in the past, Sufi dervishes would spread spirituality among the populace. The Mughals and Ottomans went to battle with spiritual men at their helm. Bonaparte, however, shook the Muslim world to its core with his new approach. As master of Egypt, he introduced the virtues of Western civilisation. He established the Institut d'Egypte for French scholars, a library, a chemistry laboratory, a health service, a botanical garden, an observatory, an antiquities museum and a zoo. Napoleon had come to challenge British naval supremacy, he claimed; Egypt was merely collateral damage. But his 'civilising mission' was more than just a matter of routing the British. The scientific and newly secular culture of the West was set to change the Muslim world for ever.

The deficits in their own knowledge, and the enthusiasm for secular enlightenment among the French, shocked the Muslims into tacitly accepting that a new, superior civilisation had emerged in the West. Worse, when Napoleon was ejected from Egypt, in 1801, this was not effected by Ottomans or Arabs but by a British fleet under Lord Nelson. In just three years Napoleon had delivered an intellectual challenge to Egypt and the Muslim world that still reverberates today. The medieval crusades had failed to have an impact on the core of Islam or trigger its worldly decline, but Napoleon's modern French ideas planted the seeds of doubt within it.

Thus began a hundred years of humiliation. By 1901, the glory days of the Muslims were over, and Russia's Tsar Nicolas I referred to the Ottoman caliphate as 'the sick man of Europe'. During the century following Napoleon's expulsion from Egypt in 1801, much was going wrong in the two greatest contemporary empires of Islam: the Ottoman and the Mughal. Failures there led to the birth of that Islamism in the 1920s that has come to haunt Muslim countries and communities around the world today.

French ideas began to spread in some of the Ottoman lands closest to the French. In February 1804 a Christian rebellion started against the Ottomans in Serbia. The Ottoman Empire had a system of 'millets', autonomous religious minority communities, giving rise to multiculturalism, religious pluralism and tolerance. Yet even this accommodation, the refuge of Europe's persecuted minorities, did not withstand French rallying cries. The Ottomans suppressed the 1804 Serbian uprising, but in 1815 a second upheaval won the Serbs autonomy within the empire. The Greeks followed, with European support, and won an independent sovereign Greek kingdom. The Christian peoples of the Balkans successively rebelled and won for themselves liberty, fraternity and equality.

The French Revolution not only sent Napoleon to become master of Egypt, but even shook the Ottomans in Istanbul, the great capital of Islam. Between 1789 and 1807, to modernise their system of government, the Ottomans responded to the French Revolution by creating a *nizami cedit*, or 'new order', by bringing in European advisers to reform the Janissaries, the sultan's military elite. The military responded by dethroning the sultan and installing their preferred monarch. This was a humiliation for the executive authority of the old caliph, Sultan Selim III (r. 1789–1807), while his short-lived successor Mustafa IV (r. 1807–8) was a mere stooge of the Janissaries. The 'new order' was killed at birth.

Sultan Selim III put the threat from the West down to European military prowess. In response, he opened a number of military schools with French instructors to teach students French, mathematics and navigation. The problem was that the Europeans could not be beaten, or even rivalled, unless the Muslims changed their intellectual approach, yet the Muslims could not go as far as the French in adopting a wholly individualistic, rational culture, and severing links with their past. This dichotomy haunted the Ottomans to their very end.

Very quickly, a new Ottoman sultan, Mahmut II (r. 1808–39), took the throne. He was more attuned to the grumblings of the population and their resentment of the machinations at the top of the empire. To seem more European, and in line with the sentiments of the time, he created a 'Charter of Alliance' (*Senet-i Ittifak* in Turkish) in 1808. This was the first agreement between ruler and ruled in Ottoman history, with local rulers demanding their rights in exchange for pledging allegiance to the sultan. It has sometimes been likened to a Turkish Magna Carta. But autocracies do not change so easily. The agreement did not last, but a precedent for change was set.

The greatest hope for change, and with it the greatest humiliation, came in the form of the Ottoman *Tanzimat* ('reorganisation') reforms. They were designed to be wholesale reforms of Muslim societies driven from the centre, and influenced fully by the secularism now in the ascendant in both France and Britain. It was no accident that the man who drove the *Tanzimat* changes, their chief architect, was the Ottoman ambassador to France in 1834 and Great Britain in 1836. Mustafa Reshid Pasha returned to Istanbul as foreign minister, and later grand vizier (prime minister). From 1839 on, he introduced a series of reforms to make the Ottoman monarchy more constitutional, more secular and more liberal – altogether more European.

While these developments earned applause from London, Paris and Vienna, they were held in deep suspicion by the Muslim populace at large. To most Muslims, particularly the leading *ulama* religious scholars, the reforms smacked of kowtowing to Europe. When, in the 1450s, the printing press was first introduced into Ottoman territories, the hard-line *ulama* successfully lobbied the Sultan and had it banned as a tool of the devil. In Europe the printing press played a role in the reformation of Christianity, as the new ideas of Martin Luther quickly spread. The availability of mass-produced bibles, translated by Luther and others into languages that people actually spoke (instead of Latin), had the direct result of creating mass interest in reading. Muslims, by contrast, kept the press at bay. Consequently, there came about a 200-year lag in the development of intellectual thought, and a Muslim stagnation in worldly matters. It was only with Napoleon that printers arrived in Cairo.

Muslims were in awe of the new and apparently superior Europeans and the Ottomans continued reforming as many aspects of government as possible in a bid to catch up. The *Tanzimat* reforms sought to Westernise fully: Napoleonic trade laws were introduced in 1850; homosexuality was decriminalised in 1858, more than a century ahead of Britain's legalisation of gay rights; sharia punishments for apostasy and adultery ended; and non-Muslims were made full citizens of the Ottoman state, ending their special taxation and *dhimmi* status. Radical changes were needed to bring the empire up to date with the modern world, and Sultan Abdul Majid (1839–61), son of Mahmut II, forged ahead.

By 1859, the hatred of Westernisation was so strong, and the humiliation of Islam felt so deeply, that unlike any other time in Ottoman history, a public assassination of the sultan was attempted, in what was called the Kuleli incident. There had been family intrigues in the past, but never before had forty-one members of the public plotted to kill an Ottoman sultan, for what they saw as his wholesale Westernisation and abandonment of Islam.

The *Tanzimat* reforms did not save the struggling Ottoman Empire, alas. By 1900, the Europeans were even further ahead, while ideas such as nationalism, Darwinism and racial superiority were finding a home among the sultan's Arab subjects. The Balkan Christians had already broken away and shown the way for others.

The humiliation from within and without was afflicting not only the heartlands of the Ottoman caliphate. Further east, in India, home of the mighty Mughals, Muslim rule was also dealt a blow from which the Mughals never recovered. Since the string of victories scored by the British East India Company, from the battle of Plassey in 1757 to the defeat of the Muslim hero Tipu Sultan in 1792, the Mughals had survived in name only. But it was survival nevertheless, and where there was life, there was hope of renewal and revival. The British destroyed that hope with a further, decisive, humiliation.

The great Indian uprising of 1857 against British rule in India was the culmination of a long simmering of grievances against imperial England. The historian William Dalrymple informs us, in his poignant and masterful *The Last Mughal*, that of the 139,000 sepoys of the Bengal army, the largest army in Asia, all but 7,796 turned against their British masters. The British had offended and abused Indians, both Hindu and Muslim, where it hurt and humiliated them most: their faith. To the Hindu, the cow was a sacred animal; to the Muslim, the unclean was defiling of ritual purity. By the mid-1850s, much like the Ottoman Empire, the British had subjected Indian troops to a process of military modernisation and adjustment. There were widespread rumours that the coating of new-issue cartridges contained cow and pig fat. Fears that the British East India Company was actively undermining India's religions had precipitated earlier mutinies in 1806, 1824 and 1852, when a regiment of largely high-caste Hindu troops refused service in Burma, since crossing the sea would have been polluting to their caste. But the 1857 rebellion coalesced around Muslims and Hindus marching to Delhi demanding full reinstatement of the Mughal emperor, Bahadur Shah Zafar.

The name Bahadur Shah Zafar still sends shivers down the spines of Indian Muslims and Hindus alike. Already eighty-two years old, he was a poet and Sufi master who spent his days at the last Mughal court in Delhi in meditation, Islamic instruction and writing verse. He had neither the stamina nor the military strength and finances to head the rebellion against the British. But he was the inheritor of Hindustan, or India, and the son of a great Muslim dynasty that included the legendary figures Babur, Humayun, Akbar, Jahangir, Shah Jahan, Jahanara, Aurangzeb and others. Powerless as Bahadur Shah Zafar was, he was the standard-bearer of Islam and India against the Christian English and their increasingly evangelical zeal. A few years earlier Emily Eden, accompanying her brother the Governor General, Lord Auckland, on a tour of India, had described Bahadur Shah Zafar's prestige even among the Governor General's own entourage, regardless of whether they were Hindu or Muslim: 'All our servants were in a state of profound veneration,' she wrote. 'The natives all look upon the King of Delhi as their rightful Lord, and so he is, I suppose.'[1] And in 1857 this revered emperor supported the uprising and the rejection of the British.

The failure of the Indian masses, together with the military, political and religious elites, was not the only degradation. It was the way the British deposed the last Mughal monarch and disposed of him that most deeply humiliated the Muslims (and Hindus). His family had ruled India for 350 years. He was born in 1775, when the British colonisers were still a relatively modest and mainly coastal power in India, at an early stage in their rise from traders to an aggressive military expansionist force. Yet the British removed Shah Zafar's name from coins, removed the Mughals from the Red Fort, their historical home, and started to control the city of Delhi itself.

Zafar was no fighter. He was a Sufi poet, calligrapher, curator of gardens, patron of the arts, and an amateur architect.

But the British could not leave this popular and intellectual Sufi emperor in peace; the direct descendant of Genghis Khan could not be allowed to die in his ancestral palaces. Instead, the British exiled him to Burma, where he died in 1862. His English captors buried him in an unmarked grave behind a prison in Rangoon, with large quantities of lime to ensure the speedy decay of both bier and body. After a week the British Commissioner, Captain H. N. Davies, wrote to London reassuring the government that news of the emperor's death had been kept secret, and armed guards kept away the crowds that arrived from the bazaar. Davies telegrammed: 'A bamboo fence surrounds the grave for some considerable distance, and by the time the fence is worn out, the grass will again have properly covered the spot, and no vestige will remain to distinguish where the last of the Great Moghuls rests.'

Britain's success in subduing and humiliating the figureheads of Islam in the nineteenth century did not stop with the disgracing of Shah Zafar. Egypt, a land at the heart of Sunni Islam, with Cairo the seat of the centuries-old Al-Azhar Mosque and University, Islam's greatest centre of learning, was similarly shamed.

The Suez Canal, cutting through Egypt from the Mediterranean to the Red Sea, provided Britain, more than any other world power, with naval advantages and a shorter route to India. Anglo-French control of the canal had been major news for almost a decade even before its opening in 1869. It continued to make global headlines, while facilitating British trade, naval and military domination, until 1956, when Egyptian President Gamal Abdul Nasser nationalised it. From the beginning, Anglo-French control of Egypt's most strategic asset, the imposition of a ministry responsible for the canal, its financial domination of a bankrupt Egyptian government, and the presence of tens of thousands of Europeans in Cairo to control Egypt's economic and political affairs, all led to deepening feelings of subjugation among Egyptians.

In 1878, Colonel Urabi Pasha led a revolt of elite Egyptians and military personnel against European control of Egyptian affairs. From constitutional liberals to landlords, and from Muslim religious leaders to the long-suffering peasantry, Egyptians of all classes joined Urabi. The uprising was portrayed in Paris, London and other European capitals as threatening the prosperity of Europe. 'Egypt crisis' headlines suggested, despite the lack of concrete evidence, that the Suez Canal was somehow unsafe in Egyptian hands. When rioting broke out in Alexandria in June 1882 and some forty Europeans died, British and French newspapers inflated the casualty toll and sensationally wrote of hundreds of Europeans dead.

In the autumn of 1882, a British expeditionary force overpowered Egyptian forces in the battle of Tel el-Kebir, not far from the canal. The British visit saw Urabi imprisoned and the uprising brought under control. British Prime Minister William Gladstone quipped: 'We have done our Egyptian business, and we are the Egyptian government.' And in order to become Egypt's government, Lord Cromer, an eminent member of the Barings banking family, was sent from London to become Consul-General of Egypt.

Nascent feelings of Egyptian nationalism were not extinguished with Urabi's rebellion, however. And it is interesting to reflect that although Urabi and his followers rose up against the European powers, nationalist uprisings in Egypt and elsewhere were actually inspired by European thinking. The nationalist movements in the Balkans against Ottoman rule were similarly motivated by ideas stemming from Europe.

The Western assumption that nation-states are a positive development was the outcome of a specifically European history of wars and compromise. That assumption, the response to a particular time and place, was destined to become a global marker of modernity and civilisation. Centuries earlier, sectarian conflict and political upheaval across Central Europe had culminated in the Thirty Years' War of 1618–48. To find peace between Europe's fanatical factions, the exhausted protagonists broke off their fighting to create a balance of power by establishing multiple political units, none of them powerful enough alone to defeat all of the others. This 'Westphalia peace', in American statesman Henry Kissinger's words, was a 'practical accommodation, not a unique moral insight'.[2] Each country was granted the sovereignty of its monarch within its territory. States would respect and acknowledge each other's domestic political and religious structures as realities, and refrain from challenging their existence. This was the balance of power that Westphalia created in 1648 – and the basis of the modern international world order, based on sovereign nation-states.

Kissinger lays this revered and oft-cited treaty bare:

> The 17th-century negotiators who crafted the Peace of Westphalia did not think they were laying the foundation for a globally applicable system. They made no attempt to include neighbouring Russia, which was then reconsidering its own order after the nightmarish 'Time of Troubles' by enshrining principles distinctly at odds with the Westphalia balance: a single absolute ruler, a unified religious orthodoxy, and a programme of territorial expansion in all directions. Nor did the other major power centres regard the Westphalia settlement (to the extent they learned of it at all) as relevant to their own regions.[3]

Yet this was the order imposed on the Muslim Ottoman territories. A Muslim civilisation born of, and sustained largely by, faith networks and scripture was now turned on its head to accommodate French revolutionary ideas, and reorganised according to the Westphalia system of nation-states. The Ottomans and Russians were not alone in their surprise. The Chinese were also out of step with this new order of national sovereignty and mutually reinforced weakness. The Ottomans, Russians, Chinese and, arguably, the Indians had for millennia operated on religious, political and cultural principles radically different from the Westphalia experiment. Would the new approach in Europe work equally well in other parts of the globe? The Europeans were in no doubt: they knew best what was right.

'The Peace of Westphalia became a turning point in the history of nations because the elements it set in place were as uncomplicated as they were sweeping,' explains Kissinger. He goes on:

> The state, not the empire, dynasty, or religious confession, was affirmed as the building block of European order ... The genius of this system, and the reason it spread across the world, was that its provisions were procedural, not substantive. If a state would accept these basic requirements, it could be recognised as an international citizen able to maintain its own culture, politics, religion and internal policies, shielded by the international system from outside intervention.[4]

The theory sounded attractive. But reality was, and remains, different. There was no precedent in the Muslim world for a European-style secular state.

The mistakes of the Muslims continued. During the First World War the Ottomans joined the wrong side. The Germans lost, and with them the Ottomans lost too. Three empires ended in 1918 with the end of the Great War: the Russian, the Austro-Hungarian and the Ottoman. The Russian end of empire produced communism; Germany produced Nazism; and Ottoman decline produced Islamism. Not, however, before the hundred years' humiliation was made worse.

The French and British imperialists carved up the Ottoman Empire in a short-sighted, arbitrary and utterly prejudicial manner, drawing lines in the desert to create new countries where nations simply did not exist before – Iraq and Jordan, for example. Out of the corpse of the caliphate were carved twenty-one separate nations. France took control of parts of Syria, Lebanon and Morocco, while Britain ruled Iraq, Jordan, Palestine and others. The 1920 Treaty of Sèvres, signed with what was left of the Ottoman Empire, created a 'Middle East' that was a patchwork of states on the Westphalia model.

By 1924, little over a century after Napoleon burst upon the scene in Egypt, Muslims were left with no caliph for the first time in their history. Worse, European powers – unbelievers – were now dominant in Muslim lands, not just across the Middle East and North Africa but also in Asia, where the Mughals had been exiled to Burma, and India was now controlled by the British.

How had the power of Islam tumbled from the heights of the minarets to the point where Atatürk, the secular president of Turkey, could now forbid the gatherings of dervishes, and the call to prayer itself? What calamity had befallen Muslims? How did they decline from being the world's most innovative, powerful people – in trade, technology and political command – to being dominated by the West? The attempt to answer this question continues into our own times.

8

Who is an Islamist?

Islamists come in many varieties, but making their version of Islam a powerful political force in the modern world drives them all. For clarity, we will define them as political activists who seek to impose their reading of the sharia as the law of the land. To Islamists, committing *Haram* acts, those forbidden in sharia, is not just a matter of having a guilty conscience for one's sins and having to face God's judgement in the next life. It means doing something that should be illegal and punished in this life on earth. He or she therefore feels a religious obligation to seek an Islamic state, or caliphate, that would enforce these laws.

The prevailing political ideology of Islamism – the zeitgeist among young Muslim activists – says that being a Muslim, a believer in Islam, is not sufficient. Islamists yearn for something deeper: to bring back the caliphate as the perceived restorer of Muslims' lost dignity and end the feelings of loss and humiliation inflicted on Muslims. Despite their ambitions, they face challenges within mainstream Islam.

For 1,400 years Muslim literature made no reference to 'Islamism'. There were very few Muslim treatises written on 'Islamic government'. There is no agreement on what constitutes 'an Islamic state'. The Prophet left no heir or designated successor, so there were leadership crises within early Islam, with the claims and counterclaims of rival caliphs, and the shedding of blood at the iconic battle of Karbala. Yet these did not give rise to Islamism or to political Islam.

In traditional Muslim societies, the family, the local mosque, seminaries, the *qadi* (sharia judge), the tribal leader, village leader or *za'eem* (mayor) all mattered more than the central government in Istanbul or Delhi. There was no ideology of statism and central state power, or any mass movement of Islamism – there was only Islam, and interpretations of it.

During the upheavals of the twentieth century, however, as world wars and political ideologies drove millions to reshape their governments in the name of Marxism, communism and socialism, activist Muslims responded by politicising their faith: after a hundred years of Muslim humiliation, loss of power and identity crisis, Islamism was born. To this day, the vast majority of the world's Muslims are not Islamists, but the slogans, discourse and political vision of Islamism nowadays dominate Muslim conversations.

Just as Marxism, communism and socialism exist across a spectrum from violent revolutionary (the Russian Bolsheviks) to democratic socialist (the British Labour Party), so it is with Islamism. Based on their geography, circumstances, history, and political leadership, Islamists range from violent nationalists (Hamas in Gaza) to rebellious and repressed opposition (the Muslim Brotherhood in Egypt), to those who have moved away from Islamism and become Muslim conservatives, much like Christian democrats. In this last category, Tunisia's Ennahda Party under the leadership of Sheikh Rachid al-Ghannouchi and Turkey's AKP are the two most prominent examples, to which we will return shortly.

Some of the earliest Islamist thought was almost entirely influenced, whether consciously or not, by the rise of communism. Abul-Ala Maududi (1903–79), in particular, opposed capitalism in the same terms as Marxism, while neglecting to examine the Prophet's own merchant background and the sharia's honouring of property, something communists abhorred and confiscated. Maududi, through his influential books and journalism in the 1930s, was among the first to describe Islam as a political ideology. His was a modern Muslim identity that was not content with praying, fasting, works of charity and pilgrimage, but actively poured scorn on Muslims who contented themselves with these things and did not work to create an Islamic state, a caliphate, with a single leader for all Muslims. In his book *Let Us be Muslims* – mandatory reading for Islamist organisations – he chides believers who are observant but do not view Islam as a contemporary political project.

Unlike Marx, Maududi was not content only with writing. He created a mass movement based on socialist party models, with a cadre and a highly ideological leadership: the Jamaat-e Islami, one of the most organised and active political parties in Pakistan, India and Bangladesh and the South Asian diaspora in the West. Maududi's Jamaat has not secured significant electoral support in Pakistan or Bangladesh, however, consistently polling well below 20 per cent of the vote in free and fair elections.

The scholar and writer Ziauddin Sardar, who met Maududi in London in 1968, describes the extent of the man's appeal:

> Today, there is hardly a corner of the Muslim world where Maududi and Jamaat-e-Islami are not influential. Pious Muslims love his simplistic diatribes. The intensity of his writing on matters of spirituality and faith, and his confidence in the virtues of Islam as a total system that will reassert itself in history, shift attention from how he conceives that Islam should operate in contemporary times. Unleashed as a political entity, his pious individuals lack self-criticism, humility and, above all, doubt about their possession of unswerving righteousness. Islamic bookshops are stocked full with his books, many of which are misogynistic and aggressively anti-Western. The end product of his thought can now be seen in the North-West Frontier Province of Pakistan, where his followers are busy closing down cinemas, banning music, locking women behind four walls, setting up religious police to monitor vice, and generally establishing an ideal Islamic society.[1]

Maududi was not alone in his new form of political activism in the name of Islam.

In Egypt a similar strain of Islam was in gestation, emerging in Ismailia on the Suez Canal just four years after the destruction of the Ottoman caliphate in 1924. The Muslim Brotherhood was launched in 1928, claiming that its aim was to reverse the decline of Muslims. The Brotherhood's answer to Muslim confusion was at once simple and all-encapsulating: '*Al-Islam huwa al-hall*' – 'Islam is the solution' – a slogan that remains popular today. When probed by other Muslims as to what such a grand statement meant in practice for improving lives, being in government, or restoring Muslim glory, the Brotherhood would respond with the oft-repeated manifesto: 'Allah is our objective, the Qur'an is our constitution, the Prophet is our leader, jihad is our path, and death in the name of Allah is our goal.'

The founder of the Muslim Brotherhood, Hasan al-Banna (1906–49), became one of the most influential Arab Muslim figures of the twentieth century. He combined Sufi influences with the methods of European mass political movements, deriving from the Muslim sense of humiliation by the West a conviction that every Muslim should prepare for jihad. The ideas, infrastructure and political aims al-Banna bequeathed to those who surrounded him in their millions continue to shape the modern Middle East and, by extension, the wider Muslim world. Despite pressure and persecution, the Muslim Brotherhood's Islamists are still a pervasive international Sunni movement, with branches or affiliated groups in over seventy countries, sometimes operating openly and sometimes acting as an unofficial underground opposition. The Brotherhood also maintains formal political parties in many Middle Eastern and African countries, including Jordan, Bahrain, Tunisia, Algeria, Iraq, Syria, Sudan, Somalia, Yemen and Israel.

Born in 1906, Hasan al-Banna was the eldest son of a pious mother who recited the Quran daily in the presence of her children. But it was al-Banna's father who exposed him to Sufism from a very young age. Sheikh Ahmad, Hasan's father, was a watchmaker and Muslim scholar who had developed a local following in the Egyptian town of al-Mahmudiyya. At that time in Egypt, Sufi orders were under public attack by a generation of modernists who blamed their obsession with litanies, tombs and superstition as a major cause of the decline of Muslims. Al-Banna's father not only adhered to the Shadhili Sufi order but also published a commentary, when Hasan was a child of six, on the litany of Sidi Ahmad Zarruq, who also belonged to the Shadhili order. The book was republished several times in Hasan al-Banna's lifetime.

Al-Banna attended his first Sufi gathering in a mosque in Damanhour, on the western edge of the Nile delta, at the age of twelve. The melody and chorus of the chanting of the names of God drew him to these men who praised God in beautiful voices in unison. This group of Sufis from the Hasafiyyah order, which remains popular in the Egyptian countryside, also studied the litanies of Zarruq, about which al-Banna's father had written.

Young Hasan returned to the gatherings of the Sufis in the mosque each week and made friends among the younger Sufis. He soon wanted to get more involved with Sufism, and became a daily visitor to a shrine not far from the mosque at the tomb of the founder of the Hasafiyyah order, Sheikh Hasanain. There he meditated and recited prayers, then returned home. Having tasted the serenity of the Sufi mausoleums, al-Banna would often walk three hours from Damanhour to al-Disuq to visit the tombs of other Sufi masters of the past. This habit stayed with him for life, to the dislike of the Salafi puritans who later joined his organisation in droves and attempted to eradicate Sufi influences from the Muslim Brotherhood.

Al-Banna's piety, regular attendance, and commitment to Sufi teachings and practice led to him being admitted into the Hasafiyyah Sufi order in 1923, aged seventeen. His creative, managerial side quickly came to the fore, as he created a Hasafi Benevolent Society to raise funds for the order and its work. The younger members of the order, with al-Banna one of the most active, were interested not just in prayers, chanting and spirituality but also in social action. Al-Banna later described the Hasafi Benevolent Society as the forerunner of his Muslim Brotherhood organisation. For al-Banna, the aims of the society were to divert Muslims away from drinking alcohol and gambling, and to encourage them to fight against the Christian missionaries who were beginning to appear in many parts of Egypt, including al-Banna's village.

That same year, 1923, al-Banna moved to Cairo to pursue further studies in order to become a schoolteacher. Every weekend he travelled home to help his Sufi brothers preach against the Christian missionaries, but every Friday night he would attend the weekly gatherings of the Hasafiyyah order at their headquarters in Cairo. Amid the Sufi chanting, litanies and warmth he would have found spiritual succour, but around him in Cairo he witnessed a different world – a world to which Sufi teachings did not speak. Sufism did not address what he perceived as the licentious culture of modern Cairo, for which he blamed the Europeans, who:

> brought their half-naked women into these regions, their liquors, their theatres, their dance halls, their entertainments, their stories, their newspapers, their romances, their phantasies, their frivolous pastimes and their insolent jokes. Here they countenanced crimes they did not tolerate in their own countries, and decked out this boisterous, frivolous world, reeking with sin and redolent with vice, to the eyes of the simple-minded deluded Muslims of wealth and influence, and to those of rank and power. They were not satisfied until they had founded schools and scientific and cultural institutions in the very heart of the Islamic realm, which cast doubt and heresy into the soul of its sons and taught them to demean themselves, disparage their religion and their fatherland, divest themselves of their traditions and beliefs, and to regard as sacred anything Western, in the belief that only what came from the Europeans served as the supreme model to be emulated in this life.[2]

Blaming the West for the evils he saw around him, without stopping to think that young Egyptians might well have willingly involved themselves in worldly pleasures, was to be a hallmark of the Muslim Brotherhood he was shortly to establish. He saw the West as being at war with Islam, and was probably the first in modern times to speak of this war with the West in the 1930s:

> I was deeply pained, for I saw that the social life of the beloved Egyptian nation was oscillating between its dear and precious Islam, which it had inherited, protected, lived with and taken pride in for fourteen centuries, and this violent Western *Ghazw* [raid], armed and equipped with all the deadly material weapons of money, status, outward appearance, indulgence, power and the means of propaganda.[3]

In keeping with Sufi etiquette, al-Banna raised his concerns with a leading Sufi in Cairo, Sheikh Yusuf al-Dijwi (1870–1946). True to Sufi form, al-Dijwi took a quietist approach and said that God was responsible for what happened in and around Cairo. Al-Banna's fury at this passivity led to him rebuking a senior Sufi in the gathering. But as was al-Banna's way, he turned his anger into action.

He and some friends from the Sufi order in Cairo decided to take Islam to the masses, rather than wait for the masses to come to their understanding of Islam. They went out, and in brief five-minute stints addressed young men in Cairo's popular coffee houses. In line with Sufi teachings, al-Banna did not threaten his audiences with hell, but spoke gently about the beauty of their religion and the cravings of the human soul for God – an approach that seemed to work. Encouraged by the fact that people listened, rather than walking away, al-Banna continued to preach on street corners in short stints, and then went from place to place calling people to God.

In 1927, his studies in Cairo at an end, Hasan al-Banna became a schoolteacher in Ismailia at the age of twenty-one. As he settled into his chosen career he continued his Sufi practices, but his experiences in the great city haunted him. His passion for preaching and proselytising, and his dedication to preserving Islam in the face of what he saw as threats from Western materialism and Christian missionaries, impressed other young men.

In the spring of 1928, six of al-Banna's admirers joined him for a series of meetings in which they lamented the state of Egypt and the perceived decline of Muslims. They asked al-Banna for ideas about what could be done to improve the situation, and their discussions led to him formulating a practical way forward.

Rather than announcing the formation of a new party with Hasan al-Banna as its president, they instead swore a pledge of allegiance (*bai'a*, in Sufi parlance, but derived from a practice of the Prophet's companions) to him. In due course he became known as the *murshid* (spiritual guide) of the group – again evidence of Sufi influence. Just as in his own order, al-Banna met with his new disciples once a week and they recited Sufi litanies. He named this small group of men '*al-Ikhwan al-Muslimeen*', the Muslim Brothers.

Within ten years al-Banna had built his organisation into a mass movement with a presence across Egypt. From university campuses to trade unions, to businesses, to mosques, to civil servants, millions embraced al-Banna's teachings on an Islam that was opposed to the West, an Islam that was a socio-political programme, that defied the humiliation brought to Egypt by the Europeans' 'war on Islam'.

In April 1934, bolstered by his success in attracting vast numbers of Egyptians from across society, he wrote in a tract entitled *To What Do We Summon People?*:

> O our people: with the Quran in our right hand and the Sunnah in our left, and with the deeds of the pious ancestors among the sons of this nation as our example, we call on you. We summon you to Islam, the teachings of Islam, the laws of Islam, and the guidance of Islam, and if this is politics for you, then it is our policy. And if the one summoning you to these principles [Islam] is a politician, then, God be praised, we are the most deeply rooted of men in politics.[4]

Islam, for al-Banna, was more than a relationship with God. In spring 1938, addressing the Brotherhood's students, he formally announced the organisation's entry into Egyptian political life:

> Tell me, Brothers: if Islam is something other than politics, society, economy and culture, what is it then? Is it only prostrations devoid of a pulsating heart? ... Did the Quran reveal a perfect, fixed and detailed system for just that? ... It is precisely

> to such a weak and narrow understanding of Islam that the enemies of Islam try to confine themselves so that they can mock and say to them: 'We left you your freedom of religion.'[5]

As al-Banna put his vision into practice, he ensured that his movement was so organised that members of the Muslim Brotherhood were engaged in programmes of 'good works' at the same time as encouraging and monitoring each other as regards the precepts of personal morality. But al-Banna was also starting to head into more uncertain, undefined and dangerous territory.

Much as he detested European influences on his country, al-Banna was aware of the effectiveness of modern European mass political movements, and so he imitated them. His Brotherhood was thus a hybrid of Sufi influences and features of the Italian fascist and German Nazi mass movements of the 1930s. Like the Italian Blackshirts and Nazi Brownshirts, he created his own paramilitary organisation within the Muslim Brotherhood.

Al-Banna personally trained a cadre known as the *Jawwala* ('Rovers') for several years in Egyptian patriotism and Islamic zeal, recalling the great Islamic past of jihad in the time of the Prophet. Nights were spent with al-Banna in collective vigils and prayers, and the opportunity to spend time with the now famous leader was enough to draw thousands of young Egyptian men. The spirit of jihad and *Futuwwa*, Islamic chivalry on the battlefield, were constantly evoked by al-Banna and this elite group. Yet even as al-Banna's organisation took on a more political and militant stance, he kept it rooted in Sufism by issuing a book of daily litanies in 1936, first for the *Jawwala* and later for the broader Muslim Brotherhood. He called this a *wird*, a practice of the Sufis – no doubt inspired by his father's commentary on the *wird* of Zarruq, and his own adoption of the Hasafi *wird* in his teens and early twenties.

The *Jawwala* were not yet involved in criminal activity or any form of terrorism. Alongside al-Banna, they became the public face of the Muslim Brotherhood, because they engaged in social work and provided a martial presence and personal security for him at Brotherhood events, lending them an air of seriousness and militancy. And all the while, the military drills and indoctrination continued for a generation of young men.

In the autumn of 1937, al-Banna went further and created the *Kata'ib* ('battalions') for select members of the *Jawwala*. Each battalion consisted of ten to forty members who had sworn the special oath (*bai'a*) of dedication to 'action, obedience and secrecy'. Al-Banna developed a tailored study programme for them, based on nightly vigils and Sufi litanies. He also wrote a series of treatises for the *Kata'ib*, which he later used as training material for the entire Muslim Brotherhood. His popular tract *On Jihad*, which is compulsory reading to this day among Brotherhood members, speaks of Muslim humiliation and the duty to pursue jihad:

> As you know, the Muslims today are forced to humble themselves before non-Muslims, and are ruled by infidels. Their lands have been trampled over, and their honour has been violated. Their enemies govern their affairs, and the rites of their religion have fallen into abeyance within their own lands, to say nothing of their impotence to spread the call [of missionary Islam]. Hence it has become an imperative individual duty for every Muslim to prepare himself for jihad until the opportunity arises and God decrees a matter that shall be accomplished ... I should mention to you that before the present age of darkness in which their pride has died, the Muslims never abandoned jihad throughout history, nor did they neglect it, not even their religious scholars, Sufis, artisans and others. All were fully prepared.[6]

All of this incendiary activism eventually spilled over into violence. In 1949 a Muslim Brotherhood member shot dead Prime Minister Nukrashi Pasha, and Brotherhood members made an attempt on the life of another politician. Al-Banna had infused the spirit of jihad into his organisation, and the genie was now out of the bottle. The Brotherhood's actions at home and abroad had made them too powerful for their own good, and this led to al-Banna's own death at the hands of the Egyptian security apparatus in 1949.

Al-Banna's teachings inspired the Muslim Brotherhood to militancy during his lifetime, and to all-out terrorism immediately after his passing. They shot and killed police officers, bombed cinemas, and often ended up in jail. This violent response came initially from the Brotherhood, but later others broke away and committed themselves solely to jihad. These included al-Gama'a al-Islamiyya and al-Jihad al-Islami, precursors to al-Qaeda. Both of them were directly implicated in terrorism, from the assassination of Egyptian President Anwar Sadat in 1981 to the first World Trade Center bombing in New York in 1993 and the Luxor massacre of foreign tourists in Upper Egypt in 1997.

Meanwhile the Muslim Brotherhood's exponential growth, from 800 members in 1936 to over 2 million in 1948, showed the power of new, politicised organisations that rivalled the old, traditional Sufi orders. The Sufis preached love and compassion, and had offered spiritual mentoring over the course of a millennium, but had no rallying call for this new age.

The political leaders of the Muslim world were admirers of the Sufis. Arab rulers regularly sat in gatherings of the Sufis, attended the annual *mawlid*, or celebration of the birth of the Prophet, or visited the shrines of saints, or endowed new mosques for ancient Sufi orders. In return the Sufi orders, with their many, many millions of members, spread good will toward the government. With the exception of the Gulf countries, every Arab and Muslim government has maintained this close, mutually beneficial relationship with the Sufis. Egypt's Sadat was a member of an order; his successor Hosni Mubarak visited Sufi sheikhs and claimed to be a descendant of the Prophet. Iraq's Saddam Hussein venerated the Naqshbandis and Qadiris, and Syria's Hafiz al-Assad regularly consulted and confessed to two leading Naqshbandi scholars.[7]

But in Iraq, Syria and Egypt this same political elite suppressed the Muslim Brotherhood as purveyors of a new Islam – or Islamism, to be precise – that refused to be co-opted and, worse, actively sought confrontation. In Egypt, the Brotherhood's hostility to Western influences put it directly in conflict with first

King Farouq and then the revolutionary military officers led by Colonel Gamal Abdul Nasser, national socialists who found Islamism abominable.

Two years after Egypt's 1952 nationalist socialist revolution, the prominent literary critic Sayyed Qutb was jailed for trying to subvert Nasser's government, or even assassinate him, as some claimed. After Qutb's return from a troublesome stay in America, he had joined the Muslim Brotherhood. In prison, he wrote his most controversial works, including *Milestones*, in which he claimed that Muslim society was now *jahili*, that is, it had reverted to the pagan Arabian days of pre-Islamic ignorance. To reverse this, he said, Muslims must take up arms against those identified by al-Banna as corroding Muslim identity and avoiding the implementation of Islamist ideology. *Haram* acts must become illegal.

The Nasser government's actions confirmed Qutb's worst fears. In prison for a decade, he was tortured, raped, humiliated. At his lowest point he was asked: 'Where is your God now?' Dogs were set on him and other Brotherhood prisoners. The furious Quran commentary that he released, *In the Shade of the Quran*, became a bestseller in the Arab world. His call in his writings was 'Rule is for God alone'. Citing Quranic verses literally, he claimed: 'Those who rule by other than what God has revealed, they are the unbelievers.'

His was the same clarion call, the same conclusion, as that of the seventh-century Kharijites who killed Imam Ali. Nasser hanged Qutb in 1966 and made a martyr of him, but the horse of Kharijite ideology had now bolted from the stables of Islamism in Egypt's prisons. The assassination of Sadat in 1981 was a direct result of Qutb's teaching that the killing of Muslim leaders could be justified on the grounds of *Takfir* – their denial of their Muslimness, which therefore rendered them apostates, deserving death.

The culture of suicide bombings, the scourge of contemporary terrorism, cannot, however, be laid at the door of these Sunni Islamists. Learning from the Tamil Tigers of Sri Lanka, it was the Shi'a Islamist group Hezbollah that was the first among Muslims to use this tactic of taking others' lives by means of suicide attacks. They struck in Lebanon in 1983 against American and French marines. Three hundred marines lost their lives, and Iran erected a memorial honouring the killers as 'martyrs'. This novel action came as a shock even to Islamist activists, who had thus far, in Afghanistan against the Soviets and in Palestine when battling Israeli forces, shunned suicide attacks, as life came from God, and God explicitly forbade suicide in the Quran. Arab media began to promote such actions as 'martyrdom operations'. Today, the Palestinian Hamas and other violent Islamist groups have made suicide bombers their weapon of choice.

So far we have only looked at Islamists from one end of the spectrum, that of Hasan al-Banna, Sayyed Qutb and the increasingly violent heirs of their tradition. But this is not the whole story. There is another, more hopeful, side to the Islamist conundrum that we ignore at our peril. Movements and ideologies, like people, change and adapt. Islamists are no different. There are shifts within these movements.

Long before Osama bin Laden's tirades, the influential Tunisian intellectual Shaikh Rachid al-Ghannouchi described the United States as 'Crusader America' and 'the enemy of Islam' because America liberated Kuwait from Iraqi occupation in 1991. Knowing what we know of Ghannouchi today, it is hard to imagine him writing, as he did in 1991:

> There must be no doubt that we will strike anywhere against whoever strikes Iraq ... We must wage unceasing war against the Americans until they leave the land of Islam, or we will burn and destroy all their interests across the entire Islamic world ... Muslim youth must be serious in their warning to the Americans that a blow to Iraq will be a licence to strike American and Western interests throughout the Islamic world.

Ghannouchi argued that the United States had waged a war against Islam, and called for a Muslim boycott of American goods, planes and ships. He genuinely believed that in annexing Kuwait Saddam Hussein had made a laudable move toward regional unity by 'joining together two Arab states out of twenty-two', and America had once again divided Arab lands.

Twenty years later, Ghannouchi's stance had evolved out of all recognition, and he went visiting New York City and Washington, DC, calling on America to invest in the Middle East and work with Arabs and Turks in the region. I met him in 2012 at the headquarters of the *Wall Street Journal* in New York, where he was lobbying for better American coverage of Tunisia and seeking to attract foreign direct investment. The change in his position epitomises the continuing changes in the Middle East, as people yearn for revival and renewal.

Whereas Sayyed Qutb once took Islamism in the direction of intolerance and violence, Ghannouchi has steered this global movement today toward pluralism and coexistence. Exiled in London in the 1990s and 2000s, he witnessed a West that was different from the America Qutb claimed to know, and opposed. Ghannouchi returned to Tunisia in 2011 to lead his country toward democracy and prosperity, free from ideology. The fact that his organisation conceded defeat in national elections in 2015, and did not seek to impose its interpretation of Islam in public, marked a significant move away from earlier Islamism. In 2016, standing before global media cameras and political representation from Arab countries, Ghannouchi declared that politics must be kept far from the mosques of the Middle East. He declared his Ennahda movement as a Muslim democratic party, and jettisoned Islamism as an ideology of the past.[8] The West mostly ignored this important change, but if understood properly and supported, then this ideological shift has the potential to give birth to free and normative politics in the Middle East. In reality, this means that Ennahda is now a sister political party to the British Conservative Party, or Germany's Christian Democrats.

I had the privilege of welcoming Ghannouchi to several high-level round-table meetings at the Council on Foreign Relations in Washington and New York. 'The mosques are open in Tunisia, and so are the beaches' was his honest answer to questions on freedom of choice in his country. His public and personal honouring of Jewish communities in Tunisia is another mark of his civility. When asked questions on law and economics, he deferred to women in his delegation, showing them a respect and recognition not normally expected of leaders in the Middle East.

On secularism, Ghannouchi did not hesitate to reject outright French-style *laïcité* as anti-religious. He said that militant secular democracy had no place in the Muslim world, and where it was enforced there was a strong backlash against it: Iran, Turkey, even Algeria. Ghannouchi then highlighted two forms of secularism or pluralism that he said were not antagonistic toward faith, and indeed accommodated devotion. In Great Britain, the Queen was the head of state and Church. In America, Christianity and faith generally were not imposed or established, but the state was not antagonistic toward piety. Both British and American models were more in line than the French with the sentiments and expectations of the Muslim world.

Ghannouchi's influence on politics and thinking extends beyond Tunisia. In Egypt, he was among a group of advisers around the first Muslim Brotherhood president of Egypt, Mohamed Morsi. But Ghannouchi's direct appeal to Morsi not to rule alone, but to form coalitions with secularists and nationalists, fell on deaf ears. Today, the leadership of the Muslim Brotherhood languishes in the same prison quarters that produced Sayyed Qutb and jihadism.

While Ghannouchi did not succeed in Egypt, his advocacy of an ethics-driven economy and centre-right politics has been more successful in Turkey, where his books and articles have shaped the thinking of the Islam-inspired AK Party. President Recep Tayyip Erdoğan and those around him readily acknowledge their intellectual debt to him. And Ghannouchi, in turn, has tried to take the best from the Turks in learning how to create jobs, attract foreign investment, build infrastructure, and provide a world-class education system and healthcare for Tunisian citizens. These are the issues that matter to governments and responsible politicians, not obsessions with confronting the West. In seeking solutions to these issues of governance, both Turks and Tunisians have shifted away from Islamist ideology and have tried to move toward free-market economics and democratic conservatism. In this, they have much in common with European or American Christian conservatives. Their Islam is expressed through their personal piety, not by imposing their view of scripture on the public or declaring *Haram* acts illegal. Who will treat yesterday's Islamists as today's conservative Muslim democrats?

The respected professor of Islamic studies Shaikh Abdullah bin Bayyah, arguably Sunni Islam's most important contemporary religious authority, to whom Ghannouchi and other political leaders defer, explains that since sharia's five overarching goals, the *Maqasid*, are the preservation of life, property, intellect, family and religion, therefore any system of government that achieves the *Maqasid* is a sharia-compliant government. In this mainstream scholarly Muslim interpretation, the secular authority of the state and its courts is completely compatible with Islam.

Although such a broad and contextualised approach to Islam, sharia, politics and power might appeal to a new generation of former Islamists and emerging Muslim political conservatives, however, it is also alienating to others, particularly those who take a fully literalist approach to scripture: the Salafis.

9

Who is a Salafi? Or a Wahhabi?

Puritanism existed in the West before it emerged in the Arab world. But whereas the Puritans ceased to exist as a movement in the West, they continue to thrive across the Muslim world. Salafism or Wahhabism is the name given to Islam's puritans: Protestants against mainstream Islam. In England, when Edward VI came to the throne in 1547 at the age of nine, the Puritans seized the opportunity to introduce evangelical reform, close down shrines because they promoted idolatry, whitewash over church wall paintings, and sell off or destroy musical instruments. They were particularly insistent that individual believers could have direct access to Christian scriptures, bypassing clerics. And all this was happening 200 years before the eerily similar puritanism of the Salafis surfaced in Arabia.

Put simply, a Salafi is a Muslim who claims to be following the example of the Salaf ('predecessors'), the first three generations of Muslims. They claim to draw their guidance from the first century of Islam (seventh century CE): the Prophet, his companions, and their immediate companions. After these three generations – the *Salaf al-Saliheen* ('the pious predecessors') – they consider that Islam grew corrupted through Christian, Roman, Persian, Greek and other influences. To be pure, therefore, Muslims must adhere only to the practices of the Salaf – hence the popular reference to them as Salafis, or more precisely as Wahhabis, after the modern revival of this puritanism by the Bedouin preacher Mohamed ibn Abd al-Wahhab (d. 1792).

Here's the rub: each and every Muslim believes in the message of the Prophet and strives to emulate him and his companions.

But not every Muslim is a Wahhabi. Salafism is a noble idea; Wahhabism is living it out in practice under the guidance of texts as interpreted by Ibn Abd al-Wahhab and his students. By focusing on Wahhabism, we examine the true nature of the modern claimants of Salafism.

Osama bin Laden was a Salafi–Wahhabi. After 9/11, there was much focus on the historic roots of Wahhabism and its deep ties with the Saudi government. Similarly, the Afghan jihad of the 1980s helped bring Salafi–Wahhabis to international attention, as droves of them from around the world went off to fight the godless Soviet enemy. On the battlefields of Afghanistan, they learned how to operate weapons and make bombs. With the destruction of the Soviet Union, this global fighting force turned on a new enemy: the West and its allies.

One of the reasons Wahhabism is a potent force today is that the kingdom of Saudi Arabia has spent an estimated $200 billion of its oil wealth in recent decades strenuously propagating its hard-line theology around the globe. The alliance between the Wahhabis and the rulers of Saudi Arabia dates back to an eighteenth-century pact between Ibn Abd al-Wahhab himself and a local tribal chieftain, Mohamed ibn Saud, forefather of today's ruling Al Saud dynasty. Ibn Saud recognised Ibn Abd al-Wahhab's puritanical creed, while the radical preacher acknowledged Ibn Saud's ambitious political leadership. In 1749, Ibn Saud pledged allegiance to the monotheistic preacher, and in return Ibn Abd al-Wahhab recognised the Saudi claim to power. That alliance still forms the basis of the political contract whereby the Saudi state upholds its clerical classes, ensuring they are well financed, immune from scrutiny, and able to impose their singular interpretation of monotheism on Islam's holiest sites.

Salafi–Wahhabism is the prevailing Islamic force in Saudi Arabia today. Its hard-line interpretation of Islam means that Christians are forbidden to build churches, Saudi women must cover up with a black face veil, a *niqab*, and near the holy cities of Mecca and Medina separate highways have been constructed for Muslims and non-Muslims. Beheadings are carried out by the state in public squares outside mosques on Fridays in the name of applying a literalist, Wahhabi, understanding of sharia as state law.

Prominent Saudi clerics, such as the popular television personality and author of school textbooks Saleh al-Fawzan, have declared in recent years that 'slavery is part of Islam. Slavery is part of jihad, and jihad will remain for as long as there is Islam'. He accuses Muslims who reject slavery of being 'apostates', for which the penalty in Saudi Arabia is execution. Those who reject slavery, therefore, deserve to be killed.

How can mainstream Muslims engage in dialogue and try to dissuade Salafis who want to kill those who disagree with them? They can't. Al-Fawzan is not a fringe figure inside Saudi Arabia. For this incitement to killing, he was neither arrested nor put on trial. The fact that ISIS and other extremist organisations practise sexual slavery can be directly linked to this normalisation of slavery inside the Saudi kingdom. Al-Fawzan is a professor at a government university in Riyadh, and has been at various times a member of Saudi Arabia's highest religious bodies. He is a prominent example, but there are several other influential clerics. They all draw their legitimacy from citing the works of the founder of Wahhabism, Mohamed Ibn Abd al-Wahhab.

His teachings and hard-line interpretation of *tawhid* (the 'oneness' of God) form the official Islam of Saudi Arabia, in opposition to that followed by most other Muslims around the world. His book, *Kitab al-Tawhid*, The Book of Oneness, dominates the global Muslim book market in cheap but well-bound editions from petrodollar-financed Gulf publishing houses. The best-funded universities in the Muslim world, in the Saudi cities of Mecca, Medina, Riyadh and Jeddah, all turn out tens of thousands of young clerics trained to travel across the Muslim world and spread the ideas in this book.

Let's take a closer look at his theology. His fundamental claim was that the vast majority of the world's Muslims had deviated from the creed of the Salaf. As Puritans opposed Catholicism, Wahhabis opposed the mainstream Islam of the Ottomans and the Mughals. The errancy of the majority of Muslims in the form of *Shirk* (idolatry, or polytheism) had to be physically purged out of Islam – hence the creation of the *Ikhwan*, a volunteer force dedicated to forcefully imposing Wahhabi ideas and behaviour. Creed, or *'aqida*, is of key importance to Wahhabis. Because the Muslim creed had 'deviated' (in their view), Muslims' actions had become un-Islamic. In his singular obsession with *'aqida*, Ibn Abd al-Wahhab focused on purity of *tawhid* as literally understood from scripture, devoid of context or the interpretations of sharia masters over the preceding millennium.

The vast majority of Sunni Muslims believe in what is called the Ash'ari creed, named after the early Imam al-Ash'ari, who was a master theologian born in Basra in 873, and who lived and died in Baghdad. His aim was to create a theological formulation that isolated Muslim belief from external influences. Where verses of the Quran talk about God's hand, knees or face, the Ash'ari school interpret this as speaking of the majesty of God metaphorically, since it is beyond human comprehension. When God says in the Quran that He descends to the lowest heaven to seek out those asking for His compassion, the majority of the world's Muslims have, for a thousand years, interpreted these verses as allegorical expressions of God's care for His creation. The Quran teaches us that the majority of its verses are *Muhkamat* (having a definite meaning), 'and these are the foundation of the book', but there are also *Mutashabihat*, 'verses that are ambiguous'. The Quran then condemns those who use the ambiguous verses to make trouble with their own spurious interpretations. To avoid the curse of that denunciation, Sunni Muslims of the mainstream have steered clear of literalism for over a millennium.

Not so the Salafis or Wahhabis. They insist on the creed that God literally has a hand, feet, knees and a face. He sits on a throne. When He descends to the lower skies, He is literally present. They view Ash'ari theologians as being swayed by the Greeks with their talk of speculative theology, rationalist theology and metaphors. Such foreign influence over Islam had to be cleansed by purity of *tawhid*, belief in God's oneness.

Imam al-Ash'ari, however, was well versed in the Arab poetry of the time of the Prophet, and therefore well equipped to make sense of metaphors in scripture. When the Quran mentioned 'God's hand' it was a reference to His power. 'God's face' should be understood as a metaphor for His essence, and 'God's sight' was an indication of His constant vigilance over His creation. His descent in the last part of the night represented His mercy and love for pious Muslims. This remained the interpretation of the majority of Muslims for more than a millennium. To modern Salafi–Wahhabis, however, all this is heresy. Herein lies the fundamental difference in methodology of understanding scripture and reaching conclusions as to creed. To Salafi–Wahhabis, most Muslims are heretics because they do not literally believe that God has a face, has eyes to see, and physically descends to earth. To test Muslims, Salafi–Wahhabis often ask: 'Where is Allah?' To which Muslims invariably answer: 'Everywhere', or 'In my heart', or 'With me'. Again, these are mainstream responses based on age-old interpretations of the Quran. For instance, the Quran says that Allah is 'closer to us than our jugular vein'. But for the Salafi, God is on His throne.

These differences, even more than attitudes to terrorism, explain how most Muslims are not Salafi–Wahhabis and are, indeed, the first targets of Salafi–Wahhabism, because Salafi–Wahhabis see a need to cleanse Islam of the stain of these ordinary Muslims. The West has not understood this theological and methodological clash, this schism between Salafi–Wahhabis and the majority of Muslims. Yet highlighting it much more clearly differentiates most Muslims from the fanatical Salafi fringe.

Despite their dictatorial ways and simplistic doctrine, Salafi–Wahhabis represent fewer than 5 per cent of the world's Muslims, and are found mostly in Saudi Arabia and the Gulf, and among imams recently exported from Saudi universities to drum up recruits in all parts of the Muslim world.[1] The vast majority of the globe's Muslims are either Ash'ari or similar in *'aqida*. With this flexibility of faith, Muslims who visit the shrine of a saint do not worship the saint or Sufi, but seek intercession with God through those whom God loves. But to the Salafi–Wahhabis, with their rigid literalism, such a practice is idolatry or *Shirk* and must be stopped at all costs.

Ibn Abd al-Wahhab's book *Kitab al-Tawhid* was essentially a literalist collection of verses of the Quran and hadiths with no commentary, either from him or other scholars. He argued that God alone should be worshipped, that shrines and saints were to be disregarded, and Sufis and Shi'a were heretics. Those who supported saints, shrines, Sufis or Shi'a were no longer Muslims, but idolaters. They were no longer committed to *Tawhid*, but were committing *Shirk*, or polytheism. In short, they were apostates and polytheists.

This theological position had serious consequences. As *Mushrikeen*, or polytheists, a despised category of humans, Muslims were no longer Muslims in the eyes of Ibn Abd al-Wahhab and his followers. The greatest polytheists became the Ottoman sultans and their local governors, patrons of mainstream Islam, shrines, churches, Sufism, music, art, calligraphy, and all that was perceived by Ibn Abd al-Wahhab as un-Islamic. In rejecting them, he was doing the same thing as his fourteenth-century mentor Ibn Taymiyya, who had risen up against the Mongols, alleging that they did not implement the sharia. Ibn Abd al-Wahhab made the same claim against the Ottomans. He saw himself as a new prophet sent to renew monotheism, and to distinguish himself from mainstream Muslims he and his followers started to refer to themselves as *Muwahhidun*, or monotheists.

He started calling upon neighbouring tribes to adopt his monotheism against the 'polytheists', the mainstream Muslims. When he destroyed a shrine and caused a local outcry, he was banished and sought refuge among the tribes of Arabia.

'Saudi' Arabia emerged in 1932, as did much of the modern Middle East, out of the corpse of the Ottoman Empire. With Wahhabism as its social glue, together with support and advice from Great Britain, it was the realpolitik of Abdul Aziz ibn Saud, a direct descendant of the Mohamed ibn Saud who allied himself with the Wahhabis, that brought the tribes together, ensured financial success, created alliances with the West, and slowly urbanised a mostly Bedouin population. As early as 1902, Ibn Saud marshalled the power of the *Ikhwan*, the volunteer force of puritans from Najd, in central Arabia, who busied themselves with ensuring that Wahhabi standards of ritual observation and creed were upheld, and all else was wiped out.

This group from Najd formed the spine of the *Ikhwan* fighters who swore allegiance to Ibn Saud and under his leadership did battle with the powerful Al Rashid tribe and the millennium-old custodians of Mecca and Medina, the Sharifs (now known as the Jordanian royal family after their expulsion from the holy cities of Islam).

Back in the 1790s, the chief *qadi* of Mecca had been convinced that the Wahhabis, or Salafis, were not even Muslims. He penned a fatwa ruling them firmly outside the fold of Islam. That view was shared by the majority of the Muslims in Mecca and Medina, and for two years they were kept away from the holy cities and the Hajj on the grounds that *kuffar* (non-believers) could not enter the city. The holy cities of Islam were then occupied in revenge by Salafi–Wahhabi fighters under the political leadership of Abdul Aziz.

The occupation persists to this day. And with it, the message of the *Muwahhid* movement is exported stridently across the Muslim world. When I visit Mecca or Medina, I am exposed to what 2 million Muslims from every part of the globe witness as the high point of our pilgrimage. In restaurants, universities and other public spaces, gender apartheid thrives, where men are superior and separate from women. The imposition of black garments, head and face covers on women comes from the same trend of Salafi–Wahhabi-dominated discourse from the headquarters of Islam.

This has now become the global Muslim zeitgeist. We see its impact on the streets of Paris, London, Vienna, Brooklyn and Berlin – men in long beards, no moustaches and trousers cut short at the ankles, wearing red-and-white chequered headscarves to mark themselves out as different. Yes, the Prophet taught that male robes should be shortened, but that was because wearing long, flowing silk robes was a sign of arrogance among the Meccan pagans. Yes, the Prophet most likely said: 'Let your beards grow, and trim your moustaches,' but he was trying to teach humility. Literalists lose sight of the spirit of the teaching, and focus on the externalities – like the English Puritans who dressed for their station in life, specifying the correct apparel for the scholar, the farmer and the merchant, rejecting fashion and avoiding sexually provocative clothing. The Salafis of the Gulf and their adherents globally have adopted the dress of the Bedouins, who were mostly goatherds and wore a rope *'igal* on their heads to hold down the *kuffiyyah*, the chequered headscarf. Yet when I visit a mosque in Turkey, which is refreshingly free of Salafi puritanism, I see women walking in and out freely, and men who are imams in Western or everyday modern dress, focusing on the state of the heart rather than the outline of the torso.

Are Salafis the only real and true Muslims? Were protestant Puritans real Christians? To say 'yes' is to worship the letter and scorn the spirit. It was in England that Puritanism began, and in England its theocracy ended. Likewise, it was in Saudi Arabia that Salafism began, and it is in Saudi Arabia that it needs to be uprooted. The 1749 alliance between the Saudi royal family and Wahhabi clerics must be nullified. Without Saudi Arabia as a financial, educational and preaching base, the Salafi–Wahhabis could not survive on the fringes of the Muslim world. Before it takes hold of other capitals, Salafi–Wahhabism must be brought to an end. Its backwardness is not limited to creed, conduct and hard-line conservatism. Its violence did not end in 1932 with the creation of Saudi Arabia, but erupts today with international jihadism.

10

Who is a Jihadi?

Just as Islamism is not Islam, so too jihadism is not jihad. To think that jihad and jihadism are the same thing would be to allow the jihadis to win their propaganda war and corrupt the teachings of Islam for their own purposes. The jihadis' tactics and branding confuse us into thinking that ISIS is different from al-Qaeda, that Boko Haram is different from the Taliban. But they all swim in the same waters; they all grow out of the same soil; and that territory is firmly Salafi–Wahhabi. That said, not every Salafi is a jihadi, but every jihadi today is a Salafi, and it is on the highway of Salafism that the intersection to jihadism lies. The more candid among the Salafi clerics accept the overlap between Salafism and jihadism. In August 2014, for example, a former imam at the Grand Mosque in Mecca with 2 million followers on Twitter, senior Salafi Sheikh Adel al-Kalbani, tweeted: 'ISIS is a true product of Salafism and we must deal with it with full transparency.'

The Quran calls Muslims to jihad – best translated as 'struggle' – but this is clearly different from *qital* (killing) or *harb* (war). The Prophet Mohamed persevered in the face of Meccan pagan hostilities for more than a decade, as God in the Quran repeatedly called for patience, kindness and gentleness in inviting the polytheist Meccans to believe in Allah. Only after thirteen long years of pagans killing Muslims, torturing, expelling, shunning and humiliating them, was the Prophet's community commanded to fight back. Muslims are not pacifists and, like the Japanese samurai or the ancient warrior cultures of Greece and Rome, Muslims believe in taking up the sword to disarm barbarians and madmen.

But there are agreed rules for undertaking jihad that distinguish it from ordinary warfare or fighting.

The sharia and the vast majority of the world's Muslim scholars have for centuries agreed that jihad has preconditions: that jihad must be declared by a Muslim head of state, not individuals or unauthorised bands of angry men; that when heading for jihad fighters must seek the permission of their parents; that only enemy combatants can be killed, not innocents; that women, children and the defenceless must not be assaulted; that wells cannot be poisoned; and that nature, cattle and livestock must not be attacked.

For over a millennium, Muslims followed the teachings of the Quran and the Prophet when engaging in warfare, and Muslim armies fought by the rules of Islam. They had with them scholars and Sufis to remind them constantly of higher ideals. In the twelfth century, the Crusader king Richard the Lionheart spoke respectfully of his Muslim enemy Saladin's chivalry and kindness in sending medical help when Richard was ill.

The violation of the rules, however, is jihadism, not jihad.

Today's jihadism, violating all the ethics of Islam, is nothing more than a continuation of the puritanism of the Salafi–Wahhabis from the deserts of Najd. They seek physically to impose their rigid *Muwahhid* worldview. The Ottomans were the focus of their grievances in the nineteenth century; now it is the Muslim rulers of our times and their Western allies.

They are connected globally today, no longer confined to the deserts of Arabia. And they will continue to spread, because they are riding a wave of Salafi–Wahhabi puritanism. Jihadism is the logical conclusion to Salafism.

As Salafi–Wahhabis, these groups believe in five key principles that give them the conviction to pursue their violent actions.

The first principle on which the worldview of jihadis rests is that of being '*Ghuraba*', a minority of 'strangers' or outsiders in modern society, different from the mainstream and seeing themselves as right and truthful in a world of wrongdoers. They wear their 'strangeness' as a badge of honour. Osama bin Laden, his successor Ayman al-Zawahiri, and countless radical Islamist organisations have cherished and advocated being *Ghuraba*. Indeed, the terrorists behind the 7 July 2005 attacks in London identified themselves as *Ghuraba* in the immediate aftermath of the bombings. The theme music of many jihadis, their global anthem from Chechnya to Yemen to Berlin, has repeatedly featured a *nasheed*, or song, called 'Ghuraba, Ghuraba'. The words, translated from Arabic, are:

> Ghuraba do not bow the foreheads to anyone except Allah.
> Ghuraba have chosen this to be the slogan of life!
> If you ask about us, then we do not care about the tyrants.
> We are the regular soldiers of Allah, our path is a reserved path.
> We never care about the chains of prison, rather we will continue for ever!
> So let us make jihad, and battle, and fight from the start.
> Ghuraba, this is how they live free in the enslaved world.
> So let us make jihad, and battle, and fight anew.
> Ghuraba, this is how they are free in the enslaved world.

A major component of extremism is the sense that being marginal, different and heterodox is a religiously blessed condition. The Salafi-jihadis base this not only on their cultish, rebellious ways but also on *Harfiyya*, literalism. The Prophet Mohamed is reported to have said: 'Islam began as a stranger, and it will once again become something strange. Blessed are the strangers.' They cling to this as a prediction of their own arrival as the true, blessed believers the Prophet spoke about. In their mental paralysis they overlook other sayings of the Prophet, including this: 'Be aware of extremism in religion, for it was extremism that destroyed those who went before you.'

Seeing themselves as 'blessed strangers', a 'saved sect' within Islam, they begin to form a psychological alienation from mainstream society. Normal Muslims are labelled 'deviants' because they do not share the supposedly faithful puritanical beliefs of those who see themselves as *Ghuraba*. Even parents and family members become deviants or disbelievers to the *Ghuraba*. The normal becomes abnormal. All are at fault.

Yet the Prophet repeatedly taught Muslims to be part of society, not to abandon it. Those who see themselves as the only true possessors of Islam, and therefore 'strangers' on a collision path with their fellow Muslims, are fundamentally wrong by the criteria of the Quran and the Prophet. The Quran warns repeatedly against going to extremes in religious observation, and against sowing *fitna* (dissension) in society. The Prophet taught that his followers would never agree, or achieve consensus (*Ijma*), on anything that is false. And yet those who claim to be *Ghuraba* break every consensus built by Muslims over a millennium in matters political and social, and now seek to divide and cause *fitna* among Muslims. According to the Quran and the Prophet, they are demonstrably wrong.

Second, not only are the Salafi-jihadis literalists and self-avowed outsiders, but they also believe and actively proclaim something that – despite their literalism – does not appear anywhere in the Quran or the sayings of the Prophet, something known in Arabic as *al-wala wa al-bara*. This can be roughly translated as 'loyalty (to Muslims) and disavowal (of, and enmity toward, non-Muslims, or infidels)'.

If a first-century Muslim, or a disciple of the Prophet, were asked what they understood by *al-wala wa al-bara*, loyalty and disavowal, they would look utterly perplexed. Although the radicals claim to be true to the text, their form of Islam would be unrecognisable to the Prophet and his disciples. Despite my being born and raised in a mainstream Sunni Muslim family, I only came across the concept of *al-wala wa al-bara* for the first time when attending Friday prayers at university. Similarly, most Muslims who come across this toxic belief do so on student campuses or in Saudi religious textbooks.

Essentially, scriptural literalists argue that Muslims should be loyal and committed in honesty and truth to one another. Disbelievers are sworn enemies of Islam and Muslims, and they should not be trusted, befriended or emulated. Believers in the *al-wala wa al-bara* principle try to enforce the prohibition of social and friendly ties between Muslims and non-Muslims. Celebrating birthdays and national holidays like Labour Day comes under the heading of 'emulating disbelievers', and it is for this reason that Saudi clerics forbid Muslims to mark Valentine's Day or celebrate birthdays. Even the birthday of the Prophet Mohamed, commemorated by most Muslims across the globe, is still officially banned by clerics in Saudi Arabia because they see birthdays as a form of 'emulating disbelievers', and thus violating the tenets of *al-wala wa al-bara*.

However odd all this may sound, Salafis justify it by citing religious scholarship from a bygone era and claiming to be trying to save Muslims' souls from hell by keeping them clear of the ways of disbelievers. Orthodox Jews have similar compunctions when interacting with the *goyim*, an often derogatory term for the non-Jewish population. More serious problems arise when this form of religious and social separatism, underpinned by theology, becomes conflated with politics.

To the most radical of anti-American militants, *al-wala wa al-bara* is not only about creed and social separatism, but also about political confrontation. Ayman al-Zawahiri wrote explicitly in December 2002 that *al-wala wa al-bara* was one of the most important pillars of his form of Islam. After explaining *al-wala wa al-bara*, and citing opinions of past Muslim scholars (while omitting to clarify that theirs was a different world), al-Zawahiri applied this notion to his reading of politics as well:

- It is Muslim governments, with their treaties and alliances with Jews and Christians, that have befriended the disbelievers and violated *al-wala wa al-bara*;
- The enemies of Islam, 'especially the Americans, Jews, French and English', have, 'through a chain of conspiracies, secret relationships, direct support, bribes, salaries, secret accounts, corruption and recruitment', put in place these governments that must be removed through jihad;
- The United Nations is 'a hegemonic organisation of universal infidelity';
- Acceptance of Israel is a rejection of jihad and shows disloyalty to the Muslims of Palestine; and

- To condemn al-Qaeda and the *mujahideen* is to be disloyal to Muslims and to side with disbelievers.

Third, based on this sense of exclusivity and separatist Muslim identity, the Salafi-jihadis invoke the concept of *Takfir*, which in practice becomes a licence to kill. *Takfir* in Arabic means literally to declare that someone is a *kafir* (pl. *kuffar*) or non-believer. The Salafis use this principle to excommunicate Muslims who disagree with their imposition of *al-wala wa al-bara*. For a Muslim to declare *Takfir* against another Muslim is already a serious undertaking and grave sin, but, when combined with the Salafis' literalist worldview, it also legitimises killing the person against whom *Takfir* has been declared.

Across the world, Salafi extremists use *Takfir* to denounce Muslims as non-Muslims and thus justify killing them on religious grounds. In their worldview, they cannot kill Muslims because it violates *al-wala wa al-bara* and is therefore a sin. They are called to be loyal to Muslims, not to kill them. But by declaring them infidels, they can justify killing them to cleanse the earth of the enemies of Islam. Modern *Takfir* of governments and then taking up arms by vigilante groups started with Wahhabi declaration of the Ottoman caliphate as deserving of jihad. That desert movement of rebellion against mainstream Islam is now known as global jihadism.

Without *Takfir*, al-Qaeda could not have declared war on the House of Saud in Saudi Arabia, or on the Muslims they killed in post-Saddam Hussein Iraq. *Takfir* was used to justify the 1981 assassination of Egypt's President Anwar Sadat. In Syria, the Muslim Brotherhood used *Takfir* in 1981 to assassinate government ministers. The Algerian Islamists and Salafis used *Takfir* from 1991 onwards to murder over 100,000 of their opponents and military personnel. Today, ISIS and other terrorist organisations continue to use *Takfir* to justify their violence.

Once belief in and use of *Takfir* ceases, the killing of other Muslims no longer has any basis in religion for Salafis. Politically, recognising the United Nations, holding senior government posts or even working for police forces in countries that are not part of a caliphate becomes acceptable. At best, Muslims who do these things are mainstream believers who simply follow a different interpretation of the faith. At worst, they are sinners – but not apostates deserving to be killed.

The fourth key Salafi principle is the belief in a religious obligation to create what they call *Hakimiyyah*, or God's government on earth, also known as a caliphate. In Arabia, the original Wahhabis of 1749 agreed that the House of Saud would serve *Hakimiyyah*. The idea that unless this obligation is fulfilled Muslims are sinful, and liable to punishment in hell, underlies not just al-Qaeda's ideology but also that of every other Salafi-jihadi group. Hence, the war against Muslim governments launched by al-Qaeda, ISIS and other violent Salafis is based not only on *Takfir* but also on the belief that these governments are apostates and must be replaced by a caliphate.

This vision of creating 'God's government' led Imam Ali, the fourth caliph of Islam, to do battle with people who claimed he was not implementing God's laws. Even the caliphate of Ali, the son-in-law of the Prophet, was not adequately Islamic for these people, a group who came to be known as the Kharijites, meaning those who went out, or made an exit, from mainstream Islam by virtue of their extremism. Muslim scholars have argued that al-Qaeda are today's Kharijites.

From the Egyptian scholar Ali Abd al-Raziq, writing in 1925 (a year after the fall of the Ottomans), to the Sudanese scholar Abdullah Naimi in our time, others have argued that 'God's government', or an Islamic state, is not a necessity today. The sharia is not a code of law that requires literal application – and it never has been. Even as early as the eleventh and twelfth centuries, Muslim scholarly giants such as Imam al-Juwayni and Imam al-Shatibi were already talking about the '*Maqasid al-Sharia*', or five Higher Aims of the sharia. For them, and for their many students through the centuries, the purpose of the sharia was essentially to preserve life, religion, property, family and human intellect. Any form of government that ensured these five key facets of human life was, by definition, Islamic government, rendering demands for *Hakimiyyah*, a literalist interpretation of God's law, null and void.

Fifth, and finally, Salafi-jihadis believe that until this caliphate is created, all Muslims are living in sin. It is therefore a collective duty on Muslims to 'lift the sin off our necks' (as they put it) by establishing God's government on earth. For as long as this government is not established, Muslims are living in what they call '*dar al-harb*', 'the abode of war'. Not only is the West part of this 'abode of war', because it is not part of a caliphate, but even most Muslim-majority countries are classified in this *Harfiyya*-driven worldview as being in *dar al-harb*. It follows that in the abode of war the rules of war are to be followed, and from such cramped and literal-minded readings of theology they derive their politics.

Based on seventh-century modes of conflict between the Arabs and Byzantines or Persians, today's violent radicals justify killing innocents, burning forests, practising deception, lying, and bringing harm to the enemy in every way possible. It was this worldview that led to Faisal Shahzad's response to a US judge when he asked: 'Didn't you swear allegiance to this country?' Shahzad, a naturalised US citizen on trial for an attempted car bombing in 2010, replied: 'I swore, but I didn't mean it.' It was this same mental state, this mixture of Salafi religion and politics, that allowed several of the 9/11 hijackers to drink, dance and visit prostitutes before carrying out their attacks. In the abode of war, such actions are permitted in order to deceive the enemy, and the rules of the sharia do not apply.

The term *dar al-harb*, like others mentioned above, does not appear in the Quran or the hadith literature. Early Muslim jurists devised this demarcation subsequently to distinguish lands in which Muslims were persecuted, or Islam could not be freely observed, from territory under Muslim jurisdiction (*dar al-Islam*, the abode of Islam). During imperial times, emperors from the Abbasids to the Ottomans used this 'abode of war' concept to expand the borders of their kingdoms, in tune with expanding *dar al-Islam*. In the modern world, however, where empires do not threaten to kill en masse or subjugate entire populations to an emperor, the notion of imperial offensive warfare is defunct.

Thanks to religious freedom, Muslims in the West are full citizens, can and do rise to high political office, have our own mosques, cemeteries and butchers for halal food, and much more. In other words, we are free as citizens and Muslims in the West. The West, therefore, is not *dar al-harb*, as early Muslims saw Rome, or later generations viewed European empires led by France, Germany, England and Italy. Contemporary Muslim clerics have suggested that such antiquated terms should be done away with in the teaching of Muslim seminaries.

What sustains enthusiasm for this entire theopolitical project is, in religious language, *yaqeen*, or certainty. The Salafis confidently believe in the literal, unilateral truth of their interpretation. There is no room for doubt – they are practically prepared to die for their beliefs. The utter certainty that suicide is martyrdom, and is rewarded (rather than punished) in the afterlife, is based on the same scriptural literalism that underpins their entire radical and violent worldview. It is this *yaqeen* that allowed Mohamed Sidique Khan, London's lead suicide bomber in 2005, to hold his baby daughter in his hands and say to her on camera that he would see her soon – that he had something important to do, but that God would let him meet her in the next life.

The above beliefs are all interconnected and interdependent, feeding off and strengthening each other to compose a worldview that is at once both political and religious. Here, there is no question of separating the secular from the sacred: they are one and the same. Whatever they call themselves – al-Qaeda or Boko Haram or al-Shabab, or some new name next year – they are all global manifestations of and adherents to this Salafi-jihadi ideology.

Today, in Libya, Tunisia, Egypt and Yemen, Salafism is on the rise again. In November 2014, for instance, there were 664 jihadi attacks in fourteen countries, killing 5,042 people. The vast majority of the victims of Salafi-jihadism are Muslims: between

2004 and 2013, about half of jihadi terrorist attacks and 60 per cent of fatalities occurred in Iraq, Afghanistan and Pakistan.

We cannot reverse the rising tide of jihadism unless we uproot its theology and ideology. The mainstream of Sunni Muslim sharia scholars believe and teach that jihad is acceptable or legitimate only in defence (*difa'i*) and cannot be initiated as aggressive (*ibtida'i*) war. In 1948 the highest authority within Sunni Islam, the sheikh of Al-Azhar Mosque and University in Egypt, Sheikh Mahmud Shaltut, pronounced that only defensive jihad is permissible, and even then it has to be in keeping with the verse of the Quran that says: 'Fight in the way of God those who fight you, but begin not hostilities. Verily God loveth not aggressors.' (2:190) Modern jihadi violence is marked by its aggression. As we have seen, however, Salafism is based on rejecting the Muslim mainstream, and its jihadi brethren are products of that approach.

Jihadis frequently cite the importance and significance of jihad in the life of the Prophet Mohamed, but theirs is a fundamental rejection of the Prophet's priorities and also of the nature of his struggle. His was not jihadism, the killing and raping of innocents, or declaring believers to be disbelievers, in the total absence of compassion and mercy. He was fighting back after a decade of torture, expulsion, persecution, boycott and violence in Mecca. His entire twenty-three-year career as a prophet calling people to God added up to 8,142 days. Of these, he spent seventy days, or 0.9 per cent, on military expeditions, and of those seventy days, only ten days were spent in actual fighting, representing just 0.1 per cent of his entire life's work in God's service.[1] How, then, is it possible to claim to be following the Prophet's example when jihadis spend decades in warfare in the name of Islam?

Let us consider an alternative and altogether more authentic model of jihad, based on a different and more consistent interpretation of the Prophet's message.

Back in the 1850s, the West African country of Senegal was controlled by the French. In 1853, in the Senegalese village of Mbacké, a woman named Maryam Bousso and her husband

Habibullah gave birth to a son, Ahmadu Bamba, who was to change his country for generations to come.

As a toddler, Ahmadu Bamba liked playing and sleeping in the prayer area of his parents' room, rather than his own bed and dedicated play area. A spiritual presence seemed to surround him. He received his basic education from his parents, both of whom were pious Muslims (his father was a *marabout*, or learned religious scholar in Africa) and who taught the child Arabic, the Quran, poetry and Muslim jurisprudence. By the age of fifteen, Bamba was writing poetry and had composed 1,600 verses in perfect Quranic Arabic.

He was also showing signs of considerable piety, and from a young age started inviting pagan African communities to worship the one God, love His creation and be of service to their fellow human beings. His humble personality, sincerity in serving people and, some say, his healing powers and miracles drew the Senegalese Wolof tribespeople away from paganism to the worship of Allah.

As he became known as a major cultural and spiritual figure in Senegal, and as a *cheikh*, a venerated religious teacher, tribal chiefs began to respond to Ahmadu Bamba's call to peace, submission to God, worship and spiritual growth. And as the number of his followers grew, along with rising resentment of French rule, so did the level of French concern. They saw that this was no ordinary African leader. His followers reported that in the small village of Touba, which he had established in 1887 for his disciples, away from the distractions of the world, the Prophet Mohamed's spirit had come to Cheikh Ahmadu Bamba. After that visit, Bamba became known throughout Senegal as *Khadim al-Rasul*, or the Servant of the Prophet. For the Arabian Prophet to bless a new village in Africa was no ordinary matter. That visit to the village still reverberates in Senegal today.

The French colonial authorities took their time, but they eventually began to worry. What if this wandering Sufi preacher declared war on Senegal's occupiers? The tribal chiefs who so revered him commanded sufficient numbers to put Cheikh Ahmadu Bamba in control. Fearing a mass outbreak of violence and rebellion against France, they decided to take pre-emptive action. In 1895 the

French exiled Bamba to Gabon, another French-occupied West African state, giving his many followers the impression that he would shortly be released. Bamba's agitated supporters wrote to him vowing that they were prepared to rise against the French and demand justice. Bamba wrote back saying that justice should be sought from God. Repeatedly, he cautioned against violence. One, two, three years went by. The French did not seem to realise that the man they held was not a man of violence.

That is not to say that others did not take up arms against the French in Senegal, but Ahmadu Bamba refused to engage in armed resistance and forbade his followers to do so, either. He wrote letters explaining to the French that he was not interested in worldly power, that his ambitions lay in the next world, but the French saw this as a ploy to deceive them. From prison in Gabon, he wrote:

> The only weapons I will use to fight my enemies are the *qalam* [pen] and the ink I use to write *qasa'id* [poems] in the glory of the Elect, the Prophet Mohamed.

Finally, after seven years, in 1902 the French released Bamba to his vast number of followers, now increased and more resilient having been trained by him to show restraint. Rather than diminish his authority through his absence, the French had only increased Bamba's stature.

Cheikh Ahmadu Bamba dressed in white, with a turban, and was remarkably serene. Word of miracles he had performed while in French custody spread like wildfire throughout Senegal, contributing to the increase in his following. It is said in Senegal to this day that the French threw him into a den of lions to scare the *Cheikh*, instil fear in the minds of his followers, and ensure their continued obedience. Bamba's soothing, tranquil presence led the lions to sit down beside him, not harming the Sufi healer in their midst.

Another story goes that on the ship to Gabon, the French denied Bamba room to pray, saying that the ship was French property and Muslim worship was not allowed on board. Bamba took his prayer mat, stepped out on to the water, and prayed on what he considered to be God's property. The millions of followers who gather to remember him in July every year face the ocean to pray, remembering the supernatural acts of their spiritual master and his commitment to serenity and worship. Three generations on, even in New York's Harlem district, where Bamba followers dominate the area called 'Little Senegal', they still hold large annual processions to remember the miracles of Africa's great son.

Noting his increased popularity and powers among the masses, the French colonial government imprisoned Bamba again, from 1903 to 1907, this time in Mauritania – another French-controlled country in Africa. It was only in 1910, after years of imprisonment and observation of him at close quarters, that the French authorities realised that Cheikh Ahmadu Bamba was a genuine pacifist, a Gandhi before Gandhi's time, and was religiously committed to non-violence even against the persecuting, imperialist French.

From where did Ahmadu Bamba's commitment to non-violence derive? Bamba himself cited the last sermon of the Prophet Mohamed in Mecca. Amid a vast gathering of his followers, the Prophet advised Muslims to abandon racism, 'superiority of black man over white, and white over black', and ensure fairness to women and adherence to regular prayers. In that same mass sermon he invoked non-violence in the phrase: 'From now on, do not shed blood.' That was a command Ahmadu Bamba refused to violate. His was a literalism of peace.

The French prison administrator Antoine Lasselves wrote of the man he saw:

> This Cheikh Bamba is gifted with some innate power whose origin the human mind cannot understand so as to explain his befriending capacity. The way people give themselves up to him is extraordinary, and their love of the Cheikh is unconditional. He seems to have some divine light and secret similar to what we read in the stories of the great prophets and their people.

Within fifty years of Bamba's release from prison, the French had left Senegal. In 1960 the country became independent, and today it is often cited as a rare model of democracy in Africa. The village he founded in 1887, Touba, is now Senegal's second-largest city. The Sufi Mouride order he left behind following his death in 1927 is one of four major Sufi movements in Senegal, with over 4 million Senegalese adherents – more than a quarter of the population. Every year, 2 million Senegalese people gather in Touba to remember Cheikh Ahmadu Bamba. In Rome, Paris and New York, the 'Muslim Rastas' with dreadlocks and tall, smiling West Africans are fans of Cheikh Ahmadu Bamba. The Senegalese musician and pop sensation Youssou N'Dour continues to sing about Cheikh Ahmadu Bamba to vast audiences.

A peaceful leader who rejected death, destruction, carnage – Cheikh Ahmadu Bamba's reputation lives on. But where is his legacy among angry Muslims claiming to resist 'Western imperialism' through violence today?

Jihadism is not the same thing as jihad.

11

Who is a Kharijite, or *Takfiri*?

The Prophet was distributing to his companions some newly acquired possessions when a man approached him and said: '*I'dil* [Be just], O Mohamed.' The one-word rebuke, the imperative *I'dil*, unsoftened by any of the polite language of the Arabs, sounded insulting to the Prophet and his disciples. 'Woe unto you,' the Prophet reproved back. 'If I am unjust, who will be just?' The Prophet's companions, visibly shocked by the man's rudeness, wanted to punish him. 'Leave him,' ordered the Prophet. 'He is not alone. He has acquaintances; he will have descendants. If you compare your prayers with their prayers, your fasting with their fasting, you will think that your worship falls short. But they will go out of this faith as an arrow darts through a game beast's body.'

The Prophet was warning about a group of people who would follow this man, Dhil Khawaisira of the Bani Tamim tribe. They would have all the external manifestations of worship to an extreme degree, but without being believers, because their actions would invalidate their faith, their hearts not being imprinted with the fairness, compassion, kindness and mercy of Mohamed's ways.

Imam Ali relayed from separate conversations with the Prophet that he had warned of 'a people who would be young in age and immature in thought, but would talk as if their words were the best among men. They would recite the Quran, but it would not reach their souls, the recitation would not go deeper than their throats; and they would pass through the religion. Kill them to cleanse your faith of them,' Ali reported the Prophet as saying.

From the very earliest days of Islam, then, there was a group of people who claimed to be within Islam but against whom the Prophet Mohamed issued a warning. The tribesman who had accused the Prophet himself of injustice was one of their forerunners, and Mohamed foresaw that their ways would lead to them leaving the mainstream body of Muslims. The Prophet's prophecies came true within only a few decades, when Ali was caliph: the Kharijite movement came to prominence – and killed him. Their modern descendants are a curse to this day, spreading death and destruction in the world, as they continue to pray, fast, and claim to be the truest of true Muslims. I am referring, of course, to ISIS and its allies.

King Abdullah of Jordan correctly identified them as Kharijites (in Arabic *khawarij*), as did even the Salafi religious leaders of Saudi Arabia, including Salafi-jihadis such as the Jordanian cleric Abu Qatadah. America's then Secretary of State John Kerry followed suit by calling them 'apostates'. But where do these people come from, and how did they emerge? What are their hallmarks, and why has their destructive worldview survived for over a millennium within Islam?

During his twelve-year reign between 644 and 656, the third caliph, Uthman, revived and reorganised the administrative structure of the caliphate. He gave the Muslim empire a sophisticated legal system, political administration and a healthy treasury. Muslims are indebted to Uthman for safeguarding and providing leadership of the early community and, more important, preserving and standardising the Quran. He also appointed several of his kinsmen as senior administrators of the caliphate. His clan, the Umayyads, had been political leaders and rulers since the time before Islam, so to some Muslims this looked like a return to the old order and power structures. From Uthman's point of view, though, his Umayyad relatives were now also Muslims, and their experience of governance was needed. He put his cousin Mu'awiya in charge of Damascus as governor of the Levant – a controversial choice, but a necessary one for Uthman, who had to keep up a balancing act between rival political factions, and needed to appoint a strongman for the potentially rebellious province. Mu'awiya was a successful, astute and wealthy governor, but he also made enemies in Syria.

By the year 654, complaints, petitioning, agitation and even peaceful sieges against Uthman had begun. In 656 matters came to a head when armed rebels and adversaries of Mu'awiya came to Medina and demanded of Caliph Uthman, among other things, that he dismiss the controversial governor. Uthman seemed to agree to this, and so these adversaries left, heading for Egypt. On the way, however, they met a man carrying a letter for Mu'awiya, which they duly intercepted: in it, Uthman gave orders for them and their tribal leader to be killed. They considered this evidence of the most heinous double-dealing, and immediately returned to Medina and laid siege to Uthman's house. (Historians absolve Uthman of blame for the letter, attributing it to his sly Machiavellian secretary Marwan.)

Uthman seemed unperturbed by the political crisis. He went ahead with leading Friday prayers and delivering the Friday sermon, determined not to be swayed by the mob. His opponents took a different attitude. Rebels in the mosque attacked Uthman with stones. Uthman's supporters killed several of the rebels. Imam Ali attempted to arbitrate, but the rebels were no longer prepared to believe what Uthman said, because they had already been double-crossed. Uthman said little, and focused his attention entirely on reciting the Quran. He was in a Zen-like state when a large crowd killed him. His Syrian wife Naila came to his defence and threw herself on to her husband to protect him. The horde attacked and killed her, too. They then chopped off her fingers and sent them, along with Uthman's bloodstained shirt, back to Damascus, sending the clear message to Mu'awiya that his cousin, caliph and protector was no more.

Amid this unrest, Imam Ali's popularity in Medina rose. People put their trust in him as the rightful heir to the Prophet's leadership of the community, and he was made caliph. But from now on, Mu'awiya in Damascus and the late Prophet's wife Ayesha, on pilgrimage in Mecca, supported demands that the killers of Uthman be brought to justice. Mu'awiya held up Uthman's shirt in the Umayyad Mosque in Damascus in front of crowds chanting 'Justice for Uthman!' One of their own had been killed too – Uthman's Syrian wife. The supporters of Mu'awiya now mobilised to oppose Ali, while Ali appealed to them for loyalty to the caliphate and unity within the ranks of the Muslims. From Mecca, Ayesha led an army, and from atop a camel she directed troops to battle Ali's forces. Ali behaved honourably and ensured that although the camel fell, the late Prophet's wife was not harmed. He sent her back to Medina with a military escort. This chivalry, however, antagonised a group among Ali's fighters, who saw what happened and resented it: to them, Ayesha should have been taken as a prisoner of war. This would be the first of the simmering grievances that the emerging Kharijites would air within the next few months.

In 657, Ali marched toward Syria with 80,000 troops to secure the allegiance of Mu'awiya. Muslim unity was essential. Ali was the caliph, and the pledged loyalty of all his governors was vital to maintaining the cohesion of the caliphate. The weekly Friday sermons that made verbal attacks on the caliph on instruction from Mu'awiya had to end. The two armies met on the banks of the Euphrates, at Siffin – eerily, in modern-day Raqqa in Syria, until recently the capital of the so-called ISIS caliphate.

Imam Ali offered peace and negotiations, but the Syrian army, numbering around 120,000, refused to recognise him as caliph and demanded that he hand over the killers of Uthman. The fighting began with Mu'awiya hoping to win back power for the Umayyads and the family of Uthman. As it progressed, Mu'awiya realised that he was losing, and that a victory for Ali would surely mean Mu'awiya losing Damascus too. A master tactician, he therefore launched a shock assault on Ali's deep sense of piety.

Mu'awiya ordered his soldiers to hold up copies of the Quran on their spears and ask Imam Ali for clemency. How could Ali continue to fight and kill those who held up the noble Quran as a shield and peace offering? Ali accepted arbitration, and the decision went against him. But a group among his forces refused to recognise his decision to seek peace. How dare he stop fighting? they demanded angrily. They cited the verse of the Quran that says: '*Hukm* [rule, or ruling] is for God alone.' To seek arbitration in his struggle with Mu'awiya meant conceding the arbitrators' right to provide *hukm*, a ruling, and that right was God's alone.

The Kharijite boil was lanced. They were now deeply hostile to Ali. As he negotiated peace terms with the governor of Damascus, the Kharijites agitated bitterly and, as the Prophet had foreseen, they left or 'went out' (*kharaja*) – the action after which they were named. Ali was keen to bring this group of approximately 6,000 extremists back within the framework of mainstream Islam, and so Abdullah Ibn Abbas, the most learned of the surviving companions of the Prophet, offered to meet them.

Ibn Abbas is venerated by both Sunni and Shi'a Muslims. He spent his entire lifetime in the service of the Prophet, keeping him constant company. The Prophet prayed for Ibn Abbas, and taught him secrets of the faith and the dynamics of the divine: 'If you seek, seek only of God. Remember Him, and you will find Him in front of you.' At first Ali was unwilling to put such a great scholar-companion of the Prophet, Islam's greatest interpreter of the Quran, in harm's way by sending him to meet the Kharijites, those who had left or 'gone out' from the Muslims. But Ibn Abbas insisted.[1]

Ibn Abbas wore his best, expensive, Yemeni robes, combed his hair, applied perfume oil and went to meet them as they lunched in their encampment. They had separated themselves from other Muslims and lived apart as their own community. Ibn Abbas was among the nearest and dearest companions of the Prophet. Moreover, he was a cousin of the Prophet and had seen the most pious of men, the Prophet Mohamed, in worship and yearning for God. And yet, upon meeting them, he wrote:

> I had entered upon a people the likes of whom I had never seen with their extremism in worship. Their foreheads were wounded due to constant prostration in prayer and their hands were rough like the feet of camels. They wore untidy shirts with their robes or trousers very short. Due to not caring for their appearance, their faces were dishevelled and tired.

Ibn Abbas greeted them, and they welcomed him. Their first question to him was: 'What is this cloak you are wearing?' Ibn Abbas's choice of clothing was not whimsical, nor intentionally lavish, but in keeping with the man he loved and learned from, the Prophet Mohamed. 'What fault do you see in me?' he replied. 'Indeed, I saw the Prophet of God dressed in the best of what we find in Yemeni clothes.' Knowing that they were not fully content with this response, he recited the verse of the Quran that says: 'Who dares forbid the decoration and blessings of God which He has produced for His servants?' Recognising Ibn Abbas's conviction, and hearing his reference to the Quran, the Kharijites moved on to other questions.

'What has brought you here?' they asked. 'I have come to you representing the companions of the Prophet of Allah,' he said, 'the migrants from Mecca, the helpers of Medina, and from Ali, the son-in-law of the Prophet. Upon them descended the Quran; they are more knowledgeable about this than you. I see not a single one of the companions of the Prophet among you.' They then conferred among themselves, and several turned to Ibn Abbas confirming their willingness to engage.

'Come forward,' said Ibn Abbas. 'What is your complaint against the companions of the Prophet and his son-in-law?' 'Three issues,' they responded. First, they complained that Ali had allowed men to be judges in arbitrating between warring sides in the recent conflict. This was polytheism and not God's law. It defied the Quranic verse that says 'Rule is for God alone.' Second, they complained that Ali had fought Ayesha and her supporters, but had not permitted his soldiers to take captives or war booty. Third, based on the above two grievances, they insisted that Ali should change his title, 'Leader of the Believers', because of his errors. He was no longer a believer. He was 'Leader of the Disbelievers'.

This was an act of *Takfir* on the part of the Kharijites – declaring someone to be a disbeliever, or an infidel. The Kharijites were the first to adopt simultaneously a number of troubling practices: excessive piety, separatism from other Muslims, literalism in reading scripture, and now *Takfir*. Soon, one more radical trait would be added to these four: intense violence. These five hallmarks of the Kharijites originated in the seventh century, and are still alive now in our times, in ISIS and others.

Ibn Abbas understood that the only language they comprehended was that of scripture. Before long, Imam Ali also realised that those who could not be dissuaded had to be destroyed. For now, however, Ibn Abbas attempted to debate, discuss and hold dialogue with them, on the agreed understanding that they would change their position and make *Tawbah*, or repent, if he could demonstrate their conclusions to be based on a false reading of the Quran.

On the question of God being the only ruler in matters of judgement, and human arbitration between people being a violation of God's command, Ibn Abbas quoted from the Quran a verse on pilgrimage that forbids hunting: 'And if a pilgrim kills an animal, then *as judged by two just men among you* the pilgrim should pay a penalty' (5:95). Was this not human judgement? God could have laid down the penalty, but He delegated the ruling to humans. Ibn Abbas quoted the Quran again on conjugal disputes, where the scripture is categorical: 'If you fear a breach between the husband and wife, appoint two arbitrators: one from his family and one from hers' (4:35). Ibn Abbas asked the Kharijites: 'Is it not better that men judge in matters regarding reconciliation of disputes rather than spill blood? Do you see how God allowed for human mediation between couples and so it is with other discord?'

True to the spirit of the sharia, Ibn Abbas used logic and reason for public benefit, drawing on Islam's primary source, the Quran. This was the normative Islam of the Prophet Mohamed at work.

As for Ali not taking captives and plunder, particularly Ayesha, as concubine according to the rules of war, Ibn Abbas asked: 'Which of you make your own mothers permissible [sexually] to yourselves? The Quran declares: "The Prophet is closer to the believers than their own selves, and his wives are their mothers" [33:6]. If you deny this verse, you are in disbelief,' he warned the Kharijites. The Prophet's wife Ayesha was therefore not to be touched, he clearly meant. He asked if they had any questions, and they fell silent.

Turning then to their final grievance – their rejection of Ali as Leader of the Believers – Ibn Abbas cited examples from the life of the Prophet of how he had compromised when his enemies insisted he no longer refer to himself as the 'Prophet of God'. If the Prophet could lay aside his rightful title for the sake of peace and security, then Ali too could compromise.

Ibn Abbas's engagement with the separatists was the epitome of scriptural reasoning with Kharijite extremists within Islam. He persuaded over 2,000 of them to repent and return to Islam. The remainder of the radicals continued to fight Ali in the most vicious ways. The caliph's army responded by annihilating the Kharijite fighters in the battle of Nahrawan, 13 miles outside Baghdad, in 658.

So the Prophet's warning about extremists and secessionists came to pass in the lifetime of Imam Ali, within the first half-century of Islam. Ibn Abbas, the best of Muslim scholars, in the noblest of ways, had limited success with the earliest sectarian radicals. The Kharijites are now back and their numbers are growing, while Muslim scholars hope that theological debates and disputes will save Islam from this internal war. Those who manifest the five *Khariji* traits – excessive piety, separatism from other Muslims, literalism in reading scripture, declaring believers to be disbelievers (*Takfir*), and intense, indiscriminate violence – are called ISIS, among other names, today, but they will inevitably fracture and spawn other groups as well. Just as ISIS is in effect a breakaway from al-Qaeda, so ISIS will produce even more extreme Kharijites.

The Prophet himself said on multiple occasions that these murderers had left ('gone out' from) Islam. Why are today's Muslims so reticent about saying the same and declaring ISIS as outsiders and disbelievers? Historically, some of the greatest Muslim thinkers, including Imams Bukhari, Ibn Taymiyya, Subki and Ibn Hajar, have considered the Kharijites to be non-believers. This *Takfir* by Muslims of the *Takfiris*, combined with decisive military action, has ensured their periodic cleansing, the necessary mowing of the lawn, throughout Muslim history. Saudi Arabia, Jordan, Egypt, Pakistan and others – both governments and religious leaders – have rightly identified the Kharijites of our time. But what will they do to win this war within Islam? On both fronts, debating and destroying ISIS and *Takfiris*, today's Muslims are proving to be weak.

PART THREE

The Rise of the West and the Loss of Muslim Confidence

Why do today's Muslims feel a loss of dignity?

How can contemporary Jews and Muslims find peace between them?

What are the challenges with the education systems of the Muslim world?

Why do Muslim women seem mistreated when compared with the West?

12

Dignity

'If the Arabs are dishonoured, Islam itself is dishonoured' is a popular saying attributed to the Prophet Mohamed. Scholars of hadith claim that along with thousands of other alleged statements by Mohamed, this one is a fake. Nevertheless, the attribution of this sentiment to the Prophet tells us of a deep desire on the part of the Arabs to clad themselves in the glory of God and the Islamic faith. Arab notions of pride, masculinity and honour run deep and can be difficult for non-Arabs to appreciate.

The images from Abu Ghraib prison in Iraq in 2003, of a woman in the US military whipping and sexually humiliating naked men, were the first that the Arab and Muslim worlds had seen of such degradation. Before that there had been reports and rumours, but here was the evidence. Not only did the woman drag naked Arab Muslim men along on dog leashes, but American military personnel also used attack dogs to torture and frighten Iraqi prisoners. How could anyone explain such a disgrace, such deep debasement of a proud people?

In the West, words such as 'shame' or 'humiliation' have limited emotional resonance, but in Arab and Muslim societies and the wider Eastern world, including China and India, the concepts of 'shame' and 'loss' have immense power to hurt and alienate. In our time we have seen ignominy visited upon powerful Arab rulers: Libya's Muammar Gaddafi chased out of the tunnel he was hiding in and killed; Iraq's Saddam Hussein captured in a dark hole and hanged; and Egypt's Hosni Mubarak brought to trial in a hospital bed before a court that had no legitimacy in his or his supporters' eyes. Whatever the rights and wrongs of the dictatorships that had been toppled, these televised images were a shattering blow to collective Arab pride.

For centuries, Muslims had always been winners. Power, glory and honour belonged to the Muslims, a people who conquered far and wide and created new civilisations in Damascus, Baghdad, Cairo, Constantinople, Delhi, Bukhara and Samarkand, and knocked on the gates of Vienna in the heart of Europe. Islam was an outward-facing civilisation, confident in its identity and resolute in its mission of calling humans to worship the one God and accept the Prophet Mohamed as His messenger. Yet this collective Muslim memory of a glorious past could no longer be reconciled with a powerful shared sense that Muslims had declined and become losers.

In 1948 the Jewish Haganah, a precursor to Israel's armed forces, defeated five Arab, mostly Muslim, armies that had launched a joint attack the very day after the creation of the State of Israel. After centuries of discrimination and being driven out of European countries, and from 1939 on being systematically annihilated in the gas chambers of the Nazis, Jews had created a Jewish state of their own, a homeland. Now they had destroyed several Arab nations' defence capabilities, as well as establishing a more formal presence in Jerusalem, Islam's third-holiest city. What had happened to Arab and Muslim might? This humiliation became known as the *Nakba* (catastrophe), and every year, across the Arab world and beyond, the *Nakba* is commemorated with heads held low in shame. To lose is terrible, but to lose so badly at the hands of the Jews, the *Yahud* – a term often used almost as a profanity in many Arab countries – was a calamity.

Over the following decades, while democracy flourished in the new State of Israel, Arab populations were humiliated further from within. In Iraq, Syria and Egypt, Arab nationalist socialists staged military coups against their countries' monarchies and confiscated the lands and homes of the wealthy. These military dictatorships, with their rural, working-class backgrounds and their left-wing politics, were not just an affront to the Arab upper classes. One set of elites had replaced another with no involvement of ordinary Arab citizens. Marginalisation of the Arab individual became the norm.

Worse still, the Arab socialists attacked the very fabric of Muslim societies, with an assault on the prestige and independence of Islamic scholarship. On Fridays, to this day, most mosques across the Muslim world are packed with worshippers. The mosque is the natural social space for most believers of all ages, and in Arab Muslim countries there is still deep veneration for the *ulama* (Islamic scholars) and their learning. Their status and dignity derive in large part from their independence – moral and financial – from the governments of the day.

The home of global Islamic learning, Al-Azhar Mosque and University in Cairo, one of the world's oldest-established universities, had been independent for a thousand years, with its own financial endowment, or *waqf*. Traditionally in Muslim societies, when a wealthy Muslim passed away she or he bequeathed their inheritance to an Islamic charity in what was known as *sadaqah jariah*, continuous charity. In other words, although the donor was deceased, their good deeds in this world continued, and they gained a heavenly reward. Often the bequest took the form of a *waqf* endowment.

Thanks to Al-Azhar's *waqf*, therefore, generations of Muslim scholars had studied in its tenth-century courtyard unbeholden to rulers or politicians, and an Islam of peace, pluralism and prosperity was able to thrive. The Arab socialists changed that when, in 1953, Gamal Abdul Nasser, leader of the Egyptian coup and later president, seized the endowment of Al-Azhar. In the West, Oxford and Cambridge universities had built their own centres of learning by emulating this enlightened Muslim model. Yet here were socialist ideologues and military dictators attacking it within the House of Islam – with tragic consequences.

I visit Al-Azhar regularly for conversations, prayers and learning. My heart aches as I see the derelict buildings, neglected learning quarters, filthy toilets, poverty among the students, and low pay of the professors. Bookshops are being shut down and replaced by butchers in the ancient neighbourhoods where writers and thinkers gave birth to ideas that upheld a civilisation for a thousand years. Where is the outcry? Where are the financiers and philanthropists who yearn to revive their civilisation by endowing knowledge and ideas?

Elsewhere in the Muslim world we can see the price to be paid for pauperising scholars and forcing them to dance to the tune of their paymasters. In Pakistan there is widespread derision of the mullah, or cleric, who is seen as backward, poor, hypocritical and constantly in need of money. This is a direct consequence of clerics holding forth on controversial politics. On Fridays a bucket is circulated at the mosque for worshippers to drop in their contributions to the mullah's weekly salary. This compromises the cleric and subjugates him to his paymasters, the congregation. Consequently, he loses the freedom to show leadership based on principled scholarship, and is instead guided by the expectations of those who pay his salary. He ends up mirroring their views.

For example, the mob might want to attack the American or Israeli embassy in Cairo or Tunis. A mullah or imam who has to keep his congregation happy will hesitate to maintain a position of rectitude and warn against attacking embassies or burning flags. To do so might make him seem to be complicit with America, and the money in the bucket might dry up. On the other hand these craven imams, fearing for their jobs, cannot compete with the strident, modern-sounding Islamists' rhetoric against Muslim governments and their Western allies.

In the twentieth century, then, the Arabs were dishonoured and Islam itself was dishonoured, as the Prophet may or may not have said. The Arabs' acute sense of *karama* (nobility, or dignity) was deeply wounded – and the wound festered. By 2004 a few candid voices among the Arabs were warning of this collapse of Arab pride and dignity:

> It's not pleasant being Arab these days. Feelings of persecution for some, self-hatred for others; a deep disquiet pervades the Arab world. Even those groups that for a long time have considered themselves invulnerable, the Saudi ruling class and Kuwaiti rich, have ceased to be immune to the enveloping sense of malaise since a certain September 11.

These are the opening words of *Being Arab* by Samir Kassir, one of Lebanon's best-known journalists and historians. For his views, and his criticisms of the Syrian occupation of Lebanon, he was assassinated by a car bomb in Beirut in June 2005 (Syrian intelligence remain the prime suspects). His life and death underscored the point he was making about the suffocation of critical thinking and writing in the modern Arab world.

Dignity, pride, self-esteem, respect are not fanciful wishes but a vital part of Arab, Muslim – human – DNA. *Karama*, in the sense of the dignity and nobility of human beings, is a major theme in the Quran, and a popular verse among Muslims is '*Laqad karramna bani Adam*': 'We have indeed ennobled the children of Adam [the human race].' An emotional sense of violation of *karama* is at the core of the contemporary Arab Muslim existential angst. And in the tiny Tunisian village of Sidi Bouzid, in December 2010, this desecration of dignity came to the fore.

Twenty-six-year-old Mohamed Bouazizi was a simple street vendor selling fruit and vegetables. His father had died when he was young, and from the age of ten he had been supporting his mother and sisters. His mother had remarried, but family poverty and the poor healthcare in Tunisia meant that his sick stepfather could not be treated and get a decent-paying job. Bouazizi tried to join the military, but he had no strong recommendations or *wasta*, connections – the magic ingredient for mobility in Arab societies. To improve his sister's prospects, he sent her to university while he sold fruit and vegetables, walking two kilometres each day to the nearest bazaar to pick up produce. Despite being poor himself, he was known to give food away to people who were even poorer.

All his life, like so many other Tunisians, he had been harassed by the police and state bureaucracy. All they wanted was bribes, but they disguised their demands as fines for spurious violations of the law and not having a vendor's licence. On 11 December 2010, a female police officer interrogated Bouazizi in public. She wanted him to pay money that he could not afford. She seized his scales and insisted he go to the police station and pay 250 dollars – more than two months' worth of his earnings. Ignoring his protests, she then slapped him in the face. This was the ultimate insult to his Arab Muslim manhood, for a female to demean him in public – and for no other reason than his efforts to earn a living and support his mother and sisters.

He went to the police station, but nobody there agreed to see him – the officials were all 'in meetings'. In Tunisia that's another way of asking for a bribe. He was up against the entire bureaucracy of the state, and had nowhere to turn. Frustrated, worn out, defeated, *humiliated*, his cry for help was to buy some paint thinner and set himself on fire in protest. He died of his burns two weeks later.

Mohamed Bouazizi's short life held meaning for millions of people across the Middle East. His story captured the injustice and indignity experienced by a generation, and the Arab Spring was born. Governments were swept from power as the Arab peoples demanded, literally, *karama*, dignity, and *adala ijtima'iyya*, social justice. These were the slogans they wrote on the walls of major cities and shouted in the mass protests that toppled dictators in Tunisia, Yemen and Egypt.

My visits to Egypt several times soon after the fall of Mubarak revealed a very different country from the land I had known for fifteen years previously. No doubt there were security challenges with the breakdown of law and order, but the pride of the Egyptians was running high. There were songs, slogans, wall paintings, and people constantly saying: '*Enta Masri, irfa' rasak!*' – 'You are Egyptian, hold your head high!' The words are more poignant in the Arabic and evoke, by contrast, the meek way in which a generation had grown up with their heads trodden under the boots of the Egyptian military and police, who controlled every aspect of their lives with fear. There was a sense that justice had finally been served.

Now, however, with the exception of Tunisia's transition to democracy, the dignity, social justice and freedom sought by the Arab uprisings has been taken away again. The Arabs' great sense of loss and defeat has been handed down to yet another generation. The general mood of despair continues and will doubtless prick the conscience of the world again, in worse form – if only in numbers – than Bouazizi's self-immolation.

What did the Arab Spring generation want? I lived and worked in their midst in Syria as a teacher and researcher for two years during the American-led occupation of Iraq. After the Arab Spring, I visited Egypt, Tunisia, Bahrain, Jordan, Morocco and Saudi Arabia multiple times as a senior fellow of a leading American think tank. I met many of the youth leaders and political and religious figureheads. In addition to their unrelenting cries for dignity, social justice and political freedom, three observations stayed with me.

First, there had been a widespread expectation that the West would come to the assistance of democracy activists. Since 11 September 2001, American political leaders had been openly calling for democracy in the Middle East. Billions of dollars had been spent on democracy promotion from Washington, DC. Surely, now that the moment had come, aid and investment from Europe and the US would follow? At the same time, governments in the region were convinced that the uprisings were Western-backed plots. But in the end the imagined help from the West never came. Massacres of protesters followed, not least by security forces in Rabaa Square in Egypt in 2013, but the blame was placed on the West. Silence in the capitals of the West reinforced perceptions of Western acquiescence in Arab degradation. Arab and Muslim lives seemed not to matter.

Second, there had been a pitched battle of ideas inside Arab societies – political ideas about democracy and freedom – that had been simultaneously repressed and exploited by governments in the region. The precise meanings of words such as 'liberal', 'democrat', 'conservative', 'right', 'left' or 'secularist' – let alone 'Islamist' – had not yet been agreed upon or even broadly defined. Dictatorships do not provide space for dignified and meaningful discussion. Meanwhile repression had led to underground Islamist movements being organised, such as the Muslim Brotherhood and the Salafists. Consequently, when the tyrants fell, the old guard proclaimed the threat of Islamist radicalism, and the West duly fell in line behind new, anti-democratic forces in government. The battle of ideas had been lost again.

Third, the activists and protesters I met across the region all spoke about their personal losses and grievances. They identified with Bouazizi's plight, but the rich middle-class kids educated at the American University in Cairo were also acutely aware that one of their own, Khaled Said, from a middle-class family in Alexandria, had died from police torture in 2010. He was not the stereotypical Islamist suspect hungering for power. The Facebook page 'We Are All Khaled Said', set up by Google executive Wael Ghonim, helped mobilise millions across Egypt. The same platform was also host to the pain that many others had felt: the Facebook pages of young Arabs are filled to this day with photos of faces in tears, thorns beside roses, and broken love hearts pierced by arrows.

Things were not working for young Muslims. They could not be in a loving relationship, because it was forbidden – and impractical, as most young Muslims, even in their twenties, still lived with their parents. If they wanted to get married, they were either too young or could not afford to do so, because buying a house and car, and providing for children, in countries with high unemployment and – even when work was available – low wages was not feasible. Everything in life seemed stacked against them.

Through my conversations I gained a strong sense of this personal loss, and young people's personal motivation to regain their dignity and improve their circumstances. These feelings are also expressed in the Arab world's music, literature and art, which all amplify the mood of despair. Seven of the all-time top ten Arabic songs are about sadness, loss and pain; only three are happy and upbeat. Earlier, too, the Arab world's most popular modern poet, the Damascene writer Nizar Qabbani, was transformed by the trauma of Arab military defeats: from writing erotic love poetry he switched to angry explorations of frustrated Arab aspirations.

The Crusaders and Mongols attacked the Muslim heartlands, yet within decades the Muslims regrouped and revitalised. But the Western onslaught led by Napoleon in 1798 destroyed the dignity of Muslims in a process sustained for two centuries. Across the Muslim world, blame is placed firmly on the West. There exists a powerful, gripping narrative of the West plotting and planning to weaken, divide and conquer the Muslims. This account is not viewed as history, from a bygone era that the modern West would like to see relegated to the annals of imperial misadventures: for the Arabs, in particular, it is a lived and everyday reality. It is the story told to Arab children in school textbooks and discussed by the general public and political circles throughout most of the Muslim world. The toxic anti-Western atmosphere that gives rise to 'Death to America' slogans in Iran, flag-burning in Pakistan, and a widespread view in Egypt that the 9/11 atrocities were committed by the CIA, is the result of a historic narrative of humiliation and indignity that is still being lived out today.

Plato best diagnosed this psycho-political condition, which has haunted sections of humanity throughout history. He identified three parts of the human soul. First, there was reasoning, the capacity to calculate, make a risk–benefit analysis, utilise logic. This element controls a person, and seeks logical means to achieve aims. Second, there was appetite, the instinct to satisfy hunger and satiate thirst. Third, there was *thymos* (pron. *thumos*), a word that is hard to capture fully in English but refers to spiritedness, togetherness, a sense of collective dignity. *Thymos* is not always in step with reason or appetite. *Thymos* deals with emotions of pride, shame, humiliation, indignation of the human soul – and the human need for justice. This was of real and fundamental importance to the ancient Greeks, as it is to today's Arabs, but seems to elude the modern Western mind.

Thymos is about a people's collective self-esteem. Honour and glory are underestimated in Western foreign policy analysis, but Russian actions in Syria or Ukraine are driven precisely by these factors that Western-trained minds find hard to grasp. Political realists stress interests and the survival instinct – Darwinist thinking is at the core of their understanding of international relations and conflict. But they fail to appreciate the emotive power of honour and glory, absent or present, in the conduct of other civilisations. Britain's Lord Palmerston was reflecting this cold, calculated view in the nineteenth century when he quipped, in what has since become a maxim of foreign diplomacy: 'Nations have no permanent friends or allies. They only have permanent interests.'

Western policymakers expect others to behave like the West, where it is claimed that reason is king. They anticipate rational actions from rational political actors, but *thymos* is often a more powerful driver, and punishing a state will not necessarily change its behaviour. Iraq, Syria, Cuba, Russia and Iran all seek to advance their *thymos* and respond according to *thymotic* calculations that are not always rational. What else explains, for example, Palestinian militants firing rockets into Israel from Gaza? And this despite Israel not only killing terrorists in retaliation, but also destroying their family homes. Israel's security wall is there to keep Palestinian radicals away from Israel's cities – without it suicide bombers could wreak murderous havoc in Tel Aviv. The Israeli wall is a consequence of Palestinians acting not from self-interest and reason but driven by *thymos*, or *karama*, to violate every law, defy every form of punishment, and continue to attack Israel to bolster feelings of Palestinian pride in resistance.

This pursuit of self-worth, the preparedness to die for dignity, also motivated the self-declared caliph of ISIS-held territory, Abu Bakr al-Baghdadi, in May 2015. Knowing full well the emotional and psychological wounds of the Arab and Muslim worlds, al-Baghdadi addressed Muslims with these words: 'We call upon you so that you leave the life of humiliation, disgrace, degradation, subordination, loss, emptiness, and poverty to a life of honour, respect, leadership, richness, and another matter that you love – victory from Allah and an imminent conquest.'[1]

Al-Baghdadi is echoing a call for *thymos*, but justified in the worst language of threats, violence, religion and invasion.

Liberal internationalism, which is the dominant paradigm in politics and international relations, argues that interests and reason are the prime motivators of state conduct. Universities and governments alike often make the mistake, however, of confusing their theoretical descriptions of rational actors and an interests-based world with the real world in which self-interest and survival are only two of several powerful motivating factors. To recognise the power of *thymos*, as Francis Fukuyama tried to do, could go a long way toward helping heal the raw wounds of Muslim disgrace and degradation.[2] We do that by treating Arabs as full, dignified humans; we help reinstate Arab *thymos* by supporting the democratic and reformist strains within governments and civil societies. We should take a longer-term view of the world's most volatile region. Revolutions may not always bring immediate benefits to oppressed peoples, but evolution toward prosperity and freedom is lacking, too. The West helped create the modern Middle Eastern nations, laws, borders, and armed forces. Where is our Marshall Plan for the Arab world? We have helped our ally Israel. What have we done for the Arabs?

Let us turn now to consider the one country that, together with its Western allies, is perceived to have dealt the heaviest blows to the *thymos* of Arabs and Muslims: Israel.

13
The Jews

In a Pew opinion poll conducted in 2011, 95 per cent of Egyptians and Lebanese expressed a 'very unfavourable' view of Jews; in Palestine the 'very unfavourable' response was 89 per cent; in Pakistan and Turkey 64 per cent. Among non-Arab Muslim nations the level of anti-Semitism was somewhat lower – 47 per cent of Indonesians felt 'very unfavourable' toward Jews – but not impressively low. It seems that the loathing of Jews among Arabs and Muslims, despite protestations that 'we are not anti-Semitic', is, lamentably, on the rise again. Yet it is not intrinsic to Islam, and has not always prevailed.

In the fifteenth century, from the city of Fez, the Marinid dynasty controlled what is today Morocco, Algeria and parts of Tunisia. A Sunni Islamic civilisation, the Marinids sponsored religious and cultural education programmes that are still vividly alive in Morocco today. There were Jews in Fez who served in successive Marinid administrations as high-ranking ministers. This matters, for in Europe at that time Jews were subjected to expulsions, pogroms and persecution. In 1290, Jews were expelled from England for nearly four hundred years. Between 1350 and 1450, provinces in France, Germany and Italy also banished this persecuted people.

When the last Muslim ruler of Spain, King Boabdil,[1] negotiated his surrender of Granada in 1491 to the Catholic monarchs Ferdinand and Isabella, he sought reassurances that Muslims would have the greatest possible freedoms. He obtained guarantees that there would be no forced conversions to Christianity, families would be protected, property rights respected, and places of worship maintained. Boabdil requested these rights not only for Muslims, but he specifically mentioned Granada's Jewish communities and stated that they 'should benefit like us from these terms'. At his weakest point in life, Spain's last Muslim ruler put Jews on a par with Muslims and set out to protect their rights.

By the spring of 1492, all Jews, not only those from Granada, were expelled from Spain, killed, or forced to convert by Ferdinand and Isabella. At their apex of power, these famed Christian rulers oppressed Jewish communities. The Ottomans welcomed in Istanbul perhaps as many as 30,000 Jews from Spain. Sultan Bayezid II commented, 'You call Ferdinand a wise ruler ... (yet) he impoverishes his country to enrich mine!'[2]

'Throughout the Middle Ages,' wrote the philosopher Bertrand Russell, 'the Muslims were more civilised and more humane than the Christians. Christians persecuted Jews, especially at times of religious excitement; the crusades were associated with appalling pogroms. In Muslim countries, on the contrary, Jews at most times were not in any way ill-treated.'[3] Russell was no friend of Islam and Muslims – his testimony was an honest assessment of the historical record.

Alas, Muslim tolerance was not to last much longer either. In 1465, the Marinids fell from power. A group of clerics, commoners and agitators declared war on the Marinid sultan Abdul Haqq and killed him while parading him humiliatingly on a donkey through the Jewish quarter of Fez. The sultan was not without supporters – many of Fez's leading merchants, professors and Muslim clerics who commanded strong support courageously gave Abdul Haqq their backing. But they could not prevail against a violent mob seeking to topple him, accusing him of corruption and 'support for the Jews'.

One honourable man in particular stepped forward amid all this political upheaval, anti-Semitism and supposed jihad, a Sufi scholar whose teachings are still thriving among Muslims in North Africa: Sidi Ahmad Zarruq. He opposed the revolution, stood up for the Jews, and was thrown out of the capital for his beliefs.

Zarruq graduated from the main Islamic college of Fez, the Madrasat al-Attarin, one of several built and maintained under the patronage of the Marinid dynasty. In its serene surroundings, he studied Islamic jurisprudence and Quranic exegesis, and took part in the rich cultural life of Islamic seminaries in the medieval period: poetry, calligraphy, and access to the royal courts.

I take comfort in the story of Sidi Ahmad Zarruq's life: I too have been called a 'Jew' for supporting a Jewish homeland in Israel, a *kafir* (infidel) for rejecting calls for a rigid sharia-based state, and much else for opposing the 'revolutionaries' of our time, the Jew-haters of our age, the jihadis of our era.

I went to Fez in 2013 to walk in the footsteps of Sidi Ahmad Zarruq. As well as the Madrasat al-Attarin, the great University of al-Qarawiyyin, founded by a wealthy Muslim woman in 859, still stands nearby, suffused with the tranquillity and mysticism that produced Zarruq. But while in Fez I also followed in the path of the greatest of Jewish scholars, who had lived in Fez and prospered there 200 years before him.

The prodigious, great Rabbi Maimonides, or Musa (Moshe, or Moses) bin Maimun, known and held in high esteem by Jews today as Rambam, came to live in Fez after being expelled from Spain. His home is still marked out in Fez, and curious visitors like me can linger in the alley outside the house to soak up a sense of the surroundings that Maimonides saw, touched and walked upon. It was during his stay in Fez from 1166 to 1168 that Maimonides wrote his renowned commentary on the Mishnah. The highly respected scholar and philosopher later travelled to settle in Cairo, where he became a trusted physician to the Muslim leader Saladin. He was also the leader of Egypt's thriving Jewish community.

Today, Jews continue to live in Morocco, but nowhere near the 300,000 who were Moroccan citizens in 1945, before the creation of modern-day Israel. In Egypt too, over the past ninety years the Jewish community that Maimonides once led has dwindled from 80,000 to fewer than forty. Only eleven Egyptian Jews remain in Cairo (all women, with the youngest in her sixties). In Yemen, a land where Jews have lived and traded since the times of King Solomon, a country where Jews settled before the arrival of Christianity or Islam, today there are fewer than seventy Jews remaining. In 1948, 45,000 of Yemen's 50,000 Jews were airlifted to safety by Israel after the rise of pogroms in that country.

Unfortunately Jews are still not safe. Leaving their homelands and congregating in Israel has not created security for this ancient people amid their Muslim neighbours. In dress, appearance, customs, habits and even beliefs and rituals, Muslims resemble Jews more closely than any other faith community. Yet the rivalry, hatred even, that exists between the descendants of Abraham risks unleashing nuclear warfare in the Middle East. It also has the effect of destroying the West's reputation in the Muslim world, viewed as biased backers of a brutal Israel.

In the twentieth century, anti-Semitism was a European cultural default position, resulting eventually in the unforgivable crime of the mass murder of Jews, the Holocaust. In this century, Jew-hatred is spreading again, but now across the Muslim world, and repeated talk of 'wiping out Israel', from multiple Arab and Muslim political and religious leaders, should not be taken lightly. This hatred is further envenomed by two other factors.

First, new migrants arriving in the West from the Middle East bring attitudes that blame Israel and the Jews for the world's ills. European difficulties with integrating Muslim populations further complicate this problem, as migrants' attitudes fester and generally go unchallenged. Second, in countries such as Great Britain, where young Muslims have integrated better than, say, in France or Germany, the virus of anti-Semitism finds a hospitable home on university campuses. In October 2015, professors from seventy-two British universities vowed to boycott Israel by refusing academic cooperation with the Jewish state. Their actions provided a boost to the widespread Boycott, Divestment and Sanctions (BDS) movement against Israel common among students in many UK institutions of higher learning. Currently, very little is being done to reverse this ethos in which young Muslim activists are made to feel that anti-Semitism is perfectly acceptable. This combination of normalising anti-Semitism, mass migration, and the fragility of Arab–Israeli politics should make us worry about what lies ahead. Europe is no stranger to this hatred.

The Holocaust was the culmination of centuries of Christian and European anti-Semitism. In the eighteenth century the philosopher Voltaire called Jews 'a totally ignorant nation' and wrote that they behaved with 'contemptible miserliness and the most revolting superstition, with a violent hatred of all the nations which have tolerated them'. Baron d'Holbach, a prominent European atheist of the same period, described Jews as 'the enemies of the human race'. A century later Karl Marx, despite his own Jewish descent, claimed that Jews were responsible for capitalism, the source of the world's evils.

In contrast to these modern European attitudes, seventh-century Arabia offered a more harmonious approach. It is recounted that the Prophet Mohamed was sitting with his companions when a funeral procession passed by, and he immediately stood up out of respect for the deceased. His disciples followed suit. The cortège moved on, and the Arabs said to the Prophet: 'That was a Jewish person who had died.' To which he responded: 'Was this not also a human soul?'

Some of the Jews of Medina had plotted with the Prophet's pagan enemies in Mecca to undermine and eradicate the new message of Islam, with its competing claim to a divine book, access to God and, unlike Judaism, a call to others to embrace the one God. When the Prophet migrated from Mecca and entered Medina, his first act after establishing a place of prayer, the mosque, was to send his companions to trade in the marketplace with Jews as equals in financial dealings, despite their earlier hostility. The pact that was agreed between the Muslims and other communities in the city included the Jews. When the Prophet spoke about the *umma* – the nation of believers – in Medina, he included Jews and Christians. The Quran even allows for Muslims to eat kosher food. In several chapters of the Quran, there is repeated praise of the Old Testament prophets. I find it hard to understand how contemporary Muslims can harbour hatred for the descendants of the prophets that are so venerated in the Quran. The Jews are the children of Noah, Abraham, Sarah, Isaac, Jacob, Rebekah, Joseph, Moses, Aaron and others.

The Prophet married a Jewish lady called Safiyya, who subsequently converted to Islam. When his other wives teased Safiyya for her Jewish ancestry, the Prophet taught her to make this riposte: 'My father is the Prophet Haroun [Aaron], my uncle is Moses, and my husband is the Prophet Mohamed. What is your problem?' To this day, Muslims honour and cherish Safiyya's memory as the earliest Muslims did: as a 'mother of the believers', a designation for the wives of the Prophet. Despite her leading role among the Muslims after the Prophet passed away, she bequeathed her wealth to her Jewish nephews.

All schools of the sharia allow Muslim men to marry Jewish women. Some Muslim scholars have also ruled that as long as a Muslim woman is allowed to practise her faith, she may marry a Jewish man.

None of this history, none of these attitudes, indicates or advocates hatred for the Jews. When Sidi Ahmad Zarruq sided with the Jews of Fez, or Saladin trusted Maimonides with his life, or Muslims protected thousands of Jews fleeing from the Nazis during the Holocaust, this empathy and fellow-feeling grew out of a strong collective memory within Islam. In 1941, King Mohamed V of Morocco confidently protected 250,000 Jews from the occupying Vichy French forces who wished to pass legislation to discriminate against Jews. In France, Muslims hid and helped hundreds of Jews by sheltering them in the main mosque in Paris. Jewish presence in a mosque was not considered to be a problem. In 1965, King Hasan II of Morocco handed over vital intelligence on Arab plans to attack Israel that helped tip the balance toward an Israeli victory in the 1967 Six Day War.

There is, however, another historical memory: one of treachery and bitterness between Jews and the early Muslims. It serves as a rallying cry for radicals from al-Qaeda, Hamas, Hezbollah and other assorted Islamists who shout: '*Khaibar, Khaibar, ya Yahud!*' – 'Remember Khaibar, Jews!' They are recalling the battle of Khaibar in 628, when the Prophet's forces killed Jewish tribal leaders from the Banu Quraizah tribe by implementing Jewish laws of punishment for betrayal of an agreement that they had previously reached with Muslims.

In the Christian tradition, Judas's betrayal of Jesus to the Romans and the alleged insistence of the High Priests of Judaism that Jesus be killed made Jews, for a long time, a focus and justification for Christian hatred of Jews. A passage, for example, in the New Testament refers to Jews as 'snakes', a 'brood of vipers', and destined to be 'sentenced to hell'.[4] Pope Leo the Great in the fifth century continued the hatred and referred to the Jewish disciple of Jesus, Judas, as 'the wickedest man that ever lived', and St John's Gospel condemns Judas as 'the son of perdition'. Something similar happened among Muslims, sadly. The word *Yahud*, or 'Jews', has become almost a profanity, bearing connotations of perennial enmity and plotting against Islam and Muslims.

None of this is helped by the existence of illogical hadiths that contradict the Quran and intensify the anti-Jewish animus. One hadith frequently cited among Islamist activists relates that before the Last Day stones and trees will say: 'O slave of God, there is a Jew behind me; come and kill him.'[5] Why are hadith scholars silent in the face of preaching in mosques based on such texts?

Another hadith allegedly claims: 'Indeed, I will expel the Jews and the Christians from the peninsula of the Arabs so that I leave only Muslims.' Literalists of the Salafi persuasion have adopted, and apply, this worldview. But the mainstream Muslim consensus is entirely different. Followers of the dominant Hanafi school allow unbelievers to live in the Hijaz, where the holy cities of Mecca and Medina are found, and even to enter those cities, including the holy mosques, and stay there as visitors. The stricter Shafi'i school allocates periods of time each year for Jews and Christians to enter Medina, the city of the Prophet.

Anti-Semitism never has been, and cannot be allowed to become, the mainstream position of Muslims globally.

It is often confused, not always benignly, with anti-Zionism. The word 'Zionist' (*Sahyouni* in Arabic) comes from Mount Zion in Jerusalem, which symbolises the Holy Land for Jews. It should do so, too, for Muslims, but instead Zionism has become the subject of global opprobrium, except in Israel and the United

States. Israel has come to be viewed as an American outpost in the Middle East in the eyes of its Arab neighbours, who obsessively link everything that happens in the region to the Jewish state. They conveniently lose sight of the fact that the people of Israel are honoured repeatedly in the Quran, which actually confirms that Jews have every right to settle in and around Jerusalem:

> And [remember] when Moses said to his people: 'O my people, call in remembrance the favour of God unto you, when he produced prophets among you, made you kings, and gave to you what He had not given to any other among the peoples. O my people, enter the Holy Land which God has assigned unto you, and do not turn back ignominiously, for then will ye be overthrown, to your own ruin.' (5:20–1)
>
> We [Allah] said to the Children of Israel: 'Dwell securely in the Promised Land. And when the last warning will come to pass, we will gather you together in a mingled crowd.' (17:104)

Today, the global Jewish population is less than 20 million. For how much longer must this great people suffer and live in fear of annihilation? There will be 2 billion Muslims worldwide within three decades. We can and must accommodate Jews in our midst in a shared Middle East of coexistence. The Jews belong in the Middle East, and deserve a dignified and safe home, as do the Palestinians who have been languishing in refugee camps for three generations.

It is simply unacceptable, indeed deplorable, that, within just a few decades of the Holocaust, anti-Semitism is once again on the rise – and in the Muslim world. Let us be honest: Jews in New York, Paris and London fear attacks from radicalised Muslims. Their schools and synagogues have armed guards and police patrols for fear of violence from extreme Muslims. The *Charlie Hebdo* murderers headed for synagogues and kosher grocers to kill Jews immediately after murdering journalists who had insulted the Prophet. And Israel is armed to the teeth and separated from the Palestinians by a wall because lowering its guard results in an immediate rise in terror attacks. This is no way to guarantee long-term security for Israelis – or dignity for Arabs.

Israel's actions, policies, intentions and very name produce a global, instantaneous response from many Muslims. Israel conducts a military operation in Gaza against jihadists lobbing rockets at its population, and there are mass protests across the Muslim world. Meanwhile the Syrian government with Iranian support can kill over 400,000 Muslims and displace millions more, and we see not a single significant rally in the capitals of Muslim nations.

After the Arab uprisings, the Israeli embassy in Egypt was attacked and the ambassador had to be evacuated. Sadat's peace deal with Israel had cost him his life in 1981, and Mubarak's warm relations with Israel had not trickled down to the Egyptian masses either. Similarly, while Saudi clerics, for all their other extremism, have been quick to condemn suicide bombings inside Israel, the message has not percolated down to the grassroots. The kings of Jordan and Morocco have behaved with dignity toward Israel, and maintain cordial relations, but their populations have yet to be won over. On the other hand, Israeli citizens are able to travel freely and safely to Turkey.

I visited Israel and the West Bank for the first time in 2013, and have done so several times since then. For many Muslims around the world, to visit Israel is to support 'the Zionist entity' and therefore risk social isolation. But this view is not only outdated; it is also self-defeating.

I wanted to see Israel for myself, and to visit the famed Dome of the Rock and Al-Aqsa Mosque in Jerusalem. What I found was depressing. On the ancient walls hung old fans that blew noisily and rattled – there was no money for air-conditioning. The carpet for worshippers to pray on was old and ragged. Here I was, inside one of the world's most beautiful and historically significant buildings, but scaffolding and general clutter prevented me from seeing the centre of the Dome of the Rock. Water leaks, rickety shoe shelves and uncleaned antique tiles all lent a sense of disharmony. And no, this was not the fault of the Jews, or of the West, but of us Muslims, we who claim to be fighting daily to 'liberate Jerusalem' and yet neglect the very heart of the city. This has to end. Old attitudes will have to change.

The Arab League began its boycott of 'Zionist' goods back in 1945, and later created a Central Boycott Office to ensure minimal Arab contact with Israel. These days the Gulf states and others have no problem circumventing this policy, but the Arab and Muslim masses have yet to break free from the burden of boycotting all things Israeli. The popular Egyptian cleric Yusuf al-Qaradawi continually rehearses his fatwas urging Muslims to avoid contact with Israel, from the platform of his regular slot on Al-Jazeera's Arabic channel. Recent attempts by European Marxist academics to boycott Israel have lent support to this counterproductive strategy.

However, the main victims of the boycott are not Israelis but Palestinians. Israel's economy is booming, while Palestinians languish in abject poverty. The decades-long Arab boycott has failed miserably. An estimated 70 per cent of Palestinian families in East Jerusalem live below the poverty line. Arabs from neighbouring countries may choose not to visit Jerusalem because of the boycott, but many Palestinians do not have that luxury: they have to take low-paid jobs as cleaners and porters in the city's hotels, or with Jewish-owned businesses, or travel to the West Bank to find work.

Many people condemn Israeli settlements and call for an economic boycott of their produce, but I saw that it was Arab builders, plumbers, taxi drivers and other workers who maintained the Israeli lifestyle. Separatism in the Holy Land has not worked, and it is time to end it. How much longer will we punish Palestinians in the name of creating a free Palestine?

I abandoned collective Muslim thinking and went to Israel because there is a new momentum building in the region. Egypt's former grand mufti Ali Gomaa, and a prominent Sufi scholar from Yemen, Habib Ali al-Jifri, broke ranks with Qaradawi and went to Jerusalem in 2013. They justified their visit on scriptural grounds, citing the Prophet Mohamed's encouragement for believers to visit the Holy Land. Their journey was facilitated by

Prince Ghazi bin Muhammad bin Talal of Jordan, the principal religious adviser to King Abdullah.

I understood why the Prophet encouraged us to visit Jerusalem. Standing beside the Jewish worshippers at the Western Wall, I could hear church bells and soon after that the Muslim muezzin's call to prayer. All three Abrahamic faiths converge in Jerusalem and, despite the political difficulties, there exists a palpable serenity. Secular pluralism inside modern-day Israel has ensured this freedom of worship for Jews, Christians and Muslims.

It is vital that religious leaders are involved in the quest for accommodation, coexistence and a durable peace in the Middle East. To be credible in Muslim eyes, any peace agreement will require backing from the major Sunni powers, including Saudi Arabia, Turkey and Egypt. The West cannot continue to ignore the religious dimension to the Arab–Israeli conflict.

By carrying Sunni Muslim opinion on the importance of a two-state solution, the West can help isolate Iran and its proxies in the region, most notably the terrorist organisation Hezbollah. While most Sunni countries are committed to finding a resolution through dialogue with Israel, Iran's theocratic government has consistently called for the destruction of Israel. Iran's long-standing Supreme Leader, Ali Khameini, declared in September 2015, 'Nothing called the "Zionist regime" will exist 25 years from now.'[6] This comes after years of the former Iranian president Mahmoud Ahmedinajad vowing to 'wipe Israel off the map'.

There is no greater touchstone of civilisation than the way it treats its minorities. And in our case, the Muslim world's treatment of Israel and the Jews, that beleaguered minority of only 20 million people, is among the greatest of tests for Muslim civilisational coexistence. The second caliph of Islam, Omar, a friend of the Prophet Mohamed, entered Jerusalem in the year 637 to receive the keys to the city from the Byzantines who had recently lost Jerusalem to the Muslims. The Christian patriarch, St Sophronius, invited Omar to the Church of the Holy Sepulchre for the key-handing-over ceremony. While there, the time for the midday Muslim prayer arrived. As the host, Sophronius insisted that the caliph pray inside the church. Omar declined, fearing and saying that Muslims of the future would demand that the church be converted to a mosque because he had prayed there. Omar excused himself and prayed on the streets nearby. Today, a mosque stands on that spot and is known as the 'Mosque of Omar'.

Upon accepting the keys to Jerusalem, as the new ruler of the city, he invited Jews back to live, pray, and be among the people of Jerusalem. After 500 years of being banished by the Romans, it was Omar and the pluralist spirit of Islam that brought Jews home to Jerusalem. Today's Muslims would do well to remember the ways of these early Muslim luminaries.

Israel has responsibilities, too.

When I visit Jerusalem and the West Bank, I frequently ask young Arabs about their views on Hamas. In almost every discussion, Christians and Muslims alike refuse to label Hamas a terrorist organisation. When I raise criticism of Hamas and its targeting of innocent civilians, my comments never register. The responses are always some variant on: 'Israel has taken our land and killed thousands of Arab civilians over the years. Hamas is only resisting occupation and fighting for our rights.'

I hear similar sentiments in Egypt, Saudi Arabia and even non-Arab Pakistan. Al-Jazeera Arabic has allowed the pro-Muslim Brotherhood Qaradawi to promote the view that suicide bombings against Israelis are not terrorism but 'martyrdom'. He used to claim that since all Israelis serve in the military, they cannot be classed as civilians. Even children, he argued, are not innocent, as they will one day grow up to serve in the military. However, when I met Shaikh Qaradawi in Qatar in 2015, he insisted that he had changed his position and no longer advocated the killing of Israeli innocents.

I can name dozens of Muslim clerics, important formulators of public opinion in a region dominated by religion, who will readily condemn acts of terrorism against the West but fall silent when it comes to condemning Hamas. From radical Iran to moderate Tunisia, Hamas's prime minister of Gaza, Ismail Haniyeh, is welcomed by vast cheering crowds during visits.

Israel is a nation in the Middle East, and it needs to find a home and place among its neighbours. To do so, the onus is on Arabs and Muslims to accept Israel and Jews as a nation that belongs firmly in the region.

Jews in Israel are accused constantly of occupation and apartheid. Granted, full equality between all citizens in Israel is yet to be realised, but the United States stands accused of similar inequalities in rights and economic opportunities between blacks and whites, southerners and northerners. Australia's treatment of its aboriginals is unjust: why is Australia not accused of apartheid? India is accused of being in occupation of Kashmir: where is the global movement to boycott India? Israel, in contrast, is forced to combat the rise of a Boycott, Divestment and Sanctions (BDS) movement in the Muslim world and parts of the West. Singling out Israel for constant criticism is the epitome of anti-Semitism.

Beyond terrorism and hostility, the Arab world desperately needs to embrace the culture of creativity and commercial flair that Israel brings to the Middle East. Between 1980 and 2000, the number of patents registered from Saudi Arabia was 171; from Egypt, 77; from the United Arab Emirates, 32; from Kuwait, 52; from Syria, 20; and from Jordan, 15 – compared with 7,652 from Israel.[7] Israel boasts the highest density of business start-ups in the world: a total of 3,850 new businesses in 2009, one for every 1,844 Israelis.[8] After the United States, Israel has more companies listed on the NASDAQ than any other country in the world, including India, China, Korea, Singapore and Ireland. Israel leads the world in the percentage of the economy that is spent on research and development.

Guarantees of peace from governments and peoples of Israel's neighbours will be reciprocated by Israel. For now, the violence of Hamas and Hezbollah has failed, but there is no certainty where their war of attrition will lead. Is there a Gandhi or a Nelson Mandela who can lead Palestine to making peace with its neighbour? To do so, what is taught in the schools and universities of the Middle East needs serious, sustained attention.

14
Education

'Knowledge and wisdom are the lost properties of the believer,' taught Imam Ali, 'so seek them even if they be with infidels.' Wherever there was new intelligence and discoveries to be made, Muslims were to have the confidence and curiosity to learn from other civilisations and cultures – all understanding and awareness was inherently the possession of a believer. This bold, self-assured mentality was borne out in reality: the Muslims absorbed with confidence new knowledge and ideas from the Greeks, Persians, Indians and Byzantines, and this cultural fusion was once the hallmark of Muslim civilisation. The seventh-century Byzantine emperor Justinian II, a Christian, was asked by Caliph Abd al-Malik to send craftsmen to cut the coloured stone and glass tesserae for the Dome of the Rock in Jerusalem. The Byzantine contribution to this stupendous Islamic monument stands to this day. An inscription 240 metres long, including Quranic verses glorifying God, runs round the base of the dazzling cupola.

'We should not be ashamed to acknowledge the truth from whatever source it comes to us, even if it is brought to us by former generations and foreign peoples. For him who seeks the truth there is nothing of higher value than truth itself,' wrote al-Kindi (801–66), the thinker with whom the history of Islamic philosophy begins.[1]

How things have changed. Today, many young Muslims memorise large tracts of the Arabic Quran, and recite prayers in Arabic, even though they do not understand the language. The average Muslim child spends three to five years in evening classes and at weekends learning Arabic, but still not learning to speak it. Memorisation is seen as more important than comprehension.

A decade ago, the Arab Human Development Report warned that 'curricula taught in Arab countries seem to encourage submission, obedience, subordination and compliance, rather than free critical thought'.[2] '*Man 'allamani harfan, kuntu lahu 'abdan*' – 'Whoever teaches me a letter, to him I am a slave' – is a popular Arabic saying. Muslim communities across the globe, like their Jewish counterparts, venerate teachers. But I am not sure if the word 'teacher' is always relevant. Too often, the correct word in Muslim educational circles might be 'transmitter'.

Modern Western education focuses on training students to ask 'how' and 'why', and teachers are seen as facilitators of learning. Continuing in the ways of instruction in ancient Greece, teaching and learning in the West take place through dialogue and mutual exchange. Education is about curiosity and asking questions, and probing multiple sources for answers: books, friends, parents, mentors and life experiences in addition to classroom teachers. The Prophet Mohamed taught his companions the same method of reciprocal questioning and reaching conclusions together. The hallmark of an open mind is to be able to ask and answer an array of questions.

Socrates preferred to understand the intellectual level of an individual or a small group of people before proceeding to impart wisdom and ideas on the meaning of life. He taught his students to avoid repeating the same concept because it could be received without full comprehension unless questions and discussions accompanied teaching. Plato built on this dialectical method. The Prophet Mohamed taught his companions *khatibunnasi 'ala qadri 'uqulihim* – 'address the people in accordance with their understanding.' Underlying that teaching was the Prophetic model of enlightening lives with knowledge and enhancing their existence. He constantly questioned and rebelled. The Quran itself testifies to the public scrutiny of Meccan life with verses such as these uttered by the Prophet in public on multiple occasions:

'Do you not think, O Pagans?'

'Why do you not reflect on the creation of the heavens and the earth?'

'For what crime do you kill the innocent?'

That spirit of asking, answering, and asking again made Muslims the greatest intellectuals of the medieval world. Aristotelian thought was preserved and further developed by the great Muslim philosophers, including most prominently Al Farabi in Damascus (872–950), and later Ibn Rushd (Averroes) in Córdoba (1126–98). The first five hundred years of early Islam welcomed this culture of questioning.

By contrast, the orthodox Muslim today adopts a position on studying theology known as '*bila kaif*' – 'without asking how' – an approach that carries over in general education into blind veneration of teachers, learning by rote, and an aversion to asking questions. Large Muslim nations such as Indonesia, Pakistan, Bangladesh, Egypt and Algeria have education systems in which students prepare for exams by memorising answers to expected questions.

I have met university students in Egypt with 8,000 students in their class – 8,000 students registered with one professor – and this is not infrequent. But no, they do not all need to attend lectures. The course textbooks on sale in the university bookshop are often solely the writings of the same professor, and they are vastly popular among the students because they can safely be memorised to guarantee favourable marks from their author. Regurgitation brings reward, and the larger the class, the higher the book sales and thus the greater the income for the professor.

The first commandment of the Quran for Muslim civilisation was: 'Read!' The archangel Gabriel conveyed the order from God to the Prophet Mohamed to 'read in the name of your Lord ...' (96:1). Reading, reflecting and writing were central to early Islam. The first generations of Muslims were taught that 'the ink of the scholar's pen is weightier and more worthy than the blood of a martyr'. The Quran reprimands those who acquire learning without comprehension for being like 'donkeys who carry the burden of books (but understand nothing of them)' (62:5).

Memorising texts was meant to be only the beginning of learning, with critical evaluation doing the rest.

Today, book-reading culture (except for religious material) is nearly absent in most Arab countries. An Arab individual reads on average a quarter of a page a year, compared with the eleven books read by an American or seven by a British person. The average Arab child reads for six minutes a year, as against the 200 hours of reading by his or her Western counterpart.[3] In European countries, 21 out of 100 people read books regularly, while in Turkey the figure is one in 10,000.[4]

The ancient Arabs were renowned for memorising vast tracts of poetry. They also memorised their genealogies, back through multiple generations to Abraham and his son Ishmael, the founder of the Arab line. These lineages are preserved in books of early Muslim biographies, but even today this culture thrives in the Gulf Arab countries and Yemen, on the Arabian Peninsula. I have met young Arabs in their twenties in Riyadh, Abu Dhabi and Qatar who can reel off their ancestry simply by saying 'my name is Mohamed, son of Ahmed, son of Ali, son of Omar of the tribe of Shammar, son of Salman, son of Fahd', all the way back to the time of the Prophet. This ease and precision of reference is particularly strong among those who are descendants of the Prophet Mohamed (*sayyids* or *sharifs* in Arabic). This is not seen as a prodigious feat, but as completely normal. The fact that women are almost entirely left out of such lists appears to be equally normal.

In addition to lineage and ancestry, the Arabs of the peninsula (the 'original' Arabs, not the peoples they conquered in Egypt and the Levant or Africa, who then adopted the Arabic language) also produced and preserved poetry by oral transmission. '*Al-shi'r diwan al-'Arab*', runs an old adage: 'Poetry is the record of the Arabs'. In the Arab world there are poetry-reciting competitions on Friday night television that attract audiences of over 70 million, rivalling *American Idol* or *The X Factor* in the West. Winners of the *Sha'ir al-Milyoon* (Millionaire Poet) show receive prizes worth up to 1.3 million dollars – more than the Nobel Prize in Literature. This kind of talent show is exactly designed to appeal to the Arabs, descendants of the proud and hospitable Bedouin people of the desert.

The richness of the Arabic language, and the ability of the Arabs to memorise so much of it, formed the basis of early Muslim culture. The 114 chapters of the Quran, more than 6,000 verses, are still committed to memory by millions of Muslims even in our time. A *hafiz*, someone who has memorised the Quran in its entirety, has a special and honoured position in the Muslim community. There is no village, town or city, no mosque or *madrasa* (Islamic school) in the Muslim world, without at least one *hafiz* helping to preserve the Quran in oral form by reciting parts of it at daily prayers. With the advance of Islam, the culture and habits of the Arabs, including that of committing the Quran to memory, spread to new lands in India, Africa, Indonesia and the Turkic sphere.

Internalising the Quran in this way has spiritual benefits for a believer standing at night in prayer before God, but to extend the technique of bulk memorisation to all spheres of learning is a mistake. When an examination system tests the capacity for rote learning rather than the ability to reflect and critically analyse, we create citizens who are not equipped for the modern world or to contribute to the global economy. That then breeds isolation and separatism.

In Pakistan, the proliferation of *madrasas* and free education is generating a mass of graduates who can memorise and transmit knowledge, but can neither understand it nor reflect on it in context. Furthermore, Islamic studies is one of the easiest subjects to study at undergraduate level, because it doesn't require very high grades for entry – and this is also true elsewhere. The absence of critical thinking skills in the curriculum is thus producing vast numbers of *ulama*, or clerics, who are ill-equipped to take on the challenges posed by their real-world congregations.

Hadith literature, collections of sayings attributed to the Prophet, forms the second-most important primary source for the sharia, after the Quran. As we have seen, each of these hadiths (traditions) consists of two parts: the *matn*, content, or actual statement, and the *sanad*, or chain of authority. The *sanad* is a list of names of those who received the saying orally, one from another, tracing it all the way back to the source, the person who heard it directly from the lips of the Prophet. Over time, scholars started paying attention only to the *sanad*, without critically examining the *matn* by cross-referencing it with the Quran, other hadiths, the historical and cultural context, logic and the public interest. Whether referring to hatred of Jews, or misogyny, or considering dogs unclean, or strange, self-serving hadiths advanced for political reasons by the Umayyad and Abbasid caliphs, the desertion of critical thinking has resulted in contemporary Muslims being willing to accept any doubtful hadith as long as it is backed by a reliable *sanad*. Critical examination of the content has been lost. Only in Turkey, under the leadership of Professor Mehmet Görmez, the country's leading Islamic authority and a longstanding hadith specialist, is there today a rigorous attempt to scrutinise hadiths and bring them into line with the Quran, human logic, and the spirit of the Prophet, thus understanding the texts in their proper contexts.

It was argued in late medieval times, and is still widely held today, especially among Sunni Muslims, that 'the gate of *ijtihad* [the scope for applying the intellect] has closed'. In the first five centuries of Islam there was no mention whatsoever of '*Insidad bab al-ijtihad*', this closure of the gate of academic endeavour and free thinking. Through the *ijtihad* of well-qualified and thoughtful scholars, Muslim values found fresh expressions and a means of renewal with the passage of time. But during the following centuries the idea of the closure of the gate of *ijtihad* gained currency; all the essential questions in life had, it appeared, already been answered, and it only remained for current and future generations to apply and hand down this fixed body of knowledge.[5] The consequence of this was that Muslims were encouraged to practise *Taqlid* (copying, or imitation) in their worship and social intercourse.

The argument for the extinction of *ijtihad* came to be widely accepted. Egyptian Muslim theologian Abd al-Rahman al-Jabarti, in his *History of Egypt* in the nineteenth century, named multiple religious freethinkers who met the specification for being called *mujtahids* (those who practise *ijtihad*), without recognising them as such. In al-Jabarti's mind, no doubt a reflection of his time, *ijtihad* had ceased, and all were now committed to blind pursuit, or *Taqlid*.

With the perceived closure of the gate of *ijtihad*, Muslims lost their zeal to question and innovate. Worse, the rise of Arab Salafism among Muslims globally reinforced the dogma that Islam's best days were over with the passing of the Prophet and the first three generations of Muslims, the *Salaf*. Literalists cited a hadith of the Prophet warning that *bid'ah* (innovation) was deviant, and all deviancy led to hellfire. If he said that, what was the context? And did it only apply as a warning against claims of new deities for worship? Among literalist Muslims the word *bid'ah* itself has become a dirty word; innovation is feared and shunned. Historically, Muslim thought leaders taught that *bid'ah* applied only to creed and matters of personal worship (not adding new compulsory prayers, for instance), and that in many aspects of life Muslims could embrace *bid'ah hasanah*, positive innovation. Celebrating the birthday of the Prophet Mohamed was one example of such *bid'ah hasanah*, agreed upon by the vast majority of Muslim scholars and observed, with joyful songs and the distribution of sweets, across much of the Muslim world, though banned in Salafi and other hard-line mosques.

The recent rise in literalism among those unwilling to interrogate texts, and dismissive of the contextual approach of most Muslims past and present, feeds and is fed by broader trends beyond religion. Today, most students in the Arab world want to pursue medicine or engineering. Scientific and technical subjects carry the highest status and attract the brightest undergraduates. Politics, sociology, history, poetry, philosophy and the liberal arts offer no future. Nuance, context, colour, metaphor and diversity of interpretation are losing ground. Creating independent minds and a pluralist outlook is seen by authoritarian governments as a threat to social and political stability.

This mentality is also being applied to matters of religion. More and more educated young Muslims approach Islam and scripture with the formulaic methodology of a trained scientist, doctor or engineer: right path vs. wrong path; heaven vs. hell; black vs. white. The subtle, spiritual ways of Rumi (see Chapter 6) or the sophistication of Ibn Arabi (see Chapter 17) risk becoming blasphemous. And from this milieu radicals and terrorists are born.

Osama bin Laden was an engineer. Ayman al-Zawahiri is a doctor. Khalid Sheikh Mohammed, mastermind of 9/11, holds a degree in mechanical engineering. The leader of the Muslim Brotherhood, Mohamed Badie, has a degree in veterinary medicine. Hizb ut-Tahrir's global leader, Ata Abu Rishta, is an engineer, as is the deputy leader of the Brotherhood, Khairat al-Shater. Hamas's chief bomb maker, Yahya Ayyash, was an electrical engineering student. It is now documented that the rank and file of Islamist and jihadi organisations are filled with doctors and engineers.[6]

Before the 1940s and Arab independence from European powers, engineering as a profession did not exist in the Arab world, except in Egypt. With decolonisation and state-led development of Arab cities and economies, and mass migration of populations to urban centres, socialist state projects were suddenly in desperate need of engineers, and they needed to come in large numbers from poor and middling backgrounds. In the 1960s, the existing city elites were established merchants, or part of a religious or political order, and had been for generations. Engineering degrees offered the new arrivals and their children funded training, access to a state-sponsored elite, security, high salaries, social advancement, and opportunities to travel to prestigious international conferences.

But within a generation, in the 1980s, engineers' prospects began to fade as socialism gave way to economic liberalisation and privatisation, led by Sadat in Egypt and widely followed in the region. States could no longer absorb the products of their own universities. Unemployment rates for Arab graduates began to soar. Many turned to protest politics to find new meaning in their lives – and Islamism and Salafism found willing recruits.

The engineering mindset is one that is ripe for jihadism. In a study of graduate jihadis, almost 45 per cent were found to be engineers. When all the 'elite degrees' were included (medicine, science, engineering), that figure went up to 56.7 per cent of the sample. If business and economics were also included, the proportion rose to 63.4 per cent of graduate jihadis.[7]

When the engineers and doctors of Salafism created their own 'state' in parts of Iraq and Syria in October 2014 (ISIS territory), they closed down the archaeology, fine arts, philosophy and politics faculties at universities in areas under their control. They banned all study of human rights, drama and novels. Women, who had to wear black face covers, headscarves and *abayas* outside their homes, had to attend separate educational facilities from men in ISIS-held territory.

In Nigeria, Boko Haram is not known by its longer, Salafi, Arabic name (Jamaat ahl al-sunnah lid-da'wah wal-jihad, the Sunni Group for Preaching and Jihad), but by its Hausa moniker, meaning 'Books are Haram [outlawed]'. 'Boko', in Hausa, the main language of northern Nigeria, is the word for 'books', and to extremist Salafi Nigerian minds these represent Western education and secular culture. (In traditional African societies, teaching and learning was conducted using hand-held slates and chalk.) Boko Haram's obsession with keeping Western-style modern education at bay through violence and killings is no accident: it is designed to force the Salafi understanding of religious purity on Nigeria's Muslims.

In Pakistan, the schoolgirl Malala Yusufzai came to global prominence because she was shot by the Taliban on her journey home from school, but there are millions of other Malalas in Afghanistan, Pakistan and elsewhere who dare not step outside their homes for fear of persecution by the *mullahs*. Educating girls and giving them the key to freedom from the control of the clerics causes fear among extremists. The primary motivation for Islamist extremists is to gain political power, and their first act in power is almost always to change the education system – particularly female education.

As well as liberal or modern education, the Salafis are also opposed to manifestations of culture, even Islamic heritage. Muslim societies once abounded in freethinking writers, poets, craftsmen and artists, architects and calligraphers. They beautified city centres with mosques surrounded by schools and universities, where students could freely debate and disagree with their teachers. This is why there exists pluralism and *ikhtilaf*, difference of opinion, within the sharia. Early Muslims believed this *ikhtilaf* to be one of God's clemencies.[8]

Hospitals and orphanages, too, found their place in this thriving cultural order, all decorated with Muslim and scriptural calligraphy and art. That heritage still flourishes in the old quarters of Baghdad, Damascus, Cairo, Istanbul and Delhi, but the descendants of the masters who created it now have no knowledge of its origins. Worse, the literalist mind of the modern engineer, shunning cultural tradition, wants to blow up these edifices and build tower blocks.

The Salafi worldview is committed to destroying, not treasuring, the past. The assault has been most sustained in Mecca and Medina, at the heart of the homeland of Islam. And an educational upbringing that does not honour its own heritage certainly has no respect for any other, as we have seen from the blowing up of the Buddhas of Bamiyan in Afghanistan and Greco-Roman Palmyra in Syria, as well as fourth-century monasteries and museums to past civilisations.

Textbooks that promote such views have gone unchanged for decades. Pakistan's hatred for minority Christians and others comes from the culture imbibed in its schools; the Saudi authorities' hatred for Shi'a Muslims is right there in school textbooks.

Against this background, private language schools are proliferating across the Muslim world. After school hours, you see young adults in Turkey, the Arab world, Bangladesh and elsewhere heading for English-language classes, hoping these will lead to better job opportunities. Within a few years they will be applying in their thousands to study in the West. But there are three disturbing factors in this leaning toward the West.

First, the Arabic language, the pure language of the Quran, is coming under pressure. In university bookshops, as we have seen, engineering manuals and medical textbooks reign supreme – and they are almost all in English. Near the medical and engineering faculties in much of the Middle East there are shops with photocopiers busy breaking copyright laws. It is through English, not Arabic, that the latest research and scientific thinking are accessed. Classical Arabic is nowadays reduced to poetry, the Quran, news, and cartoons for children. In the real, contemporary world of study, work, debate and daily encounters it is nowhere to be found. The language does not sit comfortably with modern life, and feels detached, irrelevant. What must that do to the self-esteem of young Arabs – the idea that the way to get ahead is to master the language of the British – the very people who subjugated Muslims and the Arabs, from the Crusades to the Empire?

Second, Western education carries the virus of a lack of veneration for ancient values, and the moral relativism that says nothing is absolutely right or wrong, the individual is sovereign, and religion is a cause of backwardness. When a young Muslim enters this environment, he or she is again deeply challenged. The prayer rooms in Western universities are full of Arab and Muslim students seeking refuge from the ideological bombardment of liberal individualism. Where does the contemporary Muslim belong? Neither at home nor in the West.

Amid the uncertainties for the future of Arab countries, there is the supremacy of Arabic in religion but inferiority in the sciences, the prestige of the West and the appeal of its technological innovations in daily life yet relentless verbal attacks by mosque preachers on America – all this inevitably creates cognitive dissonance. Against the confusion of identity and lack of a sense of belonging anywhere, Salafism offers an uncompromisingly clinical approach to puritanical Islam, and provides a shelter from the insecurities of living in dictatorships.

As we have seen, however, in the allocation of university places by school grades, with engineering and medicine taking the highest-achieving students and Islamic studies for those apparently least gifted, the status and prestige of traditionally trained clerics has declined. In the long term, there is a high risk that the literalist Islam of engineers and doctors will come to appear more authoritative and attractive than the more gentle, subtle and nuanced faith of the low-grade traditional *ulama*.

And third, in the formal educational setting of secondary schools and the informal cultural setting of mosques, the relegation of women to the status of second-class human beings is not preparing young Muslims to recognise the worth of half the human race. Gender segregation in classrooms, and putting women at the back of mosques or, in many countries, barring them from entering at all, is completely at odds with the early notions of Islam, and with the current and future state of the world.

An adviser to the Saudi monarchy explained to me in 2014 in Riyadh that he had made great progress in raising educational standards among Saudi students, and young women in particular. He pointed out that over 200,000 Saudi students were studying in Australia, the UK, the US and other countries at the king's expense, and highlighted the creation, to much fanfare, of nineteen new universities in Saudi Arabia.

In the West, however, the advance of education, and progress in general, was not based only on increasing the number of graduates and universities. The underlying premise of education, to train curious minds to ask questions and conquer new intellectual terrain, was once the hallmark of the Muslim world, but in most places has now been abandoned. Teaching practical skills and transmitting factual information are now seen to be more valuable than fostering an environment of freedom for ideas, innovation and inquisitive intellects.

But this freedom also requires an open society, in which a dissenting thinker is not locked up or killed. The government's view cannot be the only legitimate view in the Arab public space. Breakdowns in education are also failures of politics. The multi-layered malaise in the education systems of the Muslim world is set to produce tens of millions of young people who are torn between Islam and the West. Why should they cherish independence of thought when it results in prison or being an outcast? Why think critically about a text if the government and clergy will label you a disbeliever or a deviant? Why study politics, philosophy or history when no worth is attached to these subjects, and the courses, if available at all, are empty of critical content?

The retreat from literature and the liberal arts into the sciences and technology poses problems not only for the development of vibrant open societies but also on university campuses across the Muslim world and among Muslim communities in the West. Student bodies in engineering faculties and medical colleges are dominated by Islamists and Salafis. In large countries such as Egypt, previous generations of engineers and doctors who have turned to the Islam of Salafism now dominate the professional bodies, syndicates and unions that provide powerful networks for career advancement and job-seeking.

Meanwhile, in almost every Arab Muslim country almost half of the university student population is female, and in Saudi Arabia now more than half – the Saudi kingdom's top university has 57 female students for every 43 males.[9] What, then, are the challenges and opportunities for women in the modern Muslim world?

15
Women

Should women have the same legal rights as men? Ninety per cent of people in Indonesia and Turkey say 'yes', and in Pakistan 77 per cent agree, but in Saudi Arabia only 61 per cent concur, and 57 per cent in Egypt.

Should women have the right to vote? Turkish people are 93 per cent in favour, 80 per cent of Indonesians, 67 per cent of Pakistanis and 56 per cent of Saudis.

Do women have the right to hold any job for which they are qualified? In Egypt, 85 per cent think so, in Turkey 86 per cent, and in Saudi Arabia 69 per cent. When it comes to women holding leadership positions in cabinet and at national political levels, 50 per cent of Egyptians are supportive but only 40 per cent of Saudis.[1]

On purely religious grounds, these answers, in the largest-ever polling of Muslim nations, could and should have been above 90 per cent for every question asked. But there is an underlying attitude and a set of male assumptions, cultural impositions and interpretations of scripture that hold women back and deny them the freedom to prosper and flourish fully in the Muslim world. Taken to extremes, these views can have serious, and even fatal, consequences.

At a secondary school in Mecca, Saudi Arabia, one hot spring day in 2002, the girls had taken off their oppressive black *abayas* and headscarves as usual. Saudi men wear flowing white robes that reflect back the searing desert heat, but women and girls must wear black, the most uncomfortable of colours for the climate.

Islam sets no colour code for women's dress, but black was the traditional women's costume in the Najd region of central Arabia, from which the Al Saud tribe came, conquered the holy cities of Islam, and established its rule across the whole of what is now Saudi Arabia. Mecca was part of the colourful, urbane Hijaz region, but the puritan Najdis disliked its cosmopolitan ways. Colourful Hijazi clothing was banned in 1932, and now even these teenage girls were legally required to wear black. At least inside their all-girls school, with its all-female staff, they could take off their hijab and relax.

But on that day, 22 March 2002, a fire broke out in their school. The girls made a rush for the exit only to be met with resistance at the gates and forced by the *Mutawwa'a*, the Saudi religious police, back into the blazing building. They were not to be allowed out because they were not wearing headscarves and *abayas*. Firemen arrived at the site but were prevented from entering the building because there were teenage girls present with their hair uncovered. When parents arrived, the *Mutawwa'a* used their police powers forcibly to stop them getting in to rescue their children. Fifteen girls burned to death.

Their lives could have been saved, but Saudi Salafi Islam prioritised the rules on women's dress over the sanctity of human life. And this happened in Mecca, the home and heart of Islam. The first key principle of the sharia, first of the five *Maqasid* – preservation of life – had been abandoned. Pedantry of the literalist rule trumped the reason for the law.

Six months prior to that, in September 2001, tens of thousands of people had poured out of two collapsing buildings engulfed in fire. In New York, the firefighters and police struggled valiantly to rescue those fleeing the Twin Towers, and did everything humanly possible to get them out alive. How could Muslim men – in Mecca, of all places – have responded so completely differently, with such callousness and cruelty toward girls and women – in the name of Islam?

A minority of Salafis, with their puritanical cast of mind, now dominate Muslim discourse and control public conduct in Mecca. Their preoccupation with being 'right' and 'true' is reflected most intensely in their obsession with women. Salafi clerics from Saudi Arabia have written extensive volumes on women's periods, sexual habits and dress, whether and where it is permissible for them to work, limits on their travel, pregnancy and divorce.

Nowhere is the battle for women's identity and freedom more apparent than inside the Grand Mosque, or Sacred Mosque, in Mecca, the global nerve centre of Islam. In just 150 years the Salafis from Najd have gone from being forbidden to enter the mosque, to occupying it, then being ejected, to now being in control of it. They have knocked down ancient architecture, imposed gender segregation in prayers, removed the teaching corners of non-Salafi Muslim schools and denominations, rejected local imams from the Hijaz and imposed only Najdi prayer leaders, and forbidden gatherings of other Muslims inside Islam's holiest place of worship. Immune from international scrutiny, Salafism reigns supreme.

Within these holy precincts, my wife Faye was beaten by a Salafi with a stick for wearing a long dress that showed her ankle when we first went on pilgrimage. This was in 2005. It was only when I roared at him that he backed off, but I dare not think about the plight of any woman on her own.

When I lived in Saudi Arabia, Faye began to wear the black *abaya* out of respect for local custom. Why stand out and attract the attention of the woman-beaters? The sharia forbids women on pilgrimage to cover their faces while circumambulating the Ka'bah, the cubic structure at the centre of the Grand Mosque that Muslims face when praying. This is contradicted by the Salafi laws for Saudi women, who are still expected to wear the *abaya* and cover their faces. Faye did both, and yet, inside the Grand Mosque, in the shade of the holy Ka'bah, Saudi policemen were eyeing her up and down with determined, lustful glances. It is from the eyes of Salafi men that Muslim women must be shielded. Faye and I already despised the male advances in Saudi shops and restaurants whenever she was on her own – the dropping of business cards, the requests for her phone number, the filthy whisperings in supermarket aisles. So we had learned to be together as often as possible to ward off this lecherous behaviour. But inside the Grand Mosque?

The problem is not Saudi Arabia or the Gulf region, but the bigotry of Salafi-Wahhabism imposed on the Muslim public space. For instance, in neighbouring Bahrain, Kuwait or the United Arab Emirates, women and men are relatively free and interact with greater mutual respect in malls and mosques. Citizens of these other Gulf countries share the same language, dialect, tribes, culture and history. The distinguishing factor is that puritanism of Salafism is not powerful in their governments and therefore not imposed as law of the land.

Even before I lived in Saudi Arabia, my understanding of the hijab as purely Islamic attire was already in doubt. There is no verse in the Quran that directly calls on women to cover their heads. I saw Jewish women wearing the equivalent of the hijab in London, Arab nuns I met in Syria looking identical to Muslim women, and similar clothing depicted in ancient pre-Christian portraits I saw of the women of Palmyra. The hijab was the dress code of upper-class women in the ancient world. As a cultural residue of antiquity, it lingered in religious guise for Jews and Christians. Arabs then embraced it as they expanded their empire and encountered Byzantium and Jerusalem. The harshness of religious authorities in Mecca and Medina often encourages other Muslim institutions to imitate the 'holy cities'.

When my friend, an Italian–American journalist, walked with me and together we entered Britain's central mosque in London's Regent's Park, she was told to cover her hair or risk being expelled. In Jerusalem, my Syrian–American friend, a Middle East analyst, accompanied me to the Al-Aqsa Mosque. Across Jerusalem, she is free to be as she wants, but the moment she entered the *Haram*, or the place of security and serenity, the Arab police insisted that she must cover her head. What is so offensive about the hair of a woman? In contrast, when I was worshipping in Turkey in Konya at the mosque of Shams Tabrizi, Rumi's teacher, a beautiful woman entered in jeans and carrying a guitar. She sat, meditated, and not a word was raised to instruct her to cover her hair. I saw that same freedom for women in the shrine of Bulleh Shah in

Kasur, Pakistan, where local women came and went without men enforcing headgear on them.

'Saudi Arabia,' wrote the Lebanese historian Samir Kassir, 'has set back the entire Arab world, the most distressing proofs of which are the invisible faces of women which it has re-exported virtually everywhere.'[2] A hundred years ago, the Muslim scholars and activists Qasim Amin and Huda Sha'arawi triggered debates in Egypt by asserting that the veiling of women was neither a part of ancient Arab culture nor a requirement of Islam. Successive grand muftis of Al-Azhar in Cairo have supported even the French government's banning of the face veil.

The Saudi Salafi clerical classes, obsessed with covering up and concealing women, go so far as to argue that the *aurah* ('private parts') of a woman include her voice. Since a woman's voice can be seductive, that too is *aurah*. Once such a view is tolerated and accepted, there is no stopping it. It snowballs. Salafi clerics have argued that even a woman's name is *aurah*, and should not be mentioned in public. Most men in Saudi Arabia and the Gulf today will not speak the names of their wives, sisters or daughters. They refer to them, instead, as their *hurmah*, or honour. The first time I heard a Gulf Arab mention '*hurmati*', 'my honour', I genuinely thought I had caused him some indignity or insult. It took a while before I realised he was talking about his wife.

But there are other populations of men who wish to control the dress of women in their countries, with all the consequences that has for their lives. A Pew opinion poll found that only 14 per cent of Egyptians agree that it is up to a woman to dress whichever way she wants. In Pakistan 22 per cent thought this, and in Iraq 27 per cent. The number was somewhat higher in Saudi Arabia, at 47 per cent, Turkey 52 per cent and Tunisia 56 per cent. What has happened to undermine Muslims' confidence in ourselves to the extent that we want to constantly control and contain the beauty of women? That we feel threatened by allowing them their freedom?

This was not the Islam of the Muslim masses over their 1,500-year history. Almost every Muslim with an awareness of Islamic history and its key personalities is proud of the fact that the first person to believe in the Prophet was his wife Khadija. She trusted in his pure nature and sincere ways. Prior to their marriage, Khadija was a wealthy Meccan noble who employed the young Mohamed. She then fell in love with him and proposed to him, when he was twenty-five and she was forty. You won't find a woman proposing to a man, taking her own decisions about her love life, in today's Mecca.

The Prophet was married to Khadija for twenty-five years until her death. He later remarried a number of times, notably to a much younger woman, Ayesha bint Abu Bakr.[3] She was strong in character, and deeply involved in spreading the Prophet's message. After he passed away, she led an army against the fourth caliph, Imam Ali. The fact that a woman could lead troops in battle speaks volumes about the strong women the Prophet had around him, and early Muslim men's acceptance of them in leadership roles.

Ayesha bint Talha, a niece of the Prophet's wife Ayesha, famously refused to wear the veil, claiming that God had created female beauty and her own attractiveness, and it was too precious to hide. Sakina bint al-Husain, a granddaughter of the Prophet, also protested against the veil and refused to allow her third husband to take a second wife. She divorced him when she discovered he was having an affair. Neither woman was punished for her independence, nor did their menfolk seek to force them to cover up.

They were rooted in Quranic knowledge instinctively and understood the Prophet's disposition. They were not busy defining their identity based on opposing the modern West. A contemporary Muslim scholar has produced a forty-volume encyclopedia of Muslim professors who taught men and women.[4] The great commentator on hadith Imam Ibn Hajar al-Asqalani (1372–1449) noted that 800 of his hadith narrations included women in the chain of teaching and connecting a saying back to the Prophet. This illustrated the central role of many women in education and preserving knowledge in early Islam. In the Umayyad Mosque in Damascus, women taught in the main hall. In my own early visits to the Prophet's mosque in Medina in the late 1990s, I saw that women were allowed to gather freely near the Prophet's tomb. Now they are not allowed. Gone are the days of Imam al-Tabari (839–923), whose Quranic exegeses are still a top five must-read for scholars, whose school of thought held that women may lead men in prayer. What happened to that Islam of freedom for women?

In pre-Islamic Arabia, men bequeathed women to their sons as part of their inheritance, along with horses, camels and other livestock. The German philosopher Friedrich Nietzsche (1844–1900) also suggested, in *Beyond Good and Evil*, that we should think of women as property. The great guru of postmodernist thinking offered no evidence for this position – it was self-evident to him. In *Thus Spake Zarathustra* he went even further, concluding that women are not capable of friendship; that they are animals, like cats, birds or, at best, cows. 'Thou goest to women? Do not forget thy whip,' he advised men who sought 'the recreation of the warrior'. In contrast, the Prophet Mohamed was centuries ahead of his own time.

Every erudite Muslim in the world today believes, rightly, that the Prophet was a liberator of women. All recognise their Prophet as being a feminist of his time. Abdullah ibn Abbas, the Prophet's cousin, frequently reminded Muslims that the Prophet commanded his wives and daughters to leave their homes and join the festivals and fun of Eid gatherings with people.

The fault with many Muslims today is our failure to grasp the spirit of the Prophet's actions and the motives behind his divine sanctions relieving the plight of women. Many families buried girl babies because daughters brought shame on the household. Those of today's Arabs and Muslims who have sadly clung on to that mentality have abandoned the progressive ways of their Prophet. He abolished infanticide; he stopped the practice of passing women on to heirs by way of inheritance; and he changed the rules on dowries – now money went from the man to the woman directly, so that she owned it, and not her parents. Even in the event of a divorce, she would retain her own financial assets. Previously, divorce had been a purely male prerogative, but the Quran granted women the rights to divorce their husbands and inherit property. By the standards and in the context of the Prophet's time in seventh-century Arabia, Muslims were among the most advanced of communities in terms of recognising women's human status and granting them rights.

But somewhere in all the travails of history Muslims lost that spirit of the sharia and the Prophet. This trend grew more conspicuous as the loss of Muslim dignity became an issue. Muslim men turned inward as they lost their sense of dignity and manliness before the world. Just as a confident man feels no need to control his wife and household, neither does a confident society need to oppress its women. Even at the end of the caliphate, in the early twentieth century, the last caliph, His Majesty Sultan Abdul Majid II of the Ottoman empire, could be seen and photographed in public with his unveiled daughter and her husband, an Indian Muslim nawab.

Princess Durru Shehvar, daughter of Abdul Majid II, was by no means the only example of a confidently modest, fully Muslim woman, without hijab and yet not violating any part of the Quran. The elite Muslim families of Damascus, Cairo, Delhi, Isfahan, Baghdad and even Kabul were similar in appearance and mannerisms. They saw no contradiction between being pious believers and living in harmony with the surrounding world. The nightlife in Kabul and Cairo might not have been to everybody's taste, but it provided a symbol of freedom for millions. As Tunisia's Sheikh Rachid al-Ghannouchi says of his country today, the mosque is open for those who want it, and the beach is also open to those who want it.[5] It is not for the government to impose its reading of the sharia on people. That flexible, tolerant spirit is returning once again among leaders such as Ghannouchi in Tunisia, and soon others should follow.

This loss of confidence within Islam, of being at ease with the contemporary world, occurred some decades ago. There was no sudden rediscovery of 'true Islam', because the puritanism promoted by Egyptians, Saudis and Iranians was no more 'true' than the Islam of the recent past, or of Caliph Abdul Majid II's daughter Durru Shehvar. The rise in assertive wearing of the veil in the Muslim public space was a reaction to the Western miniskirts and sexual freedoms of the 1960s. At first, the women of Kabul, Tehran and Cairo wore miniskirts, too. Even in Jeddah,

Saudi Arabia, there were Muslim girls attending school without a headscarf.

But as the Muslim Brotherhood re-emerged on campuses in Egypt in the 1950s, King Farouq Islamised the public space as a way of attacking the Egyptian nationalist socialists; and in the 1970s the Iranian cleric Ruhollah Khomeini led a revolution against the US-backed Shah in Iran. In all instances, in Egypt, Iran and Saudi Arabia, the Islamists were fighting against symbols of the West – and what more pertinent emblem of Westernisation than the visible Muslim woman, who, once brought into line, would showcase the paradigm shift on beaches and in workplaces and homes across the Muslim world? If the West is about immodesty, then we in the Muslim world are modest. If the West exports high heels and miniskirts, then we return to the sharia of literalism and bring back the burqa. By the time of the Iranian revolution in 1979, a new dress code had been solidified. If Shi'a women could wear those chadors and fight in the armed forces, then so could Sunni women in Pakistan and the rest of the Muslim world. A new competition to out-hijab each other commenced.

With the rise of Western influence came ideas of feminism and women's liberation. Muslim societies and male clerics responded by trying to secure 'our mothers, sisters and daughters' from the corrupt West. The modus operandi shifted from differentiation to outright opposition: if Western women wore miniskirts, then Muslim women must cover up completely – face, hair, bosom, arms and legs, and all in black. Yet this was not the way Muslim women appeared historically – orientalist travellers of the eighteenth century wrote extensively about the sexual freedoms and openness of the East.

By the standards of the seventh century, the Prophet Mohamed raised the status of women. Whereas previously they had been seen on a par with camels and horses, they were now recognised as fully human. But in their determination to oppose the West, today's Islamists have flouted the spirit of the Prophet. The assumption is that the wearing of the hijab betokens a safe Muslim society. They argue that the West is home to decadence and immorality and its women are lewd and promiscuous.

However, a 2013 United Nations report found that almost all Egyptian girls and women reported being sexually harassed (99.3 per cent), 96.5 per cent said they had been subjected to unwelcome physical contact, and 95.5 per cent were verbally harassed on the streets. In Yemen, another fully veiled society, 90 per cent of women have experienced harassment, especially being pinched by men in public. In Saudi Arabia meanwhile, 86.5 per cent of men blame these experiences on 'women's excessive make-up'.

In the West, after the 9/11 attacks in America and the 7/7 London underground attacks, when hijab-wearing women were bearing the brunt of Western Islamophobia, prominent Muslim scholars including Zaki Badawi, Abdullah bin Bayyah and Hamza Yusuf Hanson called for women to be allowed to remove their veils if their safety was threatened. The same hijab that is supposed to make women safe in the East is now allegedly jeopardising women's safety elsewhere.

The ugly reality is that many Muslims, and Islamists in particular, have missed the point: it is not women's clothes and make-up but male attitudes that are the threat. And unless male attitudes change, women's lives will continue to count for little in Mecca, where girls can be burnt to death for not wearing a headscarf, with precious little outcry in the Muslim world. Forcing women to hide their hair, ears, necks, arms and legs in case they provoke lust in a man is not the way to create a healthy, free and confident society.

The assured male attitude existed among Muslim men. Take, for example, the enlightened thoughts of a tenth-century scholar from Muslim Spain on the status of women, and free love. Imam Ibn Hazm al-Andalusi (994–1064) wrote on logic, grammar, ethics, history, theology and, reflecting the interests of his time, comparative religion. His books on jurisprudence are *still* required reading in seminaries but, sadly, less attention is paid to his progressive writings on women and love. Contrary to the prevailing Muslim view of his time, Ibn Hazm argued that women were no more likely to commit sins than men. Women, he said, had the right to be leaders and hold political office, though he did not go so far as to say they could become caliphs. His views on gender equality were perhaps a millennium ahead of their time, and he was attacked for them. Some of his books were burned.

He celebrated love and attraction between women and men, rather than creating barriers between them. His acclaimed book *The Ring of the Dove* is a free-spirited guide for lovers. Based on his own experiences, Quranic stories and sayings of the Prophet, it starts with some insightful teachings on the 'signs of love'. Here Ibn Hazm reflects on the way love-struck men behave:

> How often has the miser opened his purse strings, the scowler relaxed his frown, the coward leapt heroically into the fray, the clod suddenly become sharp-witted, the boor turned into the perfect gentleman, the stinker transformed himself into the elegant dandy, the sloucher smartened up, the decrepit recaptured his lost youth, the godly gone wild, the self-respecting kicked over the traces – and all because of love![6]

Ibn Hazm lists different 'outward signs of love', from 'exceeding cheerfulness' to 'much clandestine winking', 'endeavouring to touch his hand' and 'drinking from the same cup and seeking the very spot against which his lips were pressed', noting that 'sleeplessness too is a common affliction of lovers'. How true many of these traits were for this Muslim a thousand years after Ibn Hazm! And of course they are also true for countless millions of others.

Between prose passages, Ibn Hazm interjects poetry to illustrate his thoughts and feelings. In keeping with his views on the equality of the sexes, he interchanges references between women and men, underlining the point that women also love, lust and yearn – and it is not 'devilish' or 'evil' to do so, but is fully human. Again, where do we find Ibn Hazm's broadness of mind when Saudi authorities forcibly separate the sexes in Saudi Arabia, or post Arabic warnings on dating websites today?

Here, by contrast, is Ibn Hazm reflecting on life's joys and challenging the puritans:

She sat there privily with me
And wine besides, to make us three,
While night profound o'ershadowing
Stretched out its long and stealthy wing.
A damsel fair – I would prefer
To die, than not live close with her;
And is it such a dreadful crime
To wish to live this little time?[7]

Ibn Hazm helps young lovers, with the wisdom of his own experiences and encounters, by explaining the different ways love can occur, from being asleep and dreaming of a potential lover, to falling in love with the description of someone relayed by a third party, to getting to know someone after 'long association or extended familiarity', and finally 'love at first sight' – though he thinks this last category is 'merely a kind of lust', and love requires more than just a glance.

Like Ibn Hazm's other books, *The Ring of the Dove* is known among Muslim scholars, but its message seems to have been lost. This is unfortunate, for if the spirit of that book were to be found among today's Muslims, the sexual vulture culture in today's Cairo or Riyadh or Tehran might not exist. Denying the normal human sexuality of women, and suppressing both genders' natural inclination to fall in love creates a sexual dysfunction in Muslim societies that has too often gone without scrutiny. At the core of controlling female appearance, presence, behaviour and education lies a Muslim male fixation with trying to control women's sex lives.

16

Sex

In 2013 in Saudi Arabia, a man divorced his wife because she raised her legs as he penetrated her. How dare she display such sexual confidence? He took it as a sure sign of extramarital sexual experience and therefore grounds for divorce. In 2015, a husband threw his newly wed wife off a balcony in Cairo because he concluded she was not a virgin. She did not survive the fall. These terrible instances are symptoms of a hidden problem.

A deeply harmful attitude to sexuality has emerged in today's Arab world, and what festers in the Middle East slowly spreads to other parts of the Muslim world, with migrant labourers, imams trained in Gulf universities, and the religious rhetoric pumped out through satellite television and social media. From time to time this unhealthy approach to sex displays itself in public attitudes, questions and responses, sometimes in peculiar ways.

In 2007, for example, with sex segregation increasingly being imposed in public spaces for fear of encouraging sexual freedom, an Egyptian cleric issued a controversial ruling. Dr Izzat Atiya, a mufti (specialist in issuing religious edicts, fatwas), wanted to find a way to allow women to work with men and do so without feelings of religious guilt. In his view, that could be done if a woman fed her male colleague 'directly from her breast' at least five times – this would then establish a family bond between them, and they would be able to work together. He added: 'A woman at work can take off the veil or reveal her hair in front of someone whom she breast-fed.'

Bizarre fatwas of this kind are symptomatic of the widespread sexual dysfunction in large swathes of Arab and Muslim societies. Brave and exceptional Muslim women such as the Egyptian–American leading thinker Mona Eltahawy, author of *Headscarves and Hymens: Why the Middle East Needs a Sexual Revolution*, are highlighting this pervasive problem.

On the one hand, 'protecting our morals' from being corrupted by Hollywood and the West is the rallying cry in mosques and on Arabic satellite television channels. Yet on the other hand, rates of downloading pornography from the Internet are highest in the world per capita in Muslim countries such as Pakistan and Saudi Arabia. How can we explain this hypocrisy and tension between private behaviour and public posturing? Why is it so widespread? Why is the honour of a Muslim family bound up with its female members? And when that honour is deemed to be violated by a woman's loss of virginity, or falling in love, why must her family kill her?

There have been better times in Islam's history, and turning to earlier scholarship for inspiration on how to improve matters yields some interesting material. The Sufi scholar-poet Rumi, for example, has a theory:

A certain man had a jealous wife
and a very, very appealing maidservant.

The wife was careful not to leave them alone,
ever. For six years they were never left
in a room together.
But then one day
at the public bath the wife suddenly remembered
that she'd left her washbasin at home.

'Please, go get the basin,' she told her maid.
The girl jumped to the task, because she knew
that she would finally get to be alone
with the master. She ran joyfully.
She flew,
and desire took them both so quickly
that they didn't even latch the door.

With great speed they joined each other.
When bodies blend in copulation,
spirits also merge.

Meanwhile, the wife back at the bathhouse,
washing her hair: 'What have I done!
I've set the cotton wool on fire!
I've put the ram in the ewe!'

She washed the clay soap off her hair and ran,
fixing her chador about her as she went.

The maid ran for love. The wife ran out of fear
and jealousy. There is a great difference.

The mystic flies moment to moment.
The fearful ascetic drags along month to month.

But also the length of a 'day' to a lover
may be fifty thousand years!

You can't understand this with your mind.
You must burst open!
Fear is nothing to a lover, a tiny piece of thread.
Love is a quality of God. Fear is an attribute
of those who think they serve God, but who are actually
preoccupied with penis and vagina.

You have read in the text where *They love him*
blends with *He loves them.*
Those joining loves
are both qualities of God. Fear is not.

What characteristics do God and human beings
have in common? What is the connection between
what lives in time and what lives in eternity?

If I kept talking about love,
a hundred new combinings would happen,
and still I would not say the mystery.

The fearful ascetic runs on foot, along the surface.
Lovers move like lightning and wind.

No contest.
Theologians mumble, rumble-dumble,
necessity and free will,
while lover and beloved pull themselves into each other.

The worried wife reaches the door
and opens it.
The maid, dishevelled, confused, flushed,
unable to speak.
The husband begins his five-times-a-day prayer.
The wife enters this agitated scene.
As though experimenting with clothes,
the husband holds up some flaps and edges.

She sees his testicles and penis so wet, semen
still dribbling out, spurts of jism and vaginal juices
drenching the thighs of the maid.
The wife slaps him
on the side of the head:
'Is this the way
a man prays, with his balls?
Does your penis
long for union like this?
Is that why
her legs are covered with this stuff?'

These are good questions
she's asking her 'ascetic' husband!

People who renounce desires
often turn, suddenly,
into hypocrites![1]

This is a modern translation, but a great Muslim poet and philosopher crafted these words in the thirteenth century – a sign of openness and permissiveness that seems to have disappeared in the Muslim public space. For at least the past two hundred years, no major Muslim thinker has been so explicit in their public thinking and output, a reflection of the strange prudishness forcing sexuality underground in most parts of the Muslim world. This negating of the most powerful of human impulses, thanks to the rise of the new puritanism, now finds expression in a range of unhealthy, violent and ugly ways.

The Arab Spring uprisings have, rightly, been lionised as expressing people's yearnings for freedom, social justice and dignity. But moments of liberty brought a repressed sexual culture violently to the fore. When Egyptians overthrew their dictator in 2011, one of the first celebratory acts in Tahrir Square included the gang beating and sexual assault of the American journalist Lara Logan. In 2013, a Dutch journalist was raped in the same square. Voluntary groups set up to keep women safe recorded forty-six cases of sexual assault and harassment against women on one Sunday night alone in 2013.

Victorian travel writers revelled in the sexual freedoms of the Orient. Richard Burton, famous for a written account of his 1853 pilgrimage to Mecca, also translated and published the *Kama Sutra*. Going further back, King Henry VIII caused scandal and ended up creating his own Church, breaking away from Rome, for lust and love of the women in his life. In contrast, Muslim monarchs of the time had entire quarters in their palaces, the harem, for their women. The Muslim world was renowned for being sexually liberated (at least compared with Victorian England), and the classic *Arabian Nights* was a product of this Muslim openness toward sex and the caliph's harem. The candour was set from the top.

As the West became more secular and sexual in public, the Muslim world went in decidedly the opposite direction. D. H. Lawrence's *Lady Chatterley's Lover* was once banned in Britain, but what did the book say that Rumi had not said centuries earlier? Today, however, while the West has grown freer and less censorious, *Lady Chatterley's Lover* is banned in Saudi Arabia and other countries.

It is a historical fact that in the city of the Prophet, Medina, there were women walking around bare-breasted, though it is a matter of debate whether they were all slaves or whether some free women also (un)dressed in public in this way to assert their freedom. We know this because the Quran called on 'believing women' to cover their bosoms, but declared that the polytheists, pagans and others were free to do as they wished; the Prophet and his companions, even the early caliphs, were open to such a society. Muslim scripture confirms this, but very few Muslim scholars wish to face this historical reality. Instead, there has come to be a mass culture of frowning on sexuality, the consequences of which are still with us.

Muhammad Ibn Battuta (d. 1304), often referred to as the Marco Polo of the Muslim world, travelled far and wide and wrote about his observations. He had made the pilgrimage to Mecca five times in his life, and visited frontier parts of the Muslim world to see the countries that the pilgrims came from. Once, when in Africa, he went to see the dancing of the local women by the fireside. Travelling Arab merchants came to know that the great Muslim scholar and writer Ibn Battuta was nearby, and so they sought him out. When they entered his encampment only to find him watching bare-breasted dancers by the fire, they protested that he was committing a sin. To which he responded: 'You Arabs are oversexed. This is the local way of these people.' He saw no sin in it, and instead showed openness of mind and acceptance of others.

The Arabs have a simple but profound saying that resonates more in Arabic than in English: '*Mamnou' marghoub*', or 'That which is forbidden is desired.' The forbidding by clerics and governments of public expressions of sexuality has now led to mass suppressed desire. The UN report that found that over 99 per cent of women in Egypt, the Arab world's largest country, had been sexually harassed is a worrying indicator. That in Saudi Arabia women cannot travel alone without permission from a male relative is based on the underlying premise that if left alone, women will be promiscuous or be raped by men.

Marriage has been built up as the only sexual outlet permitted by the sharia, and observant young Muslims are now being taught, based on sayings attributed to the Prophet, to venerate marriage as 'half of faith' – in other words, a substantial element in their religious life. But no marriage is perfect, and when the first opportunity to meet a woman or man comes about in the context not of friendship or dating, with the opportunity to try and fail, and learn from experience, but straightaway in marriage, then failure occurs all too often. If Twitter is any indicator of social norms, the proliferation of married couples opting for 'open marriages' in the Gulf is an instructive insight. Thousands of social media accounts have emerged in the past five years offering wife swaps and group sex.

This frustration has other, more worrying symptoms. Pent-up machismo is not directed toward women, love, lust and sexual release, but channelled into joining hard-line Islamist organisations with a global enemy that needs destroying: the West. As the West is in *dar al-harb*, the 'abode of war', non-Muslim women there are 'allowed' for the extremists. Jihadis in Iraq have been found to keep a heavy stash of Western pornography, as did Osama bin Laden in his Abbottabad hideout in Pakistan.[2]

It follows from this broader context of failure to find sex by normal routes that creating sex slaves out of non-Muslims such as Yazidis was one of the first acts of ISIS after it seized territories in Iraq in 2014. When the wider culture elevates marriage to unrealistic levels of perfection, and young Muslims then fail to find a wife or husband to match up to these ideals, or, worse, cannot afford to get married because of onerous cultural and tribal expectations, they will sometimes find themselves open to persuasion to head out to join ISIS and find the perfect partner, the *mujahid*, or fighter for God.

While Western academics and government officials may not give this sexual repression much thought, their counterparts in Saudi Arabia and Israel both recognise it as a factor helping to draw males into extremism and violence. To help deradicalise the most extreme Hamas or Islamic Jihad fighters, Israel has ensured that they are married on release from prison. In Saudi Arabia, Salafi-jihadis on official counter-extremism programmes are often provided with more than one wife by the government, to provide terrorists with a new and more immediate outlet for their sexual frustrations.

The wider world is shocked to learn of Yazidi slave girls under ISIS command, but to the literalist Salafi there is little to be frowned on. For years now young men from Saudi Arabia and the Gulf have headed to the West for summer holidays filled with drink and prostitution. Those in any doubt need only walk around London's Knightsbridge, Mayfair and Edgware Road during the summer months. Telephone booths are plastered with the calling cards of female escorts, who find lucrative business among the tens of thousands of young men who visit the British capital. The situation is so serious that for several years the imam of Mecca has felt compelled to address this issue of sex tourism in Friday sermons and forbid it.

Since the West is in *dar al-harb*, the abode of war, where sharia rules do not apply, literalist Salafi Muslims require some kind of rules for sex tourism. Some Gulf Arabs have created what they call *misyaf*, or 'summer marriages', whereby they can contract a two-month 'marriage' with a woman in Indonesia or Syria. They pay these 'wives' handsomely and then leave after the holidays, triggering divorce. Among the Shi'a there is also the practice of *mut'a* (literally 'pleasure'), short-term marriages lasting anywhere from an hour to a year or longer, but on the understanding that the arrangement is temporary.

Whether in the West or in the Muslim world, with or without any rules, the search for sex abroad because it is forbidden at home lies at the crux of this widespread malaise.

The Quran does not forbid sex, but talks about it in a matter-of-fact way in the context of marital relations. All that is required for marriage is a mutual declaration before witnesses – without the vast expense and social pressure of an elaborate wedding, lavish gifts of cars and jewellery, setting up home together and being expected to have children immediately. A man is simply supposed to give his loved one what he can afford, and at the time of the Prophet those of his companions who had no money recited *surahs* of the Quran as wedding gifts to their brides, or brought them dates to eat.

The sexual malaise in Muslim-majority societies that leads to widespread pornography use, sex tourism and so-called temporary or summer marriages results from an inability to articulate human love and sexuality for fear of sinning, being judged, and then being an outcast in society. If today's Muslims had the sexual candour of earlier writers like Hafez of Persia, with his stirring, life-affirming and unashamedly erotic – yet profoundly spiritual – poetry, our world might be a better place. With more of his spirit about, people might not feel the need to suppress human sexuality in Muslim societies around the world.

Hafez (1315–90) was a baker's apprentice who knew very little about the world beyond the cultured, gardened city of Shiraz when, one day, the baker sent him, aged twenty-one, to deliver some bread to a wealthy customer. There, at the door, Hafez caught a glimpse of a stunningly beautiful woman inside the house. That one glance was enough to capture young Hafez's pure, romantic heart, and he fell passionately in love with her. She, of course, barely noticed the poor baker's assistant – short, physically nothing special, some say of dark complexion, in a society that valued fairness. How could an impoverished apprentice court a beautiful noblewoman of the great city of Shiraz?

As the months went by, Hafez's love and lust increased, and he became completely besotted with her. He started to sing love songs and read poetry in celebration of her dazzling charms and expressing his yearning for her. Poetry is to Persians what opera is to Italians. Others heard Hafez and started to quote his emotionally powerful lines, and soon Hafez's love poetry became popular across Shiraz.

Unaware of his growing fame, he turned to oracles and magicians for help to win the attention and heart of his beloved. He was advised to keep a night vigil at the tomb of a particular saint for forty nights: it was believed that a lover who went without sleep for forty nights at this shrine would be granted his deepest desire. Willing to try anything, Hafez undertook the vigil. It is said that at dawn on the fortieth day, the archangel Gabriel appeared before Hafez and said: 'What do you wish for, Hafez?'

Hafez, stunned by the beauty of the angel in front of his eyes, wondered: if God's angel was so sublime and radiant, what could God himself be like? At that moment, a new kind of beauty entered his heart.

'What do you want, Hafez?' prompted the angel Gabriel.

Hafez kept wondering about the force that lay behind the beauty of the angel. He forgot about the elegant woman, his desires, everything. After forty sleepless nights, Hafez said: 'I want God.'

Gabriel smiled. Hafez had already reached greater spiritual depths than could have been anticipated. The woman would have been a simpler choice. But Hafez had chosen the Eternal. His life was now set to unfold in new ways.

The path that he had chosen required a spiritual teacher, a Sufi. Gabriel directed Hafez to his new teacher, whom Hafez would serve unstintingly. That teacher was Mohamed Attar, a chemist in Shiraz. Just like the Taliban and others in our time, back then religious zealots sought to contain the expression of love and longing. To defy their writ, Attar kept a low profile, and taught only a select few students. Only a limited number of people knew of his spiritual mastery. The fact that Hafez was Attar's disciple on a spiritual pathway was kept secret for the whole of both their lives.

Hafez served his guru for decades, seeking further enlightenment. Midway through his life, his desperate longing for God's loving embrace, his sworn Sufi secrecy, and soon the death of his wife and son tormented his soul. Yet he had spiritual insights that he could not share with others. The people of Shiraz, where he was born and died, were only to discover the gem in their midst after his death. Yearning to share his thoughts while he was still alive, Hafez cried out:

Who
Can I tell
The secrets of love?

Who has not confined their life
To a padded cell?

Look at
The nature of a river.
Its size, strength, and ability to give

Are often gauged by its width
And current.

God
Too moves between our poles, our depth.
He flows and gathers power between
Our heart's range of
Forgiveness and
Compassion.

Who
Can I tell,
Who can Hafez tell tonight
All the secrets of
Love?[3]

Sometimes viewed as the Sufi poet Rumi's spiritual younger brother, and writing at the same time as Geoffrey Chaucer in England, Hafez penned about 5,000 poems. Of the 700 or so that remain extant, many are still to be found on the lips of today's Iranians, not least because of the simplicity and depth of the lines that survive from six hundred years ago. Alongside Rumi's writings, Hafez's works form part of the classic literature of Muslim Sufism. His poems were introduced to the West by Johann Wolfgang von Goethe and admired by Friedrich Nietzsche, Alexander Puskhin, Thomas Carlyle and even the fictional Sherlock Holmes, who quoted Hafez in a story by Arthur Conan Doyle. To this day, many use Hafez's poetry as an oracle, opening compilations of his poems at random in the hope of finding guidance. England's Queen Victoria was said to refer to Hafez's works in this way.

Like his spiritual predecessor Rumi, Hafez was both fully Muslim and also fully critical of Islam's more extreme believers. He was called 'Hafez' because he had memorised the entire Quran; his actual name was Shamsuddin Mohamed. While working as a baker's apprentice by day to help his parents, Hafez studied theology, grammar, mathematics and astronomy by night. Again like Rumi, he was an insider among the clerical class of Muslims, so he knew full well what he was breaking away from, and what he instinctively flew towards: intimate love with the One, to become a free Sufi.

Here, Hafez draws analogies between animal and human love to reinforce his message about a greater love:

All the crazy boys
Gather around their female
Counterpart,

When her canine beauty announces to the air
'My body is ready to play its part
In this miracle of Birth.'

Look what dedicated young men will do
For their chance moment
Of dancing ecstatic on their
Hind legs.

They will forget about food for days and
Feverishly pray in their own language.

They will growl, make serious threats,
Even bite each other saying:
'She's mine, all mine – watch out,
You skinny fleabag.'

Listen, human lovers:
When did you last keep a vigil
Beseeching
Light?

When did you last fast, lose twenty pounds,
In hopes of embracing
God?

Hafez will give you unedited news today:
You will need to outdo all the noble acts
Of
Dogs' love.[4]

Lovemaking was, for Hafez, truly about love – and God. The above poem illustrates what he perceives as the sacrifices demanded by love. And then this, to his lover:

Like
A pair
Of mismatched newlyweds,
One of whom still feels very insecure,
I keep turning to God
Saying:
'Kiss
Me.'[5]

In Hafez's mind and soul, and in his verses, God and his lover become almost interchangeable; the divine and sexual lover are intertwined.

I sit in the streets with the homeless,

My clothes stained with the wine
From the vineyards the saints tend.

Light has painted all acts
The same colour

So I sit around and laugh all day
With my friends.

At night, if I feel a divine loneliness
I tear the doors of Love's mansions

And wrestle God on the floor.

He becomes so pleased with Hafez
And says:

'Our hearts should do this more.'[6]

But it is not always kisses, touches, love wrestling. Here is Hafez complaining to God, again in deeply sexual terms:

You have fathered a child with me.
You had your night of fun.
If You no longer want the love my
Beautiful body can yield,

At least take care of that
Holy infant my heart has become.

God, You sired an heir with me
When You gave birth to my soul.

I thought of complaining to all the angels
Last night

About Your treatment of this
'Homeless child',

But then I remembered they too
Have a long list of love-complaints

Because
They also know You so
Well.[7]

So much heart-aching love. What have the puritans done to the House of Islam?

PART FOUR

Islam's Global Staying Power

Why and how is God central to Muslim societies around the world?

How do we reconcile freedom of speech and blasphemy?

Does modern family life work inside the House of Islam?

What sustains a strong Muslim belief in an afterlife?

17
God is Alive

When the Prophet Mohamed entered the city of Yathrib (later renamed Medina) in July 622, the Muslims of the city, the Ansar, or Prophet's helpers, all wanted to welcome him. Rather than offend his generous hosts by accepting hospitality from any one of them, the Prophet simply indicated that his camel was being directed by God to the location of His choosing. Where the camel stopped, the Prophet purchased the land. His first act was then to allocate a plot to be the gathering place for believers to pray. The Arabic word for 'mosque', *masjid*, literally means 'place of prostration', the place where Muslims prostrate themselves and place their foreheads on the floor. This place, where the lowest met the highest in devotion to the Divine, became the centre of the city ('Medina') of the Prophet.

Within the precincts of the *masjid*, the Prophet made his home. There was an energy and language linking the very private – the home – and the very public – the mosque – that continues to resonate among Muslims everywhere. Consciously or not, every observant Muslim recognises the symbols of this language and feels at home in the mosque of any Muslim city or community.

In many ways the Muslim home is similar to a *masjid*. In most Muslim countries, shoes are removed before entering a house, or at least were until very recently. As with the mosque, the right foot is used to enter the house. In most Muslim houses, as with mosques and synagogues, no figurative art is on display. In Arab countries, even the more Westernised, such as Egypt and Syria, men and women wear the same comfortable long, loose-fitting clothes for prayers at home as they do when they go to the mosque. The *Qiblah*, the direction of Mecca, to which Muslims turn in prayer, is known in the Muslim household. The inhabitants of the home do not sleep with their feet pointing in that direction, as that would be considered disrespectful, nor place toilets facing Mecca. The food in the home will be *Halal*, procured and prepared in accordance with sharia guidelines. As in the mosque, there will be a copy of the Quran in the home, given a place of prominence. There will be some symbols of thanksgiving at the door of the house – an amulet from a Sufi sheikh, pictures of Mecca, Medina or Jerusalem, or often some combination of these.

Unlike the mosque, it is here in the home that the women of contemporary Muslim society feel fully at ease, able to remove their veils and *abayas* and wear stylish, even shocking clothes. Westerners visiting a mall in Cairo or Damascus are often amazed by the daring lingerie on display for use at home.

The home is not the only extension of the mosque, the central feature in a Muslim city. Traditionally the orphanage, hospital, library, bazaar, craftsmen's quarters and the university were all adjoined to the mosque. Homes grew organically out from the centre, and when residents could no longer easily reach the mosque, another, smaller mosque was built. Sufi shrines and gathering places (*zawiyas*) were all normal features to find among the mosques. The calligraphers, craftsmen, artists and muezzins were all engaged in external activity, but they replenished their inward spirituality, the *Batin*, in the Sufi brotherhoods.

In public and in private, behind the energy and symbolism of the city or community of Muslims, was the presence of the Divine. The environment was designed by people who were internally aware of God and sought to glorify Him in their architecture and embed reminders of Him in their cities.

In Córdoba and Granada, among the earliest of Islam's cities changed under Muslim influences in Andalusia, I saw gardens and water everywhere. Systems of water channels were also built in Damascus, Fez, Cairo and Baghdad, because the flowing water was music to the ears, and reminded the believers of verses in the Quran that refer to streams and rivers in the gardens of Paradise.

The channels were linked to the water fountain in the centre of the mosque, and carried water past the houses of the believers, bringing coolness and cleanliness. In Turkey, the last home of the caliphate, Muslims are still careful about staying clean – the Turks have hand cleansers in taxis and on their desks to kill off any germs.

Beyond hygiene and aesthetics, for Muslim households the requirements of the five daily prayers necessitate the constant availability of water. The cities of the Muslims were designed to respond to this divine daily call. In addition, Muslims have always been fastidious about washing after responding to the call of nature, and after sex they have a ritual bath. The crusaders were astonished by the standards of hygiene among the Muslims, and brought the concepts of urban water supplies, bathing and gardens back to Europe with them. Today, however, the new Muslim cities of Dubai, Abu Dhabi and Doha are being developed along European lines, with toilets where men have to urinate while standing in the presence of others. The concept of *Hishmet*, modesty, is missing; and the water is hidden away in the toilet cistern. The whole city is designed to respond to the needs of the car, not those of the believer.

Yet despite all this, the essence of God is alive and present in the Muslim public space, and God's word is read aloud daily. In shops, households and mosques, there will be copies of the Quran for blessings and recital. The sacred text, documented at the time of the Prophet Mohamed, has not undergone edits and changes, unlike other religious scriptures.

Be it in Sokoto in Nigeria, Dhaka in Bangladesh, Damascus in Syria or Istanbul in Turkey, most Muslim shop owners will start their day with a broadcast recitation of the Quran. For the first hour or so of the morning, and in the Gulf countries (where music is banned in public) for much longer, the Quran will be heard being recited by a renowned *qari* or reciter, inspiring and reminding the Muslim proprietor and his customers, even in supermarkets, of the word of God. Ordinarily, the Quran then stops and popular singers take to the airwaves – Fairouz in Syria or Lebanon, Tarkan in Turkey, Umm Kulthum in Egypt – until the time comes for the midday prayer call to sound out from minarets across cities, towns and villages. The music will halt in shops and taxis for a few minutes, while respect is shown once again for God alone.

In Muslim societies across the globe the day starts with the muezzin calling out the *adhan*. The public call to prayer, using the human voice (now assisted by microphones) rather than the church bell of Christians or the horn of the Jews, is a practice started by the Prophet, with Bilal as his first muezzin, that continues to this day. The words of the call are '*Allahu Akbar*', 'God is great', then an affirmation that Mohamed is the Prophet of God, an invitation to believers to 'come to goodness, come to felicity', and, in the morning, a reminder that prayer is superior to sleep, before the *adhan* closes with God's greatness again echoing – '*Allahu Akbar*' – across the atmosphere. To no Muslim is this divine call strange or unwelcome, and Muslims from the East who travel to the West often become nostalgic for it.

Regrettably, the order and discipline of the Ottomans, who trained muezzins, have now been lost. I once had the honour of being invited by the muezzin of the Blue Mosque in Istanbul to climb the minaret to where he normally gave the call. I had not anticipated the lung power needed; I was only twenty-five years old at the time, but I was quickly out of breath. The schools that produced muezzins are no more, and the melody is changing from the Ottoman style, which used classical musical notes and training, to the rougher ways of Najd now influencing Muslims who imitate the prayer calls of Mecca. But still, the divine remains present in the Muslim public space daily.

The modern West has lost the inner spirit that gave rise to the great cathedrals of Chartres, Winchester, Coventry, St Paul's and Notre Dame. Such sublime edifices are outer manifestations of an inner awareness of God. The dilution of faith through secularisation has produced architects who have lost the sense of the sacred in geometry. What is the theme or symbolism of Canary Wharf in London, or Freedom Tower in New York? What great truth or mystery do these structures call to mind? What will future generations think of Dubai or Kuala Lumpur?

The Taj Mahal, built by the Muslim Mughals with lavish use of calligraphy and craftsmanship, was dedicated to God by the emperor Shah Jahan in thanksgiving for the love of his wife Mumtaz. At such shrines across the Muslim world, from Morocco to Yemen to the Caucasus, a new music emerged, praising the saints and remembering God. In Turkey, this music took the form of the *Sema* of Rumi's whirling dervishes, and in India the *Qawwali* of the Chishti Sufis popularised by Nusrat Fateh Ali Khan. Those who wanted to retreat from the world took comfort in the succour of the Sufi saints and the dervishes who sang mystical songs at their tombs. These songs are top hits to this day, featuring millions of viewings on YouTube as *Qawwali* contests in Pakistan increase. In Turkey, Elif Shafak's bestselling books remind a new generation of Shams, Rumi, and the mystical ways of Muslims of the past. In songs, literature, art and calligraphy the divine permeates and is accepted by Muslims as a normal part of the human condition.

The various architects who built Córdoba and Fez, adapted Damascus and Baghdad, and rebuilt Delhi in the sacred tradition of Islam, never met, yet their designs and thinking were in such harmony that a Muslim today from Fez or Casablanca instantly recognises the spoken and unspoken language in all these cities' homes, bazaars, mosques and shrines. The esoteric and the exoteric are connected. He or she can join in the public prayers anywhere with ease, and eat without seeming a stranger, knowing the etiquette, the right prayers to say, and the appropriate modesty code.

The Muslim attachment to God is instructive and edifying in a predominantly Westernised world culture in which God has been (publicly) marginalised. But with the increasing Arabisation and radicalisation of contemporary Muslims, thanks to the Saudi-influenced Salafism now rampant across the Muslim world, it is vital that we do not forget the other, older, more rooted Muslim approach to faith in God.

'The God you worship is under my feet,' said the Sufi as he stood at the mosque door. How dare he utter such blasphemy? This was Damascus in 1240, then a centre of regional trading, political intrigue and public displays of religious observance. It was the done thing to be commonly seen in a mosque – and why not? It was where men met, networked, gossiped, prayed, rested and often studied, too. As an established commercial centre with a host of ancient mosques from Islam's earliest days, Damascus did not take kindly to freethinkers, let alone Sufi mystics who uttered inconvenient truths that upset the social order and pricked the conscience of the merchant class.

It was prayer time, and the mosque was filled with worshippers. The imam at the front was preparing to lead prayers. 'The God you worship is under my feet,' the Sufi said again. They knew this man already – it was Muhyiddin Ibn Arabi, someone who wrote far too much, they thought, and questioned too many shibboleths. And now, to claim that the God they worshipped was underneath his feet – how dare he? And to make this claim directly to a congregation preparing to kneel, bow and prostrate themselves to God?

Mob instinct combined with religious fervour almost always brings out the worst in people. The crowd turned on the lone Sufi. Without his students, disciples and defenders at his side, he sustained fatal injuries from the horde's assault. Soon afterwards, on 8 November 1240, Ibn Arabi succumbed to his injuries and died.

Like Ibn Hazm, Ibn Arabi was originally from Andalusia in Spain. Like Rumi, his esoteric statements were lost on the people of his time. And like Shams of Tabriz (who had met, admired and written about Ibn Arabi during his travels in Syria), Ibn Arabi was loathed and despised during his lifetime.

From a long line of noble Arabs, he was born and raised in Murcia in Andalusia in 1165, but due to his Arab ancestry became known as 'Ibn Arabi', or 'son of an Arab'. His vast literary output has ensured that we know much about him from his own writings. In Córdoba, as a child, Ibn Arabi encountered the great philosopher Averroes, an admirer of the Sufis. In recalling this visit, Ibn Arabi reveals much about his spiritual insight and grace from a tender age:

> I was in Cordoba one day at the home of the judge Abu al-Walid Ibn Rushd [Averroes]. He had been astonished when he heard about the illumination that God had bestowed upon me,

> and expressed a desire to meet me. Since my father was one of his friends, he found some excuse to send me to his house. At the time, I was a young boy with no hair on my face, not even a moustache. When I was led to him, he [Averroes] stood up, showed his affection and consideration, and kissed me. Then he said to me: 'Yes.' I, in turn, said: 'Yes.' His joy increased upon seeing that I understood what he was referring to. Thus, upon realising the reason for his joy, I added: 'No.' He cringed, lost his colour, and was overcome with doubt. 'So, what have you found through the lifting of the veil and divine inspiration? Is it identical to what speculative thought gives us?' I replied: 'Yes and no; between yes and no, spirits take to flight and necks are detached from their bodies.'[1]

This meeting of great minds and the incomprehensible exchange between them was the first of many such encounters for Ibn Arabi. Throughout, his life continued to twist and turn to higher planes, and to some low points as well. His regular visions and dreams of the Prophet Mohamed guided him from place to place and role to role, leading Ibn Arabi to claim that he was the 'supreme heir to Mohamed'.

And yet he had, like many Sufis, a special inclination toward the spiritual Jesus. In *al-Futuhat al-Makkiya* (The Meccan Revelations), a book of recollections of his metaphysical experiences while spending time in Mecca, Ibn Arabi wrote about Jesus: 'Jesus was my first master on the way; it was in his hands that I was converted. He watches over me at all hours, not leaving me for a second.' He stated in all candour that: 'I often met him in my visions; it was with him that I repented ... He commanded me to practise asceticism and renunciation.' Ibn Arabi went on to reveal how, step by step on the spiritual path, he took instructions from Jesus on separating himself from worldly concerns, desires and attachments, and threw himself into the fire of divine love – in Rumi's words, becoming 'burnt'.

All Muslims see Jesus as a great and beloved prophet of God, but not as God's son. Ibn Arabi, firmly within this tradition of revering but not worshipping Jesus, claimed direct guidance from

Jesus through visions and dreams. To this day, Ibn Arabi's shrine in Damascus draws Christian visitors. When I lived in Syria, I regularly spent time sitting beside Ibn Arabi's resting place, and absorbing the energy and presence that still encompass his tomb and mosque. Sometimes Christian friends came with me; at other times they were already there.

In addition to being a lover and follower of Jesus, and receiving guidance from Mohamed at key moments in his life, Ibn Arabi remains famous among Muslims for his miracles and books, and, most of all, for enunciating the controversial creed of *Wahdat al-Wujood*, 'Oneness of Being' – an attempt to explain Ibn Arabi's highly complex understanding of the relationship between 'being' and God. For centuries, scholars have debated furiously what Shaikh Muhyiddin Ibn Arabi meant by this tenet of Oneness of Being, and the debate still rages to this day.

An early Muslim polymath, Ibn Arabi is difficult to comprehend even for the most advanced philosophers. His approach to God was unorthodox, but he articulated what many Sufi Muslims believed and felt. These passages from the *Futuhat* help explain his thinking:

> The universe is neither pure Being nor pure nothingness. It is total magic: it makes you think that it is God and it is not God; it makes you think that it is creation and it is not creation, for in every respect it is neither this nor that.
>
> Regarding the realities of the universe, one cannot say that they are God nor that they are other than Him/God.
>
> If you say regarding the universe that it is real, you are speaking truthfully; if you say that it is illusory, you are not lying.
>
> Everything we perceive is the Being of God in the essences of the possible. From the point of view of ipseity, it is His Being; from the point of view of diversity of forms …

Many people who followed Ibn Arabi, whose simple minds expected God to be a 'good guy in the sky', found it difficult to accept these extraordinary statements as orthodox.

But Ibn Arabi was at a different level of Muslim spirituality – what he saw and perceived, others did not. His was the heart that the Prophet spoke about when quoting God as saying: 'My heavens and My earth do not contain me, but the heart of My believing servant contains me.' In another of his sayings the Prophet again quoted God – and Ibn Arabi's understanding of Islam reflected this Prophetic wisdom – as saying: 'I am as my servant perceives me to be.' For those who see God as near and intimate, God is so. For those who see God as far and distant, such is God.

The Prophet continued, still speaking in God's words: 'He whom I love, I am the eye with which he sees, the ears with which he listens.' Ibn Arabi explained that just as water necessarily reflects the colour of its container, so theophanies are conditioned by the container that receives them and whose form they take on. Therefore each individual knows and recognises only that god that she or he contains, the god that Ibn Arabi calls the 'god created by belief'.

For the Sufi, God is beyond belief. The Quran teaches: 'Wherever you turn, there is the Face of God', and for Ibn Arabi, based on these verses and hadiths of the Prophet, 'all sensible and intelligible forms are His places of manifestation'. To Ibn Arabi and millions of his followers, 'every reality in the world is a sign that orients us toward a divine reality, which is the basis of its existence and the place of its return'. Ibn Arabi declared: 'God possesses a face in everything that is worshipped', and, shocking to some: 'God is that which is worshipped.' Whichever religion people follow, and whatever objects they seem to worship, they never worship anything or anybody other than God, whether they are conscious of this or not.

This, then, being his theological background, Ibn Arabi is remembered to this day across the Muslim world for these verses that he wrote in Mecca – for, like Rumi, Ibn Arabi found God in love:

> My heart has become capable of all forms:
> a prairie for gazelles, a convent for monks,
> a temple for idols, a Ka'bah for the pilgrim,

the Tablets of the Torah, the Book of the Quran.
I profess the religion of Love, and regardless of which direction
Its steed may lead, Love is my Religion and my Faith.[2]

Ibn Arabi's mystical insights and unveilings led him to utter statements that upset those around him who could not see what he saw, or understand what he perceived. It was this same spiritual power that led to his being stoned and fatally injured for saying: 'The God you worship is under my feet.' Like all Sufi masters down the ages, Ibn Arabi saw not just people's bodies and behaviour but deep into their souls. Like them he looked to what lay within, rather than obsessing over 'creed' and 'practice' as the literalists do.

And so when Ibn Arabi stood at the door of the mosque, he saw people who had gathered for worldly motives: to be seen at the mosque, to impress others, to network, to earn a reputation for being an upright kind of merchant. Their ultimate aim was not to connect with the Almighty, the Divine, but to increase their profits and their wealth – a false god in Ibn Arabi's eyes, and a god that Jesus had taught him to renounce.

After his death, Ibn Arabi's students remembered the steps on which he had been standing when he insulted the gathered Muslims by saying their god was under his feet. They knew their master had spoken a transcendent truth. So they dug up the ground below the steps, and found a chest of gold, buried years previously by a merchant seeking to hide his wealth during imperial raids on Damascus. It was this chest that Ibn Arabi had seen, this wealth being treated as a god that he had spoken out against.

It is significant that today Ibn Arabi's books, written over 700 years ago, are banned in Salafi-controlled Saudi Arabia. Combined with Rumi's love for God, Ibn Arabi's powerful, religiously rooted, scripturally sound interpretation of the meaning of God helps modern Muslims come to terms with the contemporary world and lead lives of greater harmony with our surroundings, free from the burdens of formulaic faith, fear, hypocrisy and conflict.

18

Rights of the Sacred

The Prophet was returning from battle with a large group of his companions. The Muslims had suffered huge losses. As they approached their homes in Medina, the people of the city came out to welcome them. A woman walked toward the soldiers and looked at them intensely. Her son had joined the fight. Others assumed that she had come out to comfort him. The warriors saw her and were afraid to tell her news that her son had fallen in combat. Abruptly, she started to smile, and to raise her hands and face toward the heavens in thanksgiving.

'The Prophet of God is alive! The Prophet of God is with us!' she called to the people. When someone whispered to her that her son was not, she replied that she came out for the Prophet, not her son. And her son was now in paradise, and that for the next battle, her other son would join the Prophet.

She was prepared to see her own sons be martyrs rather than see harm befall the Prophet of God. Such was the love imbibed for the sacred within Islam. Muslims grow up reading about and listening to elders and preachers tell us these incidents of our glorious past. Such noble wisdom and living for a higher purpose can be elevating, but extremists can exploit it.

Our dominant global culture is that of liberal humanism, where we advance individual human rights as supreme. But other societies, particularly the Muslim world, retain and treasure a worldview that is different. Nowhere is the contrast sharper and more violent than on rights to blaspheme and insult God, the prophets and the scriptures. Muslims still place the divine above the human. When Imam Ali, the fourth caliph, was in a battle and he had subdued his enemy and was about to kill him, the angry combatant spat in his face. The affronted Imam Ali raised his sword higher for the death blow, and then all at once he stopped, and withdrew.

'What happened?' asked his opponent, getting up from under Imam Ali. 'You could kill me, but you walk away?'

Imam Ali, wiping away the foe's saliva, replied: 'I came to war to defend the honour of God. You oppose Him, not me. I was killing you as an enemy of the Creator, but when you spat at me my anger was no longer for God, but for myself. You had insulted me, and for that I cannot kill you.'

Touched by Imam Ali's sincerity, selflessness and spiritual clarity, his adversary became his ally and became a Muslim. This incident has been known and taught among Muslims for fifteen centuries. It is this same chivalry that formed the moral character of Saladin when he sent his own doctors to help Richard I. Their fight was about the sacred, not the egos of men. And in our own time, at an ugly and indefensible level, the same fight continues.

It is ugly because now there is no restraint on Imam Ali's kind, but the impulse to preserve and defend the divine remains alive. When the Prophet Mohamed built his life and city with the mosque at its epicentre, a Bedouin entered and urinated in this most sacred of places. The Prophet's companions were angered by this violation and wanted to punish the nomad, but the Prophet's response was to clean the mosque and show compassion to the Bedouin. The Prophet possessed an inner confidence in his conviction in the sacred purpose that allowed for such magnanimity. Today's Muslim world has the conviction, but lacks the confidence. How is this inner confidence to return?

Salman Rushdie's book *The Satanic Verses* did not warrant mass protests, the killing of his translators, or his going into hiding for years. The Dutch filmmaker Theo Van Gogh deserved to live, despite his anti-Islam films. Muslims should have ignored the Danish cartoons by *Jyllands-Posten*. The *Charlie Hebdo* journalists gunned down in 2015 by terrorists for its caricatures of the

Prophet were offensive, hurtful even to believers, but they had not earned death.

During the lifetime of the Prophet he faced worse insults than cartoons, accusations of witchery, forgery, lies, torture and attacks on him and his followers. When he negotiated the treaty of Hudaybiyyah with the Meccan pagans, a ten-year period of respite from their attacks, the Prophet's scribe introduced the covenant with: 'In the name of God, most compassionate, most merciful. This is an agreement between Mohamed, the Emissary of God, and the leaders of Mecca ...' The Meccans accepted reference to God, but rejected 'most compassionate, most merciful' and Mohamed as 'Emissary of Allah'. They rejected, in short, his entire *raison d'être*. His response was to accept their rejection because he sought peace in society, and not fighting and killing.

Again, he had the confidence of his convictions: he did not require constant validation from his enemies. Today, Muslim activists feel slighted when their perceived enemies among the unbelieving Danes, Dutch or Americans reject and mock the Prophet. In the past, it was the caliphate or Muslim leadership that responded to, or mostly ignored, these assaults. In modern times, it was Voltaire who initiated this tradition with his play *Mahomet*. Interestingly, it was Napoleon who defended the Prophet and Omar, the second caliph. Muslims did not send assassins to kill Voltaire because they had the confidence to ignore him and knew that the Quran forbids such vigilante violence. Now, the absence of leadership and decline has increased the sensitivity to protecting the sacred, even by going to extremes and violating the verdicts of scripture.

Muslims cling on to the kernel of their worldly identity, their treasure of faith. They have seen the successes and failures of Europe: the outcome of enlightenment and renaissance is a secularism distant from the divine, a culture that places modern man as sovereign at the centre of society. That sort of spiritual emptiness, when contrasted with the richness of religious meaning, is seen to be a life not worth living, devoid of greater purpose, but maintaining mere materialism. Amidst this, when in Muslim societies voices rise to promote atheism, mock the Muslim faith, or denigrate the Prophet, the response is fast and often violent because religious leaders fear that unless blasphemy is punished, then eventually French-style *laïcité* and godlessness may creep into the Muslim world. Worse, advocates of religious freedom are seen as agents of godlessness.

In Pakistan's Punjab in 2011, the governor of the largest region, Salman Taseer, was shot dead by his own bodyguard for supporting a Christian woman and agreeing to reverse Pakistan's murderous blasphemy laws. In 2012, a YouTube film denigrating Islam and the Prophet Mohamed led to mob attacks and arson on US embassies in Egypt and Tunisia, and deaths in Afghanistan. Turkish and Indonesian political leaders lobbied the UN with support from a fifty-seven-member bloc of countries, the Organisation of Islamic Co-operation (OIC), to create a global law forbidding criticism of religion, similar to Pakistan's blasphemy laws. A 2013 Pew poll of thirty-eight Muslim countries showed that 88 per cent of Muslims in Egypt and 76 per cent in Pakistan favour the death penalty for those who leave Islam. The number was 17 per cent in Turkey. Only 6 per cent of Russian Muslims, in contrast, felt that ex-Muslims should be killed. In Egypt in 2014, for Facebook posts criticising Islam an activist was arrested for atheism. In Saudi Arabia, a blogger was arrested and whipped. In Bangladesh, at least five bloggers have been hacked to death in 2015. In 2016, eight people were burned to death in Zamfara in Nigeria after a student made unwelcome remarks about Islam and the Prophet Mohamed.

This practice of confronting critics violently will continue unless we in the wider world disown it both intellectually and legally. Muslim activists, and particularly Islamist extremists among them, feel that this global fight for their faith is worth every drop of their blood. They wish to use the law to suppress choice. Even if there was something *Haram* or forbidden in asking questions and seeking a new or different faith, it is not the business of government bureaucrats to assist extremists by making *Haram* and *Halal* equate to legal and illegal. Those of us that oppose them must advance better arguments (see below). Currently, Islam seems strong and muscular in public life because of the real fear of death and destruction awaiting Muslim dissenters, but for how much longer can this be sustained? Without freedom, not long. The attraction of Islam lies in the simplicity of its message of worship of one God, a preserved Quran, an honoured Prophet, a celebrated family life, and emphasis on the soul's journey to a next life: these are all threatened by the brutality of the blasphemy laws.

This is not an academic argument for me. Aged thirteen, I marched against Salman Rushdie's book *The Satanic Verses* in central London, and thereby supported the Iranian fatwa calling for his death. Today, almost thirty years later, my view has changed for the following six reasons.

First, the Prophet Mohamed was the subject of the most slanderous poetry in his own lifetime – the seventh-century Arabian equivalent of today's YouTube videos, newspaper cartoons and bestselling fiction. Almost always, he ignored the popular hatred. In Medina, when he was the head of a small city-state, not only did he forgive the Bedouin who urinated in his mosque, he showed compassion to those who betrayed him. Among his greatest enemies was Abdullah bin Ubayy, a leader of factions pitted against the Prophet, and yet when Ubayy died a natural death, the Prophet mourned and offered to lead the funeral prayers. After thirteen years of oppression and eight years of war, the Prophet pardoned his adversaries, among them Wahshi, a hired spearman in war, who killed the Prophet's beloved maternal uncle, Hamza. He forgave Hind, a maddened woman who chewed the dead Hamza's liver to show public vengeance for the death of her husband in a previous battle. Among the bloodthirsty ancient Arabs, the compassion of the Prophet stemmed from a conviction and a confidence in his faith. Little wonder, then, that the Quran describes him as 'a mercy unto the worlds'.

Second, several early companions of the Prophet left Islam and Medina, and returned to Mecca to the worship of their old ways; the Prophet left them alone. A prominent example of this leaving Islam and returning to Mecca was Abdullah Ibn Abi Sarh. There were neither angry sermons, nor calls for his death. Unless there was active treachery or betrayal of state secrets, early Muslims were free to enter or leave Islam. There is no Quranic punishment for apostasy. Now, it is true that all four schools of Muslim jurisprudence, the *Madhabs*, prescribe death as punishment for apostasy; but in the medieval period in which the schools were developed they interpreted treason and apostasy as being the same. They intended to confront active subversion of early Islam and public enmity toward Muslims. In today's world, many who leave Islam do not wish it harm – they simply leave in peace. So just as the Prophet left many apostates alone, contemporary Muslims should learn to accept that people can and will leave Islam and become former Muslims, and that freedom to do so does not warrant their death.

Third, a primary motivation for the urge to kill 'non-Muslims' who offend Islam is the belief that 'the Muslim *umma*' or global community is under attack. The perceived exclusivity of the *umma* helps fuel the 'them against us' narrative. The Prophet Mohamed's notion of *umma* included Jews, Christians and others when he addressed the people of Medina.

Fourth, the age of religious intolerance and empire is now over. For centuries, Jews and Muslims did not settle in the West because as blasphemers against Christianity and Jesus Christ they would have been persecuted. Empires protected their own versions of religion: England upheld Protestantism, France and Italy Catholicism, Russia supported the Orthodox, and the Ottomans advanced Islam. That world of rival empires has now, thankfully, ended. Muslims have settled and prospered in the West in large numbers because of the end of these blasphemy laws. Muslims and others can enjoy religious freedom. Muslims are free to proselytise, as they are to apostatise. In essence, Muslims are expected to be people of *shukr*, or gratitude. The Quranic opposite to *shukr* is *kufr* or disbelief. As a community of gratitude, it is among the greatest acts of ingratitude to burn the bridges of pluralism and secularism that allow for Muslims to observe their faith in the West.

Fifth, just as Muslims are free to be pious in the West with visible signs of Islam in the building of mosques, facilitation of *Halal* butchers, establishment of cemeteries, and fulfilment of every need of communal life, so must Christians or others in Muslim countries be entitled to be free. Even in the age of empires this principle of reciprocity was often in place. In a globalised world, blasphemy laws serve no purpose but to force believers to pretend to be religious when, in fact, they have lost their convictions in faith.

Sixth, coercion does not produce piety or sincerity among believers. Wherever there is enforcement of ethics, there is ground for the breeding of hypocrisy and the creation of outlaws. I saw this when I lived in Saudi Arabia. The Quran is clear in its declaration that 'There is no compulsion in faith' – and yet the Saudi ban on distributing Bibles and forbidding Christian gatherings meant that Western embassies became bastions of a locally defiant Christianity. Young Saudis converted quietly or rejected religion altogether and became confrontational atheists. Similarly, of the many Middle Easterners I met while living and working in the United States, it was Iranians who had escaped the rule of the Shi'a clerics that were born-again, converted evangelical Christians only too keen to baptise me or any other 'infidel'. Unless Muslims stop forcing Islam through the state, then there is a serious risk of more and more Muslims leaving Islam. What the Prophet called the '*Dhawq*', or the taste of religious devotion, cannot be savoured unless it is done freely.

Among the greatest rights of the sacred within Islam is that God does not wish Muslims to kill God's creation. Human life itself is sanctified. That strength of Islam to cherish the divine deserves to be protected through freedom, not force. The argument needs to be won, and the laws in Muslim countries need to allow for pluralism.

19

The Family Table

The patriarch Abraham, or Ibrahim as Muslims know him, was renowned for his hospitality and frequent visitors. Yet Ibrahim and his family preferred his guests to be of a similar outlook to his own, reflecting broadly his own worldview. One time a middle-aged traveller stopped by Ibrahim's home. After dinner the visitor went straight to sleep with neither prayers nor thanksgiving to God. In the morning the man had breakfast, and later lunch, at Ibrahim's family table, then worshipped an idol and, after his evening meal, went back to bed without joining in Ibrahim's family worship of one God. After a week of such behaviour, Ibrahim confronted him. Disturbed by his distance from God and devotion to a statue, Ibrahim sent him away for being an ungrateful polytheist. That night, Ibrahim received a message from God: 'Ibrahim, what is with you? You could not feed My servant, My creation, for a week, for not being My worshipper? But I have fed him and protected him for over forty years.'

The Sufis tell this wisdom story to encourage Muslims to honour our guests regardless of creed or background. 'Guest is god' is a popular saying among Muslim families in south Asia and Arab countries. Hospitality is not meeting at restaurants, pubs and bars, but sharing in the eating of home-made food in family surroundings. Westerners who have travelled in Muslim societies or Muslim-influenced cultures will have noticed this widespread warmth. Despite the spread of Westernisation, this institution of family and home-oriented hospitality still stands. Even when not meeting at home, 'going Dutch' is never an option – that is seen as an embarrassment. The Muslim host always insists on paying fully.

This is a cultural manifestation of the widespread, time-tested and deeply valued institution of the family. Without the family maintaining this refinement at home, we become 'customers' at commercial institutions, rather than loved and honoured guests at homes in far-flung parts of the world as we travel away from our own abodes. The family table means nothing without the family.

Islam's deep influence on its adherents' family life is beyond doubt. It is so deeply rooted and widespread that most Muslims of all hues, from the secularly unobservant to the most pious, are raised within an enduring Islamic culture. The Arabic names of members of the Prophet Mohamed's family still dominate the choice of names given to Muslim children in Europe, Turkey, the Balkans, the Caucasus and Indonesia, and even among Uighur Muslims in China: Khadija, Ayesha, Fatima for women and Ali, Abdullah, Hasan, Husain for boys.

A test of being a liberal in the West is to not only advocate homosexual rights, but to support gay marriage. From the United States to Ireland, Western nations have legislated for same-sex unions in defiance of conservative and religious views on traditional marriage and family life. There is not a single Muslim country that has legislated for this form of matrimony. Even those who consider themselves liberal, Westernised or progressive will in the vast majority of cases oppose any aberration from the traditional nuclear family. The mother–father–child family structure remains firmly at the core of Muslim communities globally, but not without its modern trials.

There is no concept of a 'civil marriage' in the Muslim world – the ceremony is fully religious even in the most avowedly irreligious families. The imam is present. He recites from the Quran and reminds the gathering that the Prophet said: 'Marriage is from my way of life and whosoever rejects marriage is not from my community.' According to the sharia, explicit agreement is then required from the bride and groom in the presence of male witnesses. The Prophet taught that upon acceptance of the dowry by the woman from the man, sweetmeats should be exchanged.

In the Arabian peninsula the practice is to exchange dates, and in other parts of the world pastries, chocolates and other sweets are used to celebrate.

An imam normally raises his hands and prays to God, and for a few brief minutes the entire gathering joins in collective prayers for the newlyweds' health and happiness, and for pious offspring. If the wedding is public and the parents' consent has been secured, then a *walima* (feast, or banquet) is organised by the groom's family.

The husband will almost always take his new wife home to live with him and his parents, and her own parents will bid her farewell. The notion that a son or daughter must leave home on reaching adulthood is still mostly alien in the Muslim world, and often two or three generations live together.

The strongest Western influences on Muslim marriage ceremonies are seen in the wearing of Western clothes, Western music being played at the *walima* while people eat, extensive consumption of Coca-Cola and similar soft drinks, Western cars and, finally, the novel concept of a honeymoon. Young couples now travel to faraway destinations, while older Muslims look on bewildered as to why a couple would wish to leave their families and be so selfish. Taking 'moon' in the lunar sense of 'month', the word 'honeymoon' has been translated literally into Arabic as *shahr al 'asl*, 'month of honey'. The month of honey is often spent in Western capitals.

Afterwards, the couple return home to the husband's parents' house, and go to visit the bride's family with sweets and presents. Throughout, the deepest respect is shown for both sets of parents and elders. Parents are to be respected and protected partly because of the wider culture, but also because this culture has been reinforced by Islamic teachings for fourteen centuries. There is a generational contract in which the young venerate the elderly, and seniors show love to the young.

We see this on the streets, as young children are kissed, embraced and have their heads patted by complete strangers in a completely innocent and affectionate way. This ease of contact and proximity to children is now impossible in the West for fear of accusations of child molestation and paedophilia. When I first went to live in Syria, my friends would kiss young children on the hands, cheeks, head and lips. Coming from the West, that somewhat shocked me, but I soon realised that I was the one with a problem, not my friends.

Muslim societies also venerate their elders. The aged are not usually isolated or placed in old people's homes. Older members of the family and the community are revered and honoured with kisses on their hands and foreheads and the offering of seats and prime place in the mosque on Fridays. Addressing an older person by their first name is considered overfamiliar and disrespectful, so titles are in order, or just calling all elders 'uncle' or 'older brother'. This is, in essence, an extension of the deference to parents. The Quran categorically calls on believers to ensure that their parents need never utter the word *'Uff'*, an Arabic expression of pain or exasperation. The children's conduct is to be exemplary – which is, of course, hard, and demands a constant struggle. 'God, have mercy on them, as they had mercy on me when I was young' is a prayer in the Quran for young people.

The Quran describes pregnancy as *wahn 'ala wahn*, 'exhaustion upon exhaustion'. The Arabic word for 'womb', *rahm*, has the same derivation as Al-Rahman, the most compassionate, one of the key attributes of God. Something of the divine function of creation is found in the mother when she gives birth, a miracle of God.

Muslims to this day are brought up to remember that once a young man asked the Prophet: 'Who should I should respect the most?' To which the Prophet replied: 'Your mother.' 'And then whom?' asked the youth. 'Your mother,' came the reply again. 'And then whom?' he repeated. 'Your mother,' was the Prophet's further reply. Three times the Prophet emphasised the mother.

The strength of Islamic culture in Muslim societies is maintained through such ubiquitous teachings and their application in daily life and major life events such as births, marriages and deaths. But this harmony of text and context is challenged by modern life.

Until recently, the concept of an old people's home was purely Western, and care of the elderly was always, and on the whole still is, the duty of the family. Most old people still live with their families – even in refugee camps I visited in Lebanon, three generations of Palestinians lived in the same ramshackle homes – but for the first time we are beginning to see this tradition coming under strain. In some countries, such as Egypt, elderly people in large cities may be given in-home care by non-family members, or sometimes placed in nursing homes. Saudi Arabia provides some in-home care and a few nursing homes mainly for elderly people with no family to look after them – otherwise, relatives are expected to provide for their aged family members.[1]

Muslims have traditionally had large families, but the modern, Western emphasis on smaller families, reflecting later marriages, with women often in their thirties, couples' need for dual incomes and wives wanting to continue their careers, and smaller homes, secured by mortgages, are all factors influencing Muslim lives.

In the US and in Catholic societies, abortion is a major topic of controversy, but the sharia is relatively flexible on this issue: the Hanafi school permits abortions up to 120 days after conception. This issue is not widely discussed, nor is it a major obsession among Muslims, but the rise in abortions is a reality. In Indonesia, the rate of abortion is among the highest in the world at 37 for every 1,000 women – more than 2 million abortions a year.[2] In Egypt and Turkey the rate is about 15 per 1,000 women, somewhat lower than the 16.9 in the United States.

Governments in many Muslim countries are keen to promote smaller families in the interests of economic growth, development and poverty reduction. Even the clerical regime of Iran subsidises contraception to assist in family planning.

Be it the rise of divorce, the gradual increase in old age care outside the family, or the urge to Westernise and reduce the size of Muslim families, these threats are not sufficient to destabilise the core Quranic concepts that still thrive in Muslim societies. For young people, traditional marriage is still the general aspiration, and creating a family naturally is the widespread norm.

When spending time as a guest with a Muslim family, a visitor from the West will witness all of the above, and experience something more. In the poorest of homes in Nigeria, in refugee camps in Turkey – playing host to nearly 2 million displaced Syrians – the visit of a guest is felt to be an honour. The family table is lit up with additional happiness when it welcomes a guest. The sense of hospitality traditional in the deserts of Arabia has been maintained in modern homes, where a visitor is made to feel significant and special in a way with which the West cannot compete. Muslim families spontaneously offer gifts, hugs and invitations to eat in their homes. The loving spirit of Islam still holds together the family from which society derives immense benefit. But the family also prepares its young and old for what awaits us beyond this life.

20
The Next Life

Human beings instinctively seek meaning in their lives. Consciously or unconsciously, we want to know where we came from, why we are here, and where we are heading. To these existential questions, Western humanism has no definitive answers. Moral relativism and ideas such as 'There is no truth' are strange to Muslim public discourse. Islam speaks to this human search for meaning, and does so in very clear terms.

The ancient Egyptians believed in an afterlife, for which they prepared in extensive detail. The pyramids of the pharaohs and the tombs of Egyptian nobles tell us precisely that this life was spent in preparation for another existence. The ancient Greeks also understood that life in this world was a passing phase: Socrates in his last days spoke of anticipation of meeting his creator. But the ancient Arabs did *not* believe in the next life. The Prophet Mohamed's mission among the Arab tribes was to connect them to civilisations that saw beyond the here and now.

To the pagan Arabs, this earthly life was all there was. They killed their own daughters with impunity in large part because, as well as not being accountable to their contemporaries, there was also no question of having to answer for one's actions after death. The notion of being judged in the next world for one's deeds in this life was seen as an eccentric belief of the Jews and Christians who lived as minorities in the Arabian cities of Mecca, Taif and Medina. The Prophet's call to believe in only one God was revolutionary enough for idol-worshipping polytheists, but to accept that there might be another life beyond the here and now meant a change in the believer's whole approach to life.

Muslims believe that there is an *Akhirah*, another world, to which our souls travel upon our death, and throughout their lives they work toward success in the next world. This belief is reinforced with frequent reminders of the *Akhirah* in daily prayers and supplications, recitals of the Quran and maintaining purity of doing 'good deeds' that are free from ostentation or other motives. If, for instance, a conscientious Muslim gives alms or helps keep the streets clean or fights injustice, he or she tries to do so with sincerity for God and reward in this and the next life.

The greatest institutional reinforcement of *Akhirah* is the imminence of the annual Hajj gathering: every Muslim has a family member, relative or friend present. There on the great plain of Arafah, on the outskirts of Mecca, millions spend a day in repentance for the misdeeds of this life, and seeking salvation in the next. The Prophet Mohamed's last sermon was delivered on a mount in this valley, and his words echo to this day at Arafah and across the world. The day of Arafah comes approximately seventy days after Ramadan and a day before the Eid al-Adha, second of the two annual Muslim holidays. Months before the Prophet passed away, preaching on Arafah, he said to thousands of his companions: 'Remember that one day you will appear before God to answer for your actions. So beware, and do not stray from the path of righteousness after I am gone. Pass on my words to others and to others again. So the last ones understand my words better than ones present here today.'

The Hajj is an annual reminder of the Prophet's words on the preparedness for the next life. The *Akhirah* is our everlasting life: this abode is transient. Whenever I find myself in doubt about this truth, I recall the explanation provided by Imam Ghazzali (1058–1111). He wrote that just as an embryo did not know or understand birth and being a baby, and a baby does not foresee becoming a toddler and then an infant, and an infant does not understand puberty or middle age, and the able-bodied, healthy person at the peak of their lives doubts that they will ever be frail – so it is with the afterlife and us. Because we cannot scientifically comprehend the *Akhirah*, it does not mean that another realm does not await us.

This is not an abstract idea, but another lived reality of anticipation that informs many aspects of contemporary Muslim life in a way that is widely disregarded in the West. In the pre-modern West the church, both as a building and as an idea, dominated public life. Churchyards were graveyards, and there was no social taboo surrounding death. Today, many people seek to postpone death and slow down the ageing process as much as possible, by use of Botox and every other imaginable means of delaying the inevitable. Even in the megachurches of evangelical America, the dead are no longer found at rest in gardens alongside the church buildings. We have removed the dead from our cities and placed them behind high walls in cemeteries on the outskirts, unseen by the human eye.

The Prophet's city of Medina buried its dead within walking distance of the mosque. The Prophet visited the cemetery regularly, and taught Muslims to do so too. Upon his own death, he was laid to rest within the mosque itself. Both of the first two caliphs, Abu Bakr and Omar, were buried beside him. This is not something unique to Islam: in Britain's Westminster Abbey I see burial grounds of national figures such as Chaucer, Newton, Wilberforce, Dickens and Gladstone, and in the vault of St Paul's Cathedral I see John Donne, Sir Christopher Wren and the Duke of Wellington.

In Islam, entire Sufi orders were born around the burial places of saints, and continue to flourish around the tombs of saints across the Muslim world. Today the global Chishti order turns for spiritual connection to the divine at Muin ad-Din Chishti's shrine at Ajmer in India. In Africa, when I visited Ahmed al-Tijani's tomb in Fez, it was a vibrant hostel for students, teachers and worshippers.

The dead and the living, this life and the next, are all still connected in the Muslim world. Even the non-Islamist heroes of the Arab Spring – from Mohamed Bouazizi in Tunisia to Khaled Said in Egypt – who were, and are, referred to as Muslim martyrs. Martyrdom is honoured in Islam to this day, as it once was in

Christianity. The brave believers who died in the coliseums of pagan Rome inspired faith and reverence in the spectators, who slowly started to convert to Christianity. When secular leaders die in the modern Muslim world, they are still seen as martyrs even by secular political parties. Saddam Hussein's supporters claimed he was a martyr; Palestinians referred to Yasser Arafat as a martyr. Victims of the Arab Spring, secular Syrian fighters for Bashar al-Assad, Emirati soldiers in Yemen – the list goes on.

The Muslim belief in the afterlife only appears in Western public discourse as a crude caricature, when media reporting of suicide bombings perpetuates that old chestnut, the fallacy that a terrorist has killed himself to gain seventy-two female virgins in heaven. The jihadi does not need to die for sex; he can satisfy his desires in this world. He is not alone in his certainty that there is life beyond this world, but he is wrong if he thinks he is heading to heaven – as Muslim clergy were the first to highlight after the 9/11 attacks: the perpetrators were not martyrs but murderers. Only when put in those terms did the message of the al-Qaeda extremists find rebuttal in a language that resonated among Muslims.

The earliest artwork in the Muslim world outside Arabia showed how Quranic imagery of the afterlife provided the inspiration for decorating mosques and public places. The Umayyad Mosque in Damascus and the Al-Aqsa Mosque in Jerusalem still have their decoration from 1,400 years ago showing a focus on greenery, trees, gardens and water, mirroring the Quranic vision of heaven.

In Spain, first- and second-century Muslims built entire cities based on these Quranic images of gardens, flowing rivers, fountains and buildings glorifying God that are still attracting tourists to Córdoba and the Al-Hambra Palace. The spirit and values that informed that generation still inform today's Muslims.

We will meet our Maker. There is full certainty (*yaqeen*) on this among most Muslims. The Quran confirms that: 'Every individual will taste death. And We [God] test you with evil and with good as trial; and to Us you will be returned.'[1] Even if the most monumental fortresses are built, the Quran continues elsewhere, there is no escape from the reality of death and return to God. The doubt and uncertainty of liberal individualism has not yet affected this inner core of global Muslim identity and belief. When news of a death reaches a Muslim, be they Indonesian or Bengali or African, they will say in Arabic: *'Inna lillahi wa inna ilaihi raji'un'* – 'To God we belong and to God is our return', a verse of the Quran recited on these occasions by all aware Muslims. At the time of greatest uncertainty in life among families and friends, in facing the unknown of death, Islam offers clarity and solace. Life has not ended, but begun anew in a higher realm.

The language that Muslims use about death upholds the faith and convictions of an ancient community. I only became fully aware of this when my father passed away in February 2016. Amid the shock and pain of enduring loss, our Muslim family and friends, when expressing condolences, from Arab lands to India to Africa, all spoke about Dad's day of *Intiqal*, or, literally, transfer or transport. The English phrase 'pass away' now had more meaning: the soul had passed from one domain to another. This was the Muslim position of expressing the belief in relocation of the human soul from the body to another level of consciousness, the *Akhirah*. Nor was *Intiqal* of the soul a private matter for the family. The power of faith was on full display. My mother and my siblings were surrounded by extended family support: they took it in turns to provide food, prayers, money, funeral organising assistance, burial of the body, and thereafter regular visits to the grave for recitals from the Quran to assure his soul that we remember Dad. In these good deeds there was a potent reminder that life is short, and *Intiqal* to the hereafter was the unavoidable fate for all of us. What we did for Dad, others will do for us when we depart this world. And these actions of virtue will outweigh our sins and help us enter the Heavens. This is the Muslim way of approaching life and death.

Recital of the Quran takes centre stage for forty days as family and friends mourn the worldly departure of a believer. The Prophet forbade excessive crying and wailing for the deceased, however, because the believer has returned home to God. Muslims recall the Prophet on his deathbed, surrounded by his family and with his beloved daughter Fatima sadly shedding tears, as he advised his companions to be steadfast in prayer. He called Fatima over and whispered something in her ear. She came away, stopped crying and slowly started to smile. 'What did the Prophet say to you?' asked the Prophet's wife, Ayesha. 'That I will be the first to meet him in the next life,' she replied. Fatima's certainty and belief in her father's words have informed Muslims throughout the centuries, and still console today's believers, that they will meet God and the Prophet, and live in their original, heavenly home.

The Sufi scholar Rumi, writing about his death, pictured it as his wedding day, when he would return to meet his beloved God. He cautioned Muslims not to be gloomy at his funeral, and encouraged them to bring drums to celebrate. He predicted that his burial in the rose beds of the sultan's garden in Konya would draw people from East and West, and when I visited Konya I witnessed a spiritual jamboree of Japanese, Europeans, Arabs and Americans.

Rumi's whirling dervishes embody this attitude to death in their divinely inspired dance, which treats the human body as a reed flute through which our soul plays like music. The dervishes turn their right hands toward the heavens to absorb energy, which passes through their bodies and down through their left hands to Mother Earth as they twirl, while the world rotates in harmony. The dervishes' dance, symbolising this, is popular in Iran, Syria, Turkey, the Balkans and parts of Muslim India.

Yet the modern suicide bomber has subverted this sublime Muslim preparedness for eternal life, and hijacked the status of martyrs. The spiritual energy and soaring symbolism of the dervishes' dance is being marginalised.

Probably the most prominent and highly venerated female saint of early Islam was Rabia Adawiyya (d. 801) from the Iraqi city of Basra. One night she was walking with a burning torch of fire in one hand and a bucket of water in the other. When people asked her where she was going, Rabia replied: 'I want to set heaven aflame and extinguish the fire of hell.' She wanted believers to worship Allah for and through love, not out of considerations of reward and punishment.

Muslim scholars also recall that Imam Ali once prayed to God to be denied a place in heaven if he worshipped God only for hope of heaven. Love, longing and worship should not be for heaven but for God. The highest objective for the Muslim is *Wajhullah*, the Face of God. The Quran explains that a believer feeds orphans and the needy 'for the face of God', *Li wajhillah*, in order to delight in His ultimate beauty.

Islam's global staying power among its followers is and will remain strong for the foreseeable future for as long as Muslims are free to believe, and not forced to do so by fanatics enforcing Salafi sharia as state law. The centrality of God, the vibrancy of the Quran, the preservation of the rights of the sacred, the institutions of the family and the firm public belief in the afterlife all provide an unshakeable bedrock for the Muslim believer from generation to generation.

But what of the immediate future? What are we to do about the current malaise of the Muslim world being exploited by Islamists and Salafi-jihadis, the widespread feelings of diminished dignity, loss of confidence, the rise of terrorism, poor educational provision, intolerance of Jews, and the repression of women and sexuality? How can Muslims tackle these issues in a way that makes it possible to create alliances with the West, rather than breed further enmity?

Conclusion: The Way Forward

Repeated experiments with Arab nationalism, European socialism, French *laïcité*, Islamism and jihadism have all failed in the Middle East. When the Prophet Mohamed migrated from Mecca to Medina in the year 622, he sought freedom to worship without fear and violence. Upon arrival in Medina, he did not accept the land for building his mosque as a gift: he insisted that the property be bought. He guided his companions to the markets in Medina to trade freely. He created a social contract with Jews and others in Medina, known as the Constitution of Medina, to bring an end to the bloodshed between tribes and thereby established the rule of law. During a period of drought and food shortage, he refused to fix prices, and said 'These matters are in the hands of God.'

Freedom, property rights, free trade, pluralism, the rule of law and human dignity are not creations of the modern West. They are universal cravings of the human soul. The peoples of the Middle East are entrepreneurial in spirit. Political suppression, poverty, extremism, indignity, humiliation, and corruption prevent them from realising their true potential. The mass protests in 2011 were a desperate cry for help.

The Arab Spring is not over. The media caravan has moved on, but there is an undercurrent still alive and simmering. In time it will bring a generational and geostrategic shift in the region. Unless we understand and respond to the emotions and ideas of the young people of the Middle East, there will be yet more chaos and carnage, which will also eventually be visited upon streets and neighbourhoods in the West with greater ferocity. Too much blood has been spilled for the yearnings of the Arab uprisings to die. We may soon be caught off guard again, with millions pouring into Arab urban centres to face the tanks, terror and tyranny of their governments. The trauma of having witnessed shootings and killings, the loss of friends and family, and the dashing of high hopes for dignity and justice hangs over a generation. Their grandfathers failed in the revolts of the 1920s. Their fathers failed after the coups of the 1950s. Did they fail too in 2011? What will their children do?

Five years on from the beginning of the Arab revolutions, four countries in the Middle East are now failed states, with daily loss of human life: Iraq, Syria, Libya and Yemen. Several others are fragile. The same forces that gave rise to the Arab revolutions in 2011, and to the 'Green Movement' in Iran in 2009, are still simmering away and could boil up again in Saudi Arabia, Egypt, Lebanon, Jordan, Iran or a number of other places. Turkey is no longer a home of democratic stability – military coups and ethnic tensions rumble. Pakistan and Afghanistan are teetering on the brink, with poor governance, security lapses and economic failures. Iran is meddling in the affairs of its neighbours in Yemen, Saudi Arabia, Bahrain, Syria, Iraq and Lebanon. And then there is the abiding Arab–Israeli conflict. The world outside of these areas will not remain immune from the fires spreading in their neighbours' houses.

Instability and ineffective governance in the Middle East, as the historical, religious and emotional epicentre of the Muslim world, feed a global narrative of Muslims wallowing in victimhood and failure. Islamists amplify this state of loss with their networks on social media, universities, workplaces, and mosques. This then provides a breeding ground for Salafi-jihadi recruits, who blame the West and unleash violence rationalised by Salafi literalism, seeking victory or martyrdom. If they can expect, through self-destruction as suicide bombers, to find dignity in the afterlife, then the appeal of suicide missions will continue to spread. What do they have to live for? They see glory only in the next life.

Globally, feelings of ignominy and betrayal are not confined to Muslims. The Germans, Russians, Indians and Chinese have all lost territories and empires. In the case of India, two large Muslim countries have been carved out of its land: Pakistan and

Bangladesh. Why are Indians not becoming suicide bombers in a quest to restore the united, glorious India of old? Why are Russians not seeking to recapture their national sense of self-worth by hijacking aeroplanes or bombing Western public transport systems? Why are Africans, mass sufferers of poverty, corruption and injustice, not resorting to terrorism?

When I wrote *The Islamist* in 2007, I warned about the rise of ideological extremism and the cravings for a caliphate among Islamists who are driving global Muslim opinion. I was accused at the time of being an alarmist. I wish I had been wrong. Today the West and ordinary Muslims are on a more dangerous and devastating trajectory. We must all realise that our direction of travel must change, or else it will certainly lead to more destruction. Largely unreformed and mostly failing Arab governments cannot keep the West and its populations secure from future threats.

Ahmed El-Derawi, a PR executive, democracy activist and then parliamentary hopeful, looked elsewhere for dignity when the revolution in Egypt failed. He disappeared for a long time after President Morsi was toppled, and then resurfaced with this comment on Twitter in late 2015: 'I have found justice in Jihad, and dignity and bravery in leaving my old life forever.' He died as a suicide bomber for ISIS. El-Derawi is not alone in seeking dignity through death after failing to find meaning and worth in life.

The prisons of the Arab world are full of Islamists and Salafists. Our Arab allies incarcerate their dissenters, and all of us pay the price through increased radicalisation. The ordinary Arab's feeling of powerlessness needs to end. The Arab Spring was powerful because it granted agency to new peoples. Samir Kassir, in *Being Arab*, nails the problem:

> As a system of thought, jihadist Islamism is far from being the dominant ideology it is often portrayed as in the Western media. Yet it is powerful, no doubt because it is the only ideology that seems to offer relief from the victim status the Arabs delight in claiming (a status that in fact Islamism, jihadist or otherwise, is only too happy to confirm).

There are lessons from other parts of the world – notably, but not uniquely, post-war Western Europe – that are instructive when it comes to seeking answers on how to reverse this collective cultural trend. It can be done. Peace can be found.

In parallel to the contemporary Middle East, the anti-American narrative in South Korea was once tied up with American foreign policy and a US troop presence on South Korean soil. As in the Middle East, feelings were widespread of being 'America's pawn', not least because of the American military presence in the region. The troops are still there today, yet South Korean attitudes have shifted. In 2002, leading South Korean musicians performed in a vast concert to protest against America, with fans furiously stamping on cardboard models of US military tanks. The concert and other anti-American protests were, on the face of it, in response to an incident in which a US military vehicle struck and killed two teenage girls on a road outside Seoul, and a US court martial acquitted the American soldiers involved.

Like Arabs, South Koreans were sensitive to the honour of their women being violated, and, like Arabs, they raised claims of a new American empire dominating their country, as other powers had done in the past. A poll in 2002 found that 75 per cent of young Koreans said they hated Americans – unusually for the time, given the international sympathy toward America after the 9/11 attacks. However, the opinions of a nation, a people, can change in a decade. South Korea, before the election of President Trump, was one of the most pro-American countries in the world, where eight in ten people have confidence in the US government's international leadership.[1]

Henry Kissinger captured the Middle East conundrum best when he wrote in *World Order* in 2014:

> A profusion of prophetic absolutisms has been the hallmark of a region suspended between a dream of its former glory and its inability to unify around common principles of domestic or international legitimacy. Nowhere is the challenge of the international order more complex – in terms of both organising

regional order and ensuring the compatibility of that order with peace and stability in the rest of the world.

Kissinger's warning was serious. He was highlighting the failure of nation-states. But the catastrophe is compounded by the proliferation of Islamist and Salafist groups across the region: Hamas, Hezbollah, al-Qaeda and ISIS are only a shadow of what is yet to come if we do not open up pluralist political spaces and wider economic participation.

Terrorist groups, their tactics, new names for breakaway groups, must not distract us from the fact that they are also becoming more successful as the effectiveness of state military forces weakens. Hezbollah, Hamas, al-Qaeda may have been losing to date, but their war of attrition is not over. Unless we, their opponents, including most Muslims around the world, shift the grounds on which they stand, then they can sustain a long war in a way in which liberal democrats cannot.

A Harvard study[2] has shown that in asymmetric conflicts between 1800 and 1849, the weaker side in terms of soldiers and arms achieved its aim in 12 per cent of cases. In the wars between 1950 and 1998, the weaker side won in 55 per cent of cases. Moisés Naím, in *The End of Power*, concludes that 'when nation-states go to war these days, big military power delivers less than it once did'. It looks particularly impotent in the face of amateur lone attackers – and in 2015, 450 of the 452 suicide bomb attacks across the world were by Islamist extremists.

The Arab masses cannot be bombed into submission by governments and their armies. Terrorist organisations will continue to be born claiming to want to restore dignity and honour to their imagined form of Islam. The more we delay, postpone, contain or block the cry for dignity and participation in government, the messier, bloodier and more protracted the conflicts of the Middle East will become. We need a long-term, comprehensive strategy to unpick the webs of warfare in the region.

But what will that new order be? Hoping for the best, the comfortable refuge of relativists, is not an option. We cannot leave matters to the Middle Easterners themselves, for fear of giving offence or facing accusations of renewed colonialism. What happens in the region has an impact upon the West. On the other hand, intensive European and American meddling, imposing Westphalia-style nation-states, empire, world wars, secular liberalism and dictatorships has not worked in a part of the world that holds true to its conservative heritage on faith, family, and a future world beyond this one. Treading a careful line between ignoring and fuelling the fire, we can all assist in organising regional order and contributing to global peace and security.

There are major challenges facing our world over the coming decades: the actuality of a changing climate, rapid population growth, resource scarcity, a resurgence of ideology, and shifts in power from West to East.[3] In all of these, the Muslim world generally, and the Middle East specifically, is at the sharp end. Water shortages and record temperatures are occurring across the Arabian Gulf. Rising water levels in Bangladesh, literally inch by inch each year, threaten to obliterate that country. Muslim birth rates are higher than in every other faith and non-faith community. Islamist ideology is on the rise, and all the more so now because of government crackdowns in several countries. And the West-to-East shift in power is likely to concentrate on India and China, again bypassing the Middle East – unless the region changes, and changes fast.

Western governments have been pursuing policies that ignore concrete realities. Leftist activists and NGOs help spread the secularising and revolutionary ideas of Voltaire, Rousseau and Marx, but not the conservative, faith-accommodating philosophy and economics of Burke and Adam Smith. Yet the latter resonate among peoples who were traders and merchants for millennia, and maintained a conservative balance between monarchs, merchants, mullahs and the masses in their political systems.

Edmund Burke's genius in Britain and relevance in today's Middle East was that he was both religious and a conservative, but also understood and held in balance the forces of past, present and future. He balanced the monarchy, aristocracy and commons while reining in the iconoclastic temptations of the French Revolution. And yet he supported the American Revolution, the

Irish cause and Catholic emancipation; he took the British East Indian Company to task for its injustices; and he believed in a constitutional monarchy for Great Britain with checks and balances. This compromise and consensus of conservatism is based on centuries of coexistence. To oppose this with abstract ideas of human rights while endorsing attacks upon and killing of police officers (as happened during the Arab Spring in Bahrain and Egypt) is to sow the seeds of destruction. Governments and revolutionaries wanting all or nothing have repeatedly resulted in Arab failures. Mubarak, Assad and Gaddafi battled street protesters; business elites lost out and capital took flight; and the rule of law suffered further setbacks in countries where the legal culture had been lost. To address this, the Burkean compromise was to include all in power – monarchy, aristocracy and commons, which would nowadays translate into head of state, opposition, and religious, military and business elites all working together.

'A state without the means of some change is without the means of its conservation,' Burke wrote. The changes that the Muslim world in general, and the Middle East in particular, will need in order to conserve what is best in those societies include religious faith, family values, a sense of the sacred in the public space, and maintaining a belief in life beyond this world. But where must the changes be made? Based on the themes identified in this book, there are three areas that can be worked on to help heal the increasing rifts and rancour in the Islamic world.

1. CREATE A MIDDLE EAST UNION (MEU) – URGENTLY

In 2015 alone, a million migrants entered Europe, most of them from the war-shattered lands of the Middle East. Since 2012, over three million Syrian refugees have fled to Turkey. The conflicts in several Arab countries have yet to peak. Refugee flows will continue to increase, not decrease. Tens of thousands of Muslims and others have already died at sea trying to enter Europe. What does it say about societies and governments when their people are, literally, dying to leave them for Europe?

There are urgent steps we need to take in partnership with, not by dominating, the Middle East. First, we need to respond to the calls from the region and assist in the creation of a Middle East Union. Not long ago, Europe was a continent that looked the way the Middle East looks today. It was full of dictators and stalked by political extremists. Its intolerance of minorities led to the horrors of the Holocaust. Perpetual contests over its national borders triggered two world wars. This depressing picture is now being repeated across the Middle East, from Morocco to Syria to Yemen. The rise of religious sectarianism in Iraq and Syria, as well as the repression of Islamists in Egypt, produces the magnetic narratives of radicalism that find adherents among young Muslims in the West.

Europe's past and present can inform the future of the Middle East. Ironically, despite current fractures over its future direction, the European Union's history and stability offer a model for putting the Middle East back together in a way that reinstates *thymos*, a sense of pride in their place in the world, the political desire for recognition and respect as dignified ancient peoples. Just as a warring continent found peace through unity, by creating what became the EU, so Arabs, Turks, Iranians, Kurds and other groups in the region could find relative peace in ever closer union. Most of its problems – terrorism, poverty, unemployment, sectarianism, refugee crises, water shortages – require regional answers. None of the countries concerned can solve its problems on its own. The rule should be simple: we need to face in common that which we cannot do alone.

Egypt's President Abdel Fattah el-Sisi, in full recognition of regional challenges, has at several junctures called for the creation of a joint Arab military force. A Middle East Union could hold the key to a common security response to the shared threat of regional jihadism. Egypt describes this as 'one of the most important tools of integration of the Arab world to defend the causes of Arab nations', alongside the economic integration of Arab countries.

Such regional amalgamation and assimilation would have other benefits, and meet other needs too. For example, Egypt has low-cost labour but high youth unemployment. Neighbouring Libya has excess capital, huge infrastructure projects and an insatiable demand for workers. Turkey has the expertise to build airports, bridges and roads. These dots need connecting.

For more than a millennium, the Middle East was broadly united under different monarchical dynasties. Free movement of people, goods, tribes, ideas and armies was the norm. There was a common religion for most and, compared with other regions of the world, there were fewer languages and more commonalities of culture and history. When Europe's medieval pogroms were unleashed, it was the Muslim Mamluks and Ottomans who welcomed Jews. Minorities were protected when the majority had confidence in themselves.

Most people in the Middle East today no longer feel the dignity of their ancestors. *Thymos* is desperately missing. This is something an MEU could recreate. Through a sharing of resources and policies, the necessary corrections could be made in the education systems of the Middle East to promote critical thinking and develop open minds that honour women as equal human beings in the workplace and in families.

Conflict in Europe was eroded by Europeans growing more interdependent on each other for trade, security and prosperity, and joining their governments and peoples closer together. During Britain's referendum to exit ('Brexit') the EU, the strongest warning not to leave came from the then Conservative prime minister, David Cameron: 'The European Union has helped reconcile countries which were at each other's throats for decades.' He talked about 'maintaining common purpose in Europe to avoid future conflict between European countries'. It is the absence of any such architecture of unity in the modern Middle East that creates fertile grounds for fanatics.

In a special report on the Arab world entitled 'The War Within', the *Economist* put forward a similar argument:

> Arab states could do with more supranational integration to open markets and spur growth. As a political body, the Arab League is a failure. But many Arabs admire the European Union,

even as it loses its appeal to a growing number of Europeans, not least because of Arab refugees. European history provides some solace to Arabs: before the continent united, it waged wars even bloodier than those Arabs are enduring.[4]

Israel, meanwhile, should be an ally and trading partner of this regional union, and eventually a member. Palestinians must be allowed to travel and trade across the Middle East rather than languish for further generations in refugee camps as recruitment fodder for Hamas and the jihadis. Israel's technological, educational and innovative advantages over its Arab neighbours should be motivational: why does Israel have more patents and Nobel Prize winners than the entire Arab world combined? Israel is a magnet for global investors – peace with Israel would ensure that capital is spread across the region. Per capita venture capital investments in Israel in 2009 were 2.5 times higher than in the United States, more than 30 times greater than in Europe, 80 times higher than in China, and 350 times larger than in India. In absolute terms, Israel, a small nation of only 7 million people, attracted almost 2 billion dollars in venture capital, as much as flowed to the UK's 61 million people. For how much longer must there be conflict rather than cooperation?

Regional thinkers and leaders have made calls for unity for almost a century. This is not, therefore, a Western project. Intellectuals of the past sowed the seeds of regionalist thought long ago.[5] In polls, most people in the Middle East have been found to see themselves primarily as Arab or Muslim before, say, Jordanian or Saudi. Pan-Islamic identity still has more resonance than nationality.

Such calls for closer regional collaboration have been echoed by former president of Turkey Abdullah Gul, the Saudi king, the president of the United Arab Emirates, Jordan's monarch – and also by more threatening voices among Hamas, Egypt's Salafists and the Muslim Brotherhood. On a visit to Egypt in April 2016, King Salman of Saudi Arabia, addressing the Egyptian parliament, called for regional issues to be addressed through regional unity. This did not make headlines in the West, but it reflected the instincts of the peoples and politicians of the Arab world's two most powerful nations. The commitment of both sides to building a new bridge across the Red Sea to connect their countries is a symbol of this urge for greater Arab unity.[6]

ISIS already operates beyond nation-states, and its transnational outlook and ideology are spreading fast worldwide. Is the West going to wait until the Islamists and radicals are powerful enough to create a Middle East in their own image, one hostile to the rest of us? Or will it help its Middle Eastern partners in government to harness this momentum for greater unity? This is the moment to create multilateral institutions that could embed pluralism across the region as firmly as Mustafa Kemal Atatürk's constitution did in Turkey almost a century ago. An MEU would not be the caliphate of the literalists or the secular democracy of liberals, but a pluralistic political and economic union true to the reality of the region, where the sharia is honoured through the *Maqasid* of preserving life, freedom, intellect, family and property. Yearning for the sharia will not vanish. 'Human beings will no more cease to be religious than they will stop being sexual, playful or violent,' warns John Gray.[7] But the *Maqasid* approach to the sharia, being at once rooted in history and scholarship dating back nine hundred years and at the same time readily applicable to the modern world, is the most constructive way forward for Muslim activists.

In short, conservatism, capitalism and coexistence should be the forces behind creating a new Middle East order that provides dignity, security and stability for the region and the wider world.

2. IMPLEMENT A MUSLIM MARSHALL PLAN

As well as closer regional political and security cooperation, economic integration is essential to create prosperity and meet the rising generation's aspirations. After the demolition of Europe's infrastructure and depletion of its capital reserves at the end of the Second World War, the United States deployed $130 billion in today's money to rebuild Europe. The Marshall Fund aimed to minimise state barriers, eradicate red tape that prevented business growth, and facilitate business productivity and economic growth. In recent times the West has fought multiple wars in the Middle East, at enormous expense – the Iraq War cost the United States 2 trillion dollars – but no such economic reconstruction plan for the region has been conceived. A Marshall Plan for the Middle East, which could help to fund and facilitate a Middle East Union, is urgently overdue. The nearest we have come to this so far is the Deauville Partnership floated by the G8 in 2011 after the Arab uprisings, but none of the promises made were kept. France's President Nicolas Sarkozy is said to have made up the figure for the amount of aid to be pledged just thirty seconds before it was announced.[8]

During the past three decades, the Middle East region's per capita income has grown by a mere 0.9 per cent per year (the lowest of all regions in the world except sub-Saharan Africa). In a region of 450 million people, only 3.2 million jobs have been created per year in the past ten years – fewer than half the number needed. In 2008–10, 76 per cent of the region's exports were primary commodities, largely oil and gas – not products created by the people. Manufactured goods accounted for only 11 per cent of exports. Only 20 per cent of small and medium-sized businesses have a loan or line of credit, much lower than anywhere else in the world.

In August 2015, Jordan's Queen Rania warned that 100 million new jobs were needed in the Middle East by 2020. What regional and strategic steps are in place to meet this desperate need? None. Two in three Egyptians live on less than 2 dollars a day. The situation is only set to get worse unless an international economic plan for the region, linked to creating a Middle East Union, is crafted and implemented with speed.

In May 2012 the World Bank had released a report[9] highlighting the vital need for Arab economic integration, 'for without strong economic underpinnings, and without growth and quality employment for the millions of young Arab men and women who seek jobs and a decent life, the Arab democratic transition indeed faces a grim future'.[10] It said the region was the least integrated in the world, despite having the strongest ingredients for integration, including the sharing of a common religion, heritage, language, culture and history.

A regional union, with economic integration, would promote greater movement of people, capital and enterprises. It would turn Arabs and Muslims inwards to help raise the status of their people from impoverishment to one of dignity, political rights, and a role in the global economy. Almost 70 per cent of Middle Eastern trade at present is with the EU. Free trade agreements with the EU and US would help incentivise entrepreneurship. Just as China and the US negotiate agreements with the EU and not its member states, so too the West would deal with the Middle East Union as a bloc. And just as Germany and Britain have footed the bill for subsidising poorer EU members, Arab states with higher GDPs should share their resources with Egypt, Jordan, Syria and other poorer nations. Failure to do so creates conflicts that then consume the peoples of the entire region and beyond.

China, India, Europe and America are all organised today as political and economic unions and federations of various kinds. Globalisation, free trade and the pooling of sovereignty and resources minimise internal wars and loss of life. In Europe, Germany is no longer at war with France. In a united America, the Civil War ended two centuries ago and has not been reignited. But Saudi Arabia and Iran are continuing to fight old sectarian wars by new proxies – and the consequences, seen in Syria, Lebanon, Iraq and Yemen, are growing annually.

If Arabs, Turks, Kurds and Iranians do not expedite the creation of a Middle East Union, then responsibility for the breakdown will be theirs. The West cannot be held accountable for the failings of a divided people. Currently, blame for Middle Eastern catastrophes is placed firmly on the West. A move away from addressing one nation at a time to taking a regional approach to regional problems would shift the blame, and show that the West understands the impulses and instincts of the region. Success would be a win–win outcome. Failure would not be the fault of the West.

3. EXPEL VIOLENT EXTREMISTS FROM WITHIN ISLAM

The House of Islam is on fire – and the arsonist still lives there. Neighbours can bring water to put out the fire, but Muslims must also expel the fire bombers in their midst. It is no longer enough simply to condemn terrorism. Muslims deserve no applause or special recognition merely for condemning murderers. That is the least we can do, not the most. The measure of civilisation is not that low. From the earliest days of Islam, the Kharijites were so called because they were exactly that: outsiders, people who had 'gone out', beyond the pale. The greatest of Muslim scholars declared them to be non-Muslims. And the earliest violent Salafi-jihadis were banned from Mecca by the *qadi* and the Ottoman rulers because they were considered to be infidels.

As long as the House of Islam provides shelter for Salafi-jihadis, the rest of the world will attack Islam and Muslims. A poll carried out in the Netherlands in 2013 disclosed that 73 per cent of respondents said that 'a relationship exists' between Islam and terror attacks.[11] In France in the same year, 74 per cent of people polled said that they considered Islam as intolerant, and 73 per cent viewed Islam negatively.[12] In Germany in 2012, 64 per cent of Germans associated Islam with violence and 70 per cent connected Islam with fanaticism and radicalism.[13]

As long as Muslims tolerate their presence, we will give licence even to the ideologues in both the East *and* West to conflate Islam with Salafi-jihadism. More Muslims will turn to jihadism, and another generation will be lost. We need to cleanse our mosques, publishing houses, schools, websites, satellite TV stations, *madrasas* and ministries of Salafi-jihadi influences. Unless we do, Islamophobia will continue to rise and we cannot complain when the West repeatedly suggests that Muslims are suspect. Unless we do, no matter how much Muslims protest, they will continue to share the opprobrium heaped on those who claim to represent us. Unless we do, we cannot credibly claim that 'they have nothing to do with us'. Sadly, they *do* come from within us.

Islamists and Salafists seek to suppress thoughts of coexistence not only with Israel but also with other Muslims, particularly

Shi'a believers. If mainstream Sunni Islam does not expel the killers of Shi'a, it will continue to allow Salafi-jihadis to claim that they are acting in the name of Sunni Islam, and further fuel the inferno of Sunni–Shi'a clashes in the Middle East. Entire countries are already in the grip of this sectarian crisis, and it has probably not yet peaked in Syria, Iraq, Saudi Arabia, Lebanon, Iran and elsewhere. Once these people have been ejected and identified as the chief foes of Islam, both Sunni and Shi'a can then turn their attention to isolating and eradicating the Salafi-jihadis, the Kharijites of our time. This is not happening at present, so they exploit the privilege and enjoy the protection of being within the House of Islam and can claim that their *ijtihad*, or sharia-based reasoning, is as valid as that of mainstream Muslims.

To deny their claim to Islam, to oust them from the faith, offers three immediate advantages: first, their *yaqeen*, or certainty, comes into question, for the majority of the world's Muslims cannot be wrong. Second, although those who are already jihadis or Kharijites may not repent and return to the fold of mainstream Islam, the vast majority of young Muslims, potential recruits in the decades ahead, are forced to reconsider. You cannot be fighting for Islam if the majority of Muslims do not even consider you Muslim. Currently, no such fork in the road exists, and both options – jihadism and mainstream Islam – are presented, at least in the early stages of radicalisation, as equally Muslim. Third, declaring the Kharijites' apostasy from Islam is a solidly theological and scriptural argument, and therefore defeats them on the very ground that they seek to claim as their prerogative.

As matters stand, Islam and ordinary Muslims are not responsible for terrorism, but have *something* to do with Salafi violence. Just as Pakistan was held in deep distrust for harbouring Osama bin Laden, the role of its *madrasas* and for assisting North Korea with nuclear technology, today the Islamic world is considered suspect for including murderers, beheaders, rapists, slave owners and terrorists. There needs to be a global declaration by all fifty-plus Muslim governments and their Islamic leaders, disowning these theological brigands as disbelievers. This should start with a summit in Mecca and then amplified in multiple Muslim capitals over a sustained period of time.

In Islam, if a Muslim drinks alcohol, consumes pork or steals, he or she is still considered a Muslim, albeit a sinful believer who is expected to have to face God to account for these acts in the next life. If, however, that same person then attempts to justify those sins, then she or he becomes a disbeliever, a *kafir*, because they have committed an open act of disbelief (known as *kufr bawah*) by denying and defying the basic precepts of Islam. Actions and faith are detached. Sinful actions do not nullify a Muslim's belief. But the opposite is true for Salafi-jihadis or the Kharijites. They believe and vehemently insist that Muslims not praying, or drinking alcohol, are not sinful, but in fact are disbelievers. On these grounds they make *Takfir*, or excommunicate Muslims.

By their own definition, what then of someone, nay an entire movement, committed to the worst acts of inhumanity – killing innocents, enslaving women, murdering Muslim believers and destroying historical sites? If consuming and defending the consumption of a bacon sandwich puts a Muslim outside the faith, then why not murder, rape, enslavement and the demolition of antiquities?

By their own measure, Salafi-jihadis are disbelievers and behave and belong outside the fold of Islam. When will more Muslim governments and leaders again have the courage to say so?[14]

Just like the Kharijites, Salafi-jihadis claim to be the truest of true Muslims, and they cite chapter and verse in support of their claim. They inject *yaqeen*, total certainty, into the minds of their adherents, so that they would be prepared to kill millions if they could. It is not lack of intent, or compassion for God's creation, that prevents them, merely the inability thus far to do so. For as long as Salafi-jihadis or Kharijites are allowed to wear the mantle of Islam, they will continue to win more and more of the Muslim masses over to their side. 'True Muslim brothers are being killed' and 'War is being waged on Islam' will continue to be their rallying cries.

Killing them will not solve the problem on its own. This is only dealing with the visible symptom of a disease. Keeping them within the fold of Islam for over thirty years since the assassination of Egyptian President Anwar Sadat in 1981 has transformed the Kharijite threat from an Egyptian problem into a global security threat. This failed policy needs to end, or else, within a century, Kharijite extremism will claim millions more adherents within the Muslim world and beyond. In an age of pressurised attention spans, sound bites and tweets, the nuance, context and caveats of mainstream Muslim scholarship cannot compete with the simplistic clarity of extremists speaking the language of the engineers, scientists and doctors who dominate the elite of Arab societies. An organised minority is now in control of the discourse of the disorganised majority of Muslims. We cannot, in the name of pluralism and tolerating different views within Islam, tolerate intolerance.

For how much longer will we blame the West and take comfort in conspiracy theories? Expelling extremists is fully within Muslim control. When the Wahhabi sect first came into being in the eighteenth century, Suleiman Abd al-Wahhab, the *qadi* of Mecca who was the brother of the founder of the sect, kept Salafi-jihadis out of the city. In India, Muslim scholars have issued a fatwa against the Taliban, al-Qaeda and ISIS, ruling that they are 'not Islamic organisations'. And leading Pakistani scholar Muhammad Tahir-ul-Qadri has issued an extensive edict calling them disbelievers of the Kharijite strain within Islam. In Egypt, the grand imam of Al-Azhar has called for them to be punished.

Takfiris only understand this language of *Takfir*. Only this may force them to reconsider their Islamic credentials, repent and return to the fold of Islam by denouncing their un-Islamic acts of killing, raping, enslaving, and destroying Islam from within. Historically, some of the greatest of Muslim scholars, including Imams Bukhari, Ibn Taymiyya, Subki, Ibn Hajar and others, have said that these are not people from within Islam. So what stops today's Muslims from expelling the jihadis from within our ranks, denying them the platform that they seek to hijack?

Jordan, Britain, Turkey, Egypt and America have made the point, identifying the extremists as Kharijites and apostates, but more Muslim governments and scholars in positions of leadership still need to organise, mobilise, speak, and then take active measures to deny all putative Islamic, scriptural, justifications of Salafi-jihadism. For how much longer will they first remain silent, and then complain that the West and others are falsely blaming Muslims?

The House of Islam is on fire. Anger and hate are fanning the flames from room to room. We must act before it suffocates us. We all need to bring buckets of water to douse the flames, and then support the task of renovating after the fire we helped to set. Unlike climate change or natural disasters, we can make a real difference in our lifetimes, and create peaceable alliances in the Muslim world. And to do that, we must turn our urgent attention to the battle of ideas raging across the Middle East.

Appendix: Middle Eastern Thinkers' Calls for a Regional Union

The calls for Arab unity or regionalism discussed below represent a range of ideologies – some pan-Arab and others pan-Islamic, some secular and others religious – but all call for a regional architecture that transcends the nation-state. Some authors were Christian, some Muslim. Remember that this is not an exhaustive list; rather, I chose to highlight those who were most representative of the major political trends.

AFTER THE ARAB UPRISINGS

Recep Tayyip Erdoğan, Turkey (1954–)

In September 2011, Erdoğan departed on his 'Arab Spring tour' to Egypt, Tunisia and Libya, during which he emphasised Turkish–Arab unity and positioned Turkey as a model for these countries' futures.

In April 2016, as Turkish president, Erdoğan called on Muslim-majority states to unite in fighting terrorism and overcoming sectarian divisions in an opening speech at the annual summit meeting of the Organisation of Islamic Cooperation (OIC) in Istanbul.

'I believe the greatest challenge we need to surmount is sectarianism. My religion is not that of Sunnis, of Shi'as. My religion is Islam,' he said in his opening speech.

'Why are we waiting for help from outside to solve our problems and put a stop to terror?' he asked.

'Sectarianism is the biggest source of danger facing the Muslim world. We must unite to solve these problems ourselves,' he said.

Abdullah Gul, Turkey (1950–)
Abdullah Gul was president of Turkey from 2007 to 2014. He stated in November 2011, addressing the British Foreign Office's Wilton Park think tank, that the Middle East lacked 'an efficient regional economic cooperation and integration mechanism'. President Gul noted the role of the European Union in Europe's development after the fall of the Berlin Wall to indicate the potential for such a union after the Arab Spring.[1]

I invited President Gul to address a Westminster audience in 2017, when he reiterated his calls for deeper regional integration through a political and economic union that addressed the challenges of the Middle East.

GCC (Gulf Cooperation Council)
King Abdullah bin Abdul Aziz al-Saud, Saudi Arabia (1924–2015)

King Abdullah, reigning King of Saudi Arabia, called in 2011 for the transition of the Gulf Cooperation Council from a cooperative agreement towards a single entity.

Prince Mutaib bin Abdullah al-Saud, Saudi Arabia (1952–)
In 2013, the Saudi King Abdullah promoted his son, Prince Mutaib bin Abdullah, to head the Saudi national guard; almost immediately following, Prince Mutaib announced that the GCC would create a 100,000-strong defence force over the next few years.[2]

Prince Khalifa bin Salman al-Khalifa, Bahrain (1935–)
Prince Khalifa bin Salman al-Khalifa, the current prime minister of Bahrain, has made many statements in support of both Gulf and Arab unity projects. In April 2013 at the Gulf Press Association Conference, he stated: 'unity will protect our future and make us

a strong entity in the international arena'.[3] In January 2014, he echoed the same sentiments and added that a Gulf union could be 'the core of the Arab unity' and would be a means to protect against 'the schemes being plotted against us', referencing the unrest in Bahrain that could be a 'gateway through which terror could be spread into the entire region'.[4]

Sheikh Zayed bin Sultan al-Nahyan, United Arab Emirates (1918–2004)

Sheikh Zayed bin Sultan al-Nahyan, former ruler of Abu Dhabi and president of the UAE, said in a February 2000 meeting with Jordan's King Abdullah: 'Without building solidarity and closing their ranks, the Arabs will have no weight and strength in the world. They will lose nothing if they pursue the path of solidarity, unity, and joint action.'[5] Sheikh Zayed's political vision of unity among Arabs led to the creation in 1973 of the United Arab Emirates, a confederation of seven Arab political entities.

Sheikh Mohammed bin Rashid al-Maktoum, United Arab Emirates (1949–)

Sheikh Mohammed bin Rashid al-Maktoum, current ruler of Dubai and vice president and prime minister of the UAE, in August 1987 as defence minister met with PLO chairman Yasser Arafat to discuss Arab unity and Palestinian political aims. Sheikh Mohammed stated that: 'Arab unity is essential,' and that the UAE would always support any joint Arab action aimed at promoting Arab interests.[6] In November 2000, he stated in a broadcast Internet chat with other UAE rulers that progress had been made in the 'much sought-after unity among Arab states'.[7]

ANTI-COLONIALIST

Jamal al-Din al-Afghani (1838/9–97)

Jamal al-Din al-Afghani is considered a founder of Arab nationalism. He campaigned for pan-Arab/pan-Islamic unity starting in the 1860s to challenge European encroachments into the Middle East and beyond. Though he was born in either Iran or Afghanistan – scholars disagree despite the *nisba* 'al-Afghani' – he spent his life travelling, living for a time in India, Egypt, the Ottoman Empire, Europe, Persia and Russia. Afghani aspired to create a strong state to protect Muslims from European ambitions. However, the concern with Muslim, rather than Arab unity does not indicate an interest in religious doctrine or spirituality in Afghani's project; he considered Islam to be a civilisation, rather than a religion.[8]

Muhammad 'Abduh, Egypt (1849–1905)
Muhammad 'Abduh, a student of Afghani, was more focused on the religious nature of Islam than on his teacher's political activism. 'Abduh served as Mufti of Egypt and is considered a founder of Islamic Modernism. He believed that Islam could only be revitalised through cultural activity, not politics, and he preached brotherhood and unity between all schools of Islamic thought. He was a supporter of the rebellion against the British in Egypt, and he made popular a more hopeful attitude toward unitarian politics that led faithful Egyptians to engage in politics.[9]

Muhammad Rashid Rida, Syria (1865–1935)
Muhammad Rashid Rida, a student of Muhammad 'Abduh, built upon his teacher's philosophy in the religious direction, toward the establishment of the caliphate. Rashid Rida's writings influenced the modern political philosophy for an 'Islamic State'.[10]

Abd al-Rahman al-Kawakibi, Syria (1849–1902)
Abd al-Rahman al-Kawakibi was also a student of Muhammad 'Abduh, though his ideology focused on Arab nationalism, rather than pan-Islamism. To Kawakibi, Arabs were the only legitimate representatives of Islam,[11] and he championed Arabs against the Turks. He argued for a spiritual caliphate, whose ruler would exercise no political authority.[12]

PRO-OTTOMAN

Sultan ʻAbd al-Hamid II, Ottoman Empire (1842–1918)
The Ottoman ruler Sultan ʻAbd al-Hamid II adopted Afghani's call for pan-Islamism in an attempt to draw Arab peoples and territory under Ottoman influence. Afghani rejected the Sultan's confluence of Ottomanism and pan-Islamism.[13]

ANTI-OTTOMAN

Negib Azoury, Syria (1870–1916)
Negib Azoury, an Ottoman Christian, built upon Kawakibi's theology and called for both a spiritual caliphate and a secular Arab empire from the Euphrates and Tigris rivers to the Suez Canal. Azoury intended this Arab empire to separate from the Ottoman Empire. His book *Le réveil de la nation arabe* was published in 1905.

Shukri al-'Asali, Syria (1868–1916)
Shukri al-'Asali, a supporter of the 1908 Young Turk revolt, was elected to the restored Ottoman Parliament in 1911. As a Member of Parliament, he called for the reform of the Syrian socioeconomic and education systems and was a strong opponent of Zionism. Unlike Azoury and other Arab nationalists of his time, 'Asali supported a combined Arab and Turkish project under the Committee of Union and Progress (CUP) to rebuild the Ottoman Empire, with improved status and quality of life for Arabs. However, he eventually rejected CUP, because Arabs' condition had not improved; in April 1911, he spoke in Parliament, describing the lack of Arab representation in senior ministry positions. Despite these grievances, 'Asali maintained that he was loyal to the Ottoman project, yet some historians argue that his views had changed by the time of his death.[14]

Abd al-Hamid al-Zahrawi, Syria (1855–1916)
Abd al-Hamid al-Zahrawi, like 'Asali, began his political career supporting the Young Turks, then becoming a member of the

reinstated Ottoman Parliament. He condemned the CUP as too tyrannical and not supportive of Arab rights. Though he was a member of the Ottoman Parliament, he was motivated by pan-Islamic impulses and supported 'a strong Ottoman entity in which Arabs would prosper'. Al-Zahrawi was president of the First Arab Congress, held in Paris in 1913, and eventually adopted the goal of Arab independence.[15]

Aziz Ali al-Misri, Egypt (1879–1965)

Aziz Ali al-Misri served in the Ottoman military and originally supported unity within the Ottoman Empire; however, he later left the CUP due to their radicalism and instead became a supporter of the Arab nationalist cause. Misri was an important force in turning Egyptians away from purely Egyptian nationalism toward pan-Arab nationalism.

Sati al-Husri (1879–1967)

Sati al-Husri was originally a supporter of the Young Turks, but – like so many of his peers – eventually abandoned Ottomanism for Arab nationalism. He stressed the importance of language and history for Arabs to embrace unity. Husri held a variety of positions in the Syrian government after 1908, where he worked to reform the education system.[16]

Husain bin Ali, Sharif of Mecca (early twentieth century)

Sharif Husain bin Ali was the head of the Hashemite dynasty in the early twentieth century. With the support of Sir Henry McMahon, British High Commissioner of Egypt, Sharif Husain intended to overthrow Ottoman rule in Arab lands and restore Mecca and Medina to their former glory; this plan is outlined in the McMahon–Husain Correspondence. Sharif Husain envisioned himself as Caliph following the Arab victory, in a territory spanning from Aleppo to Aden. Though this was an Arab national movement in a sense, it was based more on political aims than social or humanitarian ones. Ultimately, the Arab Revolt was a failure; though Sharif Husain declared himself Caliph of all Muslims after the Kemalist revolt in 1924, he was driven out of Mecca by Wahhabis shortly thereafter.[17]

George Antonius (1891–1942)

George Antonius, a Lebanese–Egyptian scholar who lived in Palestine, is considered the first historian of Arab nationalism. In his book *The Arab Awakening*, he argued that the Arab nation – which consisted of racial and cultural-linguistic elements – had been 'dormant' for centuries.

BA'ATH PARTY AND UNITED ARAB REPUBLIC

Michel Aflaq, Syria (1910–89)

Michel Aflaq, a Christian, co-founded the Arab Ba'ath Party[18] in 1940 with Salah al-Din al-Bitar. 'Ba'ath' means 'renaissance' or 'rebirth'. Through the party, which combined elements of nationalism and socialism, Aflaq worked with Gamal Abdul Nasser to create the United Arab Republic (UAR). Although he was Christian, Aflaq believed that there was a special relationship between Islam and Arab nationalism that Arabs of any religion could and should respect.[19]

Salah al-Din al-Bitar, Syria (1912–80)

Salah al-Din al-Bitar co-founded the Arab Ba'ath Party with Michel Aflaq in 1940. Bitar served as prime minister in several early Ba'athist governments in Syria, and he expected to be appointed the vice president of the UAR. Instead, he was appointed the minister of state for Arab affairs, and later minister of culture and national guidance. He was dismayed over the dominant role Nasser gave the Egyptians in administrating the UAR. In 1966 he fled the country, after which he lived mostly in Europe and remained politically active until he was assassinated in 1980, most likely by an agent of Syrian president Hafez al-Assad.

Zaki al-Arsuzi, Syria (1899–1968)
Zaki al-Arsuzi founded a separate Arab Ba'ath party in 1940, which eventually merged with Aflaq and Bitar's party in 1947. Arsuzi aimed to establish the identity of the Arab nation through his philosophy of the Arabic language; he believed the foundation of Arab nationalism was brotherhood – fraternity by nature and proximity of their descent. He conceded in 1966 that the creation of a single Arab nation was untenable at that time, and he instead suggested a federated order through which borders might eventually disappear.[20]

Gamal Abdul Nasser, Egypt (1918–70)
Gamal Abdul Nasser was president of Egypt from 1956 until his death. His socialist and nationalist ideas were broadcast throughout the Arab world on the Cairo-based Voice of the Arabs radio station. Despite his popular appeal, by mid-1957 his only governmental ally in the region was Syria. In January 1958, Nasser acquiesced to repeated calls from Syria to unify, creating the United Arab Republic.[21]

Taha Hussein, Egypt (1889–1973)
Although the author Taha Hussein was originally a pharonist, meaning he did not want Egypt involved in Arab nationalism, he eventually came to support the Arab nationalist project, publishing the article '*al-Udaba hum bunat al-qaumiyaa al-arabiyya*' in the late 1950s.

Constantin Zureiq, Syria (1909–2000)
Constantin Zureiq was a Christian academic and supporter of Arab nationalism. He sought to transform Arab society by emphasising rational thought. Like Michel Aflaq, he saw an important relationship between Islam and Arab nationalism.[22]

Abd al-Rahman al-Bazzaz, Iraq (1913–73)
Abd al-Rahman al-Bazzaz became a proponent of Arab nationalism while studying law in Baghdad and London in the 1930s. He later supported the 1941 failed Iraqi rebellion against the

British, and eventually served as prime minister of Iraq. While in government, Bazzaz aimed to reduce military salaries and privilege – an unpopular goal. He was charged by the Ba'athist government with participation in activities against the government. Bazzaz argued that Arab nationalism and Islam were compatible in every respect.[23]

Notes

INTRODUCTION

1. North Korea calls itself the 'Democratic People's Republic of Korea', but we know that it is not a democracy, so our media is confident in referring to it as undemocratic. Our lack of knowledge about Islam renders our press unable to refute ISIS's claim to being Islamic.
2. John Gray, *Black Mass* (Allen Lane 2007).
3. Edmund Burke, *Reflections on the Revolution in France* (Penguin 2004), p. 195.
4. Ibid.
5. Ibid., p. 172.
6. Esposito, J. & Mogahed, M., *Who Speaks for Islam? What a Billion Muslims Really Think* (Gallup 2007), pp. 6, 7.
7. Burke, op. cit., p. 11.

CHAPTER 1 WHAT IS ISLAM?

1. Karen Armstrong, *Fields of Blood: Religion and the History of Violence* (Penguin Random House 2014), pp. 2–3.
2. Inhabitants of two towns on the outskirts of Damascus in Syria, Ma'lula and Sednaya, still speak Aramaic. I have visited both.
3. I have mostly used my own translations of the Quran from the Arabic original.

CHAPTER 3 WHO IS A MUSLIM TODAY?

1. John Darwin, *After Tamerlane: The Global History of Empire since 1405* (Allen Lane 2007).

2. While Turks, Persians and Muslim civilisations in India did not use the Arabic language orally, they did use the Arabic script for their own languages. Today, Urdu and Persian still use Arabic script. In Turkey, the secular Muslim reformer Kemal Atatürk abolished Arabic use in writing, and Turks now use Latin script.
3. Muslims follow a lunar year with a different calendar. The calendar commenced from the day that the Prophet settled in Medina. By that measure, the year 2017 in the Gregorian calendar will be 1438. Known as the Hijri calculation, derived from the *Hijrah* (often anglicised as Hegira) or migration of the Prophet from Mecca, this dating is still important to Muslims, but not widely used. Only in Saudi Arabia, Iran and among Islamic organisations is the Hijri dating cited.
4. Genesis 22:17.
5. Peter Frankopan, *The Silk Roads* (Bloomsbury 2015), pp. 85–6.

CHAPTER 4 THE SUNNI–SHIʿA SCHISM

1. The Umayyads gave birth to the first dynastic monarchy within Islam. After the first four caliphs, they ruled for almost a century from their headquarters in Damascus, Syria. They were known for their luxuries, conquests, grand palaces, political intrigue, corruption, murders, and attempts at mass control. They were widely seen by Muslims to be the old order, representing the pre-Islamic Meccan elite. The original Umayyads (with the exception of the caliph Omar bin Abdul Aziz) were mostly perceived as the off-spring of those who had persecuted the Prophet, and had converted to Islam only after making the calculation that becoming Muslim could yield new power.
2. Steve Coll, a Pulitzer prize-winning journalist, documents that the CIA were encouraging Sunni *mujahideen* in Afghanistan to launch suicide bombings against the Soviets, but that the Sunni fighters refused on religious grounds, as committing suicide is forbidden in the Quran. That God alone gives and takes life is the mainstream Sunni Muslim position. Thirty years later, Hezbollah's invention has become a weapon of choice among both Sunni and Shiʿa terrorists. See *Ghost Wars: The Secret History of the CIA, Afghanistan, and Bin Laden from the Soviet Invasion to September 10, 2001* (Penguin 2004).

3. Cited in Margaret Macmillan, *The Uses and Abuses of History* (Profile 2010), p. 24.
4. Sayyida Zeinab, a granddaughter of the Prophet, is buried on the outskirts of Damascus. The site is a regular target of ISIS and al-Qaeda attacks. Hezbollah and Iranian pressure has ensured its protection. When I lived in Damascus, I used to visit this shrine regularly for its ethos of spiritual splendour and serenity.
5. Tweet by the popular English-speaking Shi'a scholar Sayed M. Modarresi on 10 December 2015.
6. Every year, Shi'a Muslims celebrate this occasion as Eid e Ghadir, named after the well beside which the Prophet stopped while travelling back to Medina after the last pilgrimage. There, he pointed to Imam Ali as a protector of those the Prophet had protected in life. Shi'a Muslims claim that this was an indication of Ali becoming the successor of the Prophet. Sunni Muslims dispute that conclusion.
7. The Abbasid caliph al-Mansur conducted an inquisition of beliefs to eliminate Shi'a attitudes during the years 754 to 775. *Taqiyya* was developed to maintain secretly Shi'a identity and avoid persecution.

CHAPTER 5 WHAT IS THE SHARIA?

1. *The World's Muslims, Religion, Politics and Society* (Pew Research Centre 2013).
2. http://www.telegraph.co.uk/news/worldnews/islamic-state/11414646/To-defeat-our-foe-we-must-first-define-him.html; To Defeat Our Foe, We Must First Define Him, *Telegraph*.
3. A *sanad* is a chain of narrators that transmitted a hadith from the Prophet. Famously, Imam Bukhari collected over 100,000 hadith but recorded only 7,000. His criterion was the soundness of the *sanad* or chain. If a narrator was of doubtful character, then he rejected the hadith. But if the chain of narrators included men of good repute, then no matter how questionable the actual text of the hadith, Imam Bukhari would include it in his authoritative collection.
4. Most prominent among these scholars were Imam Abu Bakr al-Jassas and Abu Ja'far al-Tahawi.
5. It is a mistake committed in many Muslim societies today to seek to judge the liberalism of a Muslim by testing to see if they drink alcohol or not. Muslims who avoid alcohol are not extremists, and those who drink are not liberals – such crass differences betray ignorance. The 9/11 murderers drank alcohol, for example.

CHAPTER 7 A HUNDRED YEARS OF HUMILIATION

1. William Dalrymple, *The Last Mughal* (Bloomsbury 2006), p. 21.
2. Henry Kissinger, *World Order* (Penguin 2014), p. 3.
3. Ibid. p. 4.
4. Ibid. p. 27.

CHAPTER 8 WHO IS AN ISLAMIST?

1. Z. Sardar, 'Great thinkers of our time – Maulana Sayyid Abul-Ala Maududi', *New Statesman*, 14 July 2003.
2. Quoted in Gudrun Kramer, *Makers of the Muslim World: Hasan al-Banna* (Oxford, One World, 2010), p. 21.
3. Ibid.
4. Ibid., p. 51.
5. Ibid.
6. Ibid., p. 102.
7. Sheikh Ramadan Al-Bouti (d. 2013) and Sheikh Ahmad Kuftaro (d. 2005).
8. 20 May 2016, Ennahda summit in Tunis.

CHAPTER 9 WHO IS A SALAFI? OR A WAHHABI?

1. *The Muslim 500* published in 2010 by the Royal Aal al-Bayt Institute for Islamic Thought in Amman, Jordan, defined Salafis as Islamic fundamentalists and estimated their population to be 3 per cent of Muslims.

CHAPTER 10 WHO IS A JIHADI?

1. As analysed and cited by Shaikh Hamza Yusuf at the annual conference of Muslim scholars gathered at the Global Forum for Promoting Peace in Muslim Societies, held in Abu Dhabi, UAE, in 2015.

CHAPTER 11 WHO IS A KHARIJITE, OR *TAKFIRI*?

1. Taken from hadith sources cited on Salafi websites including www.answering-extremism.com (accessed on 26 December 2017).

CHAPTER 12 DIGNITY

1. Quoted in *Foreign Policy*, 14 May 2015.
2. See Francis Fukuyama, *The End of History and the Last Man* (New York, Avon, 1992).

CHAPTER 13 THE JEWS

1. King Abu Abdullah Muhammad XI was known as Boabdil, the twenty-third Muslim king of Granada.
2. B. Hughes, *Istanbul: A Tale of Three Cities* (Weidenfeld & Nicolson, 2017), p. 426.
3. Bertrand Russell, *A History of Western Philosophy* (London, Routledge, 1996), p. 303.
4. Matthew 23:33.
5. The banality is redoubled by the suggestion that a specific tree, the *gharqad* (boxwood), will protect Jewish people and not call out to Muslims. These claims of hadith are popular among those who oppose Jewish people being in Israel.
6. http://www.jpost.com/Middle-East/Iran-News/Iran-continues-to-call-for-Israels-destruction-despite-nuclear-deal-481659; Iran Continues to Call for Israel's Destruction Despite Nuclear Deal, *Jerusalem Post*, 16 February 2017.
7. Dan Senor and Saul Singer, *Start-Up Nation: The Story of Israel's Economic Miracle* (New York 2009), p. 209.
8. Ibid., p. 11.

CHAPTER 14 EDUCATION

1. See Albert Hourani, *A History of the Arab Peoples* (London 1991), p. 76.
2. UNDP, Arab Human Development Report, *Building a Knowledge Society* (NY 2003), p. 53.
3. Arab Thought Foundation, Fourth annual cultural development report, 2012.
4. UNESCO report, 2012.
5. In 'Was the Gate of Ijtihad Closed?', *International Journal of Middle East Studies*, Vol. 16, No. 1, March 1984, Wael Hallaq illustrates how, among the highest echelons of the Sunni *ulama*, both in theory and in practice, the gate of *ijtihad* was not closed, but the prevailing perception was that it was from roughly the twelfth century onwards.

6. A study of 4,000 political radicals operating across the Muslim world and the West found that among Islamist radicals, 44.9 per cent had studied engineering, compared with only 11.6 per cent of the general populations in their countries. They did not all contribute bomb-making expertise: only 15 per cent of the engineers worked as terrorist bomb-makers, while 26 per cent had communication roles. Steffen Hertog and Diego Gambetta, 'The Surprising Link Between Education and Jihad', *Foreign Affairs*, March 2016.
7. Gambetta and Hertog, cited in Martin Rose, *Immunising the Mind* (British Council 2015).
8. A popular hadith claims that the Prophet said: 'Disagreement among my community is a mercy.' Hadith scholars disagree on its authenticity, but the prevalence of it reflects Muslim communal attitudes.
9. *The Economist*, 2–8 April 2016.

CHAPTER 15 WOMEN

1. Gallup poll, Mogahed, Esposito, 2007.
2. Samir Kassir, *Being Arab* (Verso 2006).
3. There is a historical debate on how old she was at the time of her marriage to the Prophet. Some suggest nine, others twelve, and some seventeen.
4. See M. A. Nadwi, *Al-muhaddithat: The Women Scholars in Islam* (2013), a summary of the Arabic forty volumes.
5. Sheikh Ghannouchi in conversation with the author at a round-table meeting organised by the author in 2013 at the US Council on Foreign Relations, Washington DC.
6. A. J. Arberry (Trans.), *The Ring of the Dove: A Treatise on the Art and Practice of Arab Love* (Luzac, London 1951), p.16.
7. Ibid., p. 21.

CHAPTER 16 SEX

1. C. Barks (Trans.), *Rumi: Selected Poems* (Penguin, 1996), p. 178.
2. *Washington Post*, 10 June 2015.
3. D. Ladinsky (Trans.), *The Gift: Poems by Hafiz, the Great Sufi Master* (Penguin, 1999), p. 253.
4. Ibid., p. 282.
5. Ibid., p. 40.

6. Ibid., p. 191.
7. Ibid., p. 107.

CHAPTER 17 GOD IS ALIVE

1. Ibn Arabi, *The Voyage of No Return* (Cambridge, Islamic Texts Society, 2000), p. 16.
2. C. Addas (Trans.), *Ibn Arabi: The Voyage of No Return* (Islamic Texts Society, 2000), p. 100.

CHAPTER 19 THE FAMILY TABLE

1. Radwa S. Elsaman and Mohamed A. Arafa, 'The Rights of the Elderly in the Arab Middle East: Islamic Theory Versus Arabic Practice', in *Marquette Elder's Advisor*, Vol. 14, Issue 1.
2. *Boston Review*, 6 November 2014.

CHAPTER 20 THE NEXT LIFE

1. Quran, 21:35.

CONCLUSION: THE WAY FORWARD

1. Max Fisher, 'Anti-American countries can become pro-American. Here's how South Korea did it', *Washington Post*, 7 May 2013.
2. See Moisés Naím, *The End of Power* (New York, Basic, 2013), p. 5,
3. UK Ministry of Defence, *Strategic Trends Programme: Global Strategic Trends – out to 2040* (London 2010).
4. *Economist*, 14–20 May, 2016.
5. See Appendix.
6. http://www.bbc.co.uk/news/world-middle-east-35999557; BBC, 8 April, 2016, Saudi Arabia and Egypt announce Red Sea bridge.
7. See John Gray, *Straw Dogs* (London, Granta, 2002).
8. Source: senior European diplomat present at the declaration.
9. Jean-Pierre Chauffour, *From Political to Economic Awakening in the Arab World: The Path of Economic Integration* (Washington, DC, World Bank, 2013).
10. Economic integration is defined as elimination of tariff and non-tariff barriers to the flow of goods, services and factors of production within a group of countries.

11. Poll commissioned by Geert Wilders's PVV party and undertaken by Maurice de Hond's research organisation in June 2013. Cited by Douglas Murray in *The Strange Death of Europe* (Bloomsbury, 2017), p. 236.
12. Ibid.
13. Ibid., p. 237.
14. Great Muslim scholars and imams of the past, including Abu Bakr Ibn al-'Arabi and Imam al-Qurtubi, ruled that the *khawarij* were not Muslims. In the modern era, even Saudi Arabia's most prominent religious authority, the late Shaykh Abd al-Aziz bin Baz, declared the *khawarij* disbelievers. In Pakistan, Shaikh Tahir al-Qadri has been vocal in declaring the *khawarij* and modern-day imitators such as al-Qaeda and ISIS to stand altogether outside the fold of Islam.

APPENDIX: MIDDLE EASTERN THINKERS' CALLS FOR A REGIONAL UNION

1. 'Turkey Says Mideast Needs Own EU', *Financial Times*, 23 November 2011.
2. 'Saudi Arabia Moving Ahead with Gulf Union', *Al-Monitor*, 22 December 2013.
3. 'Bahrain PM: Unity Only Option for GCC Success', *Arab News*, 17 April 2013.
4. 'Bahrain PM Says Arab Unity "Strongly Needed"', *Gulf News*, 7 January 2014.
5. Media Office of the Government of Dubai, www.sheikhmohammed.com, 10 February 2000.
6. Media Office of the Government of Dubai, www.sheikhmohammed.com, 2 August 1987.
7. Media Office of the Government of Dubai, www.sheikhmohammed.com, 26 November 2000.
8. Sylvia G. Haim, *Arab Nationalism: An Anthology* (Berkeley, University of California Press, 1962), pp. 6–10.
9. Bassam Tibi, *Arab Nationalism: A Critical Enquiry* (New York, St Martin's Press, 1997), pp. 90–4.
10. See Rida's article from *Al Manar* in Haim, *Arab Nationalism: An Anthology*, pp. 75–7.
11. See his pamphlet 'Umm al-Qura' in Haim, *Arab Nationalism: An Anthology*, pp. 78–80.

12. Haim, *Arab Nationalism: An Anthology* (University of California, 1974), pp. 26–7.
13. Tibi, *Arab Nationalism: A Critical Enquiry* (Palgrave, 1990), p. 91.
14. Samir Seikaly, 'Shukri al-'Asali: A Case Study of a Political Activist', in *The Origins of Arab Nationalism*, pp. 73–96.
15. Ahmed Tarabein, 'Abd al-Hamid al-Zahrawi: The Career and Thought of an Arab Nationalist', in *The Origins of Arab Nationalism*, pp. 97–119.
16. Tibi, *Arab Nationalism: A Critical Enquiry*, pp. 161–97.
17. See Husain's demands to the British government in Haim, *Arab Nationalism: An Anthology*, pp. 89–93.
18. See the Arab Ba'ath Party Constitution in Haim, *Arab Nationalism: An Anthology*, pp. 233–41.
19. See Aflaq's article 'Nationalism and Revolution', in Haim, *Arab Nationalism: An Anthology*, pp. 242–50.
20. Dalal Arsuzi-Elamir, 'Nation, State, and Democracy in the Writings of Zaki al-Arsuzi', in Cristoph Schumann, ed., *Nationalism and Liberal Thought in the Arab East* (Abingdon, Routledge, 2010), pp. 66–91.
21. See Nasser's essay 'The Philosophy of Revolution' in Haim, *Arab Nationalism: An Anthology*, pp. 229–32.
22. See Zureiq's essay in Haim, *Arab Nationalism: An Anthology*, pp. 167–71.
23. See al-Bazzaz's essay in Haim, *Arab Nationalism: An Anthology*, pp. 172–88.

Acknowledgements

My greatest debt is to my parents, *Abba* and *Amma*, for teaching me about the ways of Muslim believers through love, *suhbet* or companionship and living their faith rather than preaching it. Had they not taught me Islam, I would not have the linguistic and cultural tools with which to access the Muslim world. Their *murshid*, or spiritual master, Saheb Qiblah Fultali and his disciples taught me Arabic, the Quran, and about the spirit of the Prophet.

My wife, Faye, has been my greatest support as I travelled, read and wrote. Faye has been my constant companion in life, my first port of call, my critic. In writing this book, she and our two daughters have been a source of love, understanding and encouragement.

This book was born after a *New York Times* opinion editorial I wrote in August 2014. The unrivalled and far-sighted Andrew Wylie contacted me and we began a conversation that led to this book. I am grateful to Andrew's candour when providing thoughtful and speedy feedback. James Pullen, at the Wylie Agency, has been a great conversant and judge of ideas.

At Bloomsbury, I have been privileged to work with Michael Fishwick, a discerning and instinctive editor who has flair and feel for excellent content; he wanted *The House of Islam* to 'not be a book of the hour'. Michael's high standards, holidays in Andalusia and readings on Luther all provided food for thought as we worked through the iterations of the manuscript. Sarah Ruddick, Jasmine Horsey, Emma Bal, Genista Tate-Alexander and Marigold Atkey have all been wonderful and helpful throughout.

Among my friends, 'Her Majesty's *Shura*' have been invaluable as true brothers and musketeers. While we may not always agree, their love, loyalty, and roaring laughter mean the world to a writer in his aloof world. They have tolerated my questions and provided erudite answers again and again. To the *Shura*, my deepest thanks.

His Eminence Shaikh Abdullah bin Bayyah, Cheikhna bin Bayyah, and Zeshan Zafar have always encouraged me to write, and never sought to censor. That sort of freedom among religious leaders is rare, and hence precious. Generations to come will appreciate the Shaikh's efforts in teaching the *Maqasid* of the sharia and helping reconcile the West and Islam. It was from Shaikh bin Bayyah that I learned of the House of Islam being on fire – and the duty of us all to extinguish the blaze.

I am forever grateful to Ceylan Ozgul for re-introducing the heritage of the Ottomans to my life, and helping me question the premise of many Muslim assertions. She is the epitome of multiple civilisations: Greece, Judea, the Ottomans, Islam and the modern West. Her feedback on the book and its main ideas were beneficial.

Nathan Feldman has been a source of brotherhood and abiding friendship. His invitation to visit Jerusalem and see Jewish, Christian and Muslim co-existence and his sincere conversations about a more peaceful world for all the children of God reassures me that goodness exists. His feedback on several chapters helped me.

Rula Jebreal, a true friend, was always an inspiration. Our intriguing conversations in Rome, London and New York guided me to ponder on ideas mentioned in chapters that I would have ordinarily overlooked.

Heba Youssry in Cairo is a true Sufi who inspired me with the wisdom of Ibn Arabi and others. Such sensible and delicate souls are rare.

Ambassador Sheikh Fahad al-Atiyya and I may not always agree on politics, but his impeccable manners, *adab*, generosity, and criticisms of modernity gave me cause for reflection. Conversations with him in Qatar and London on the importance of tradition, re-thinking art, architecture and Muslim cities were always deeply meaningful.

Ambassador Omar Ghobash always asked the questions that others missed in Muslim gatherings. In New York and Abu Dhabi, his wit, humour, intelligence and sincere concern for the future of the Muslim world were heartening.

Stephanie Hare kindly dissected parts of the book and helped make it stronger.

Nidhi Sinha never stopped believing that the book was a top priority. Each time we met or talked, her asking about the writing always propelled me to work harder.

Fatima Mullick's soulful conversations on Shi'as and Sufis always leave me wanting more. Her words and thoughts helped with chapters.

Sue Eedle and Alona Ferber helped tidy up and question early drafts. Their diligence and attention to detail was truly admirable.

Peter Welby's grasp of theology, philosophy and politics are hard to match in one so young. His detailed reading of the manuscript and feedback was valuable.

William Neal is a strategic mind that can foresee where an argument is landing before it is concluded. His wisdom and anticipation helped map the contours of the book as I discussed it with him.

Finally, to all those good people in planes, hotels and restaurants across the world who gave me a pen and paper when a sudden, new thought gripped me: thank you.

Any mistakes in the book are entirely mine – goodness, truth, and knowledge belong to my teachers.

Index

A Note on the Type

The text of this book is set in Linotype Stempel Garamond, a version of Garamond adapted and first used by the Stempel foundry in 1924. It is one of several versions of Garamond based on the designs of Claude Garamond. It is thought that Garamond based his font on Bembo, cut in 1495 by Francesco Griffo in collaboration with the Italian printer Aldus Manutius. Garamond types were first used in books printed in Paris around 1532. Many of the present-day versions of this type are based on the *Typi Academiae* of Jean Jannon cut in Sedan in 1615.

Claude Garamond was born in Paris in 1480. He learned how to cut type from his father and by the age of fifteen he was able to fashion steel punches the size of a pica with great precision. At the age of sixty he was commissioned by King Francis I to design a Greek alphabet, and for this he was given the honourable title of royal type founder. He died in 1561.